Mometrix

TEST PREPARATION

FTCE

Humanities K-12 Secrets Study Guide

Dear Future Exam Success Story

First of all, **THANK YOU** for purchasing Mometrix study materials!

Second, congratulations! You are one of the few determined test-takers who are committed to doing whatever it takes to excel on your exam. **You have come to the right place.** We developed these study materials with one goal in mind: to deliver you the information you need in a format that's concise and easy to use.

In addition to optimizing your guide for the content of the test, we've outlined our recommended steps for breaking down the preparation process into small, attainable goals so you can make sure you stay on track.

We've also analyzed the entire test-taking process, identifying the most common pitfalls and showing how you can overcome them and be ready for any curveball the test throws you.

Standardized testing is one of the biggest obstacles on your road to success, which only increases the importance of doing well in the high-pressure, high-stakes environment of test day. Your results on this test could have a significant impact on your future, and this guide provides the information and practical advice to help you achieve your full potential on test day.

Your success is our success

We would love to hear from you! If you would like to share the story of your exam success or if you have any questions or comments in regard to our products, please contact us at **800-673-8175** or **support@mometrix.com**.

Thanks again for your business and we wish you continued success!

Sincerely,
The Mometrix Test Preparation Team

Need more help? Check out our flashcards at:
http://mometrixflashcards.com/FTCE

TABLE OF CONTENTS

INTRODUCTION 1
SECRET KEY #1 – PLAN BIG, STUDY SMALL 2
SECRET KEY #2 – MAKE YOUR STUDYING COUNT 3
SECRET KEY #3 – PRACTICE THE RIGHT WAY 4
SECRET KEY #4 – PACE YOURSELF 6
SECRET KEY #5 – HAVE A PLAN FOR GUESSING 7
TEST-TAKING STRATEGIES 10
VOCABULARY AND CONCEPTS BASIC TO THE HUMANITIES 15
- MUSIC HISTORY AND LITERATURE 15
- COSTUMES AND MAKEUP 26
- STAGES AND SET DESIGN 28
- STAGING A PLAY 31
- BACKSTAGE PROCEDURES AND PRODUCTION CREWS 32
- CRAFT AND COMPREHENSION 34
- ELEMENTS OF STORY 41
- CHAPTER QUIZ 53

HISTORICAL PERIODS, STYLES, AND MOVEMENTS AND PROMINENT AESTHETIC PRINCIPLES 54
- ARCHITECTURE 54
- ART FROM AROUND THE WORLD 71
- WESTERN ART THROUGH THE AGES 80
- CHAPTER QUIZ 109

INTERRELATEDNESS OF ARTS AND IDEAS 110
- CHAPTER QUIZ 116

CULTURAL BELIEFS AND VALUES AND THEIR EXPRESSION IN THE HUMANITIES 117
- GENRES IN FICTION 117
- TYPES OF STORIES 118
- HISTORICAL FORMS OF PROSE 119
- POETRY 121
- STRUCTURE AND MEANING IN POETRY 123
- DRAMA 126
- WORLD LITERATURE 130
- LITERARY PERIODS AND MOVEMENTS 133
- PUBLIC SPEAKING 136
- CHAPTER QUIZ 137

INSTRUCTIONAL TECHNIQUES, ASSESSMENT, AND RESOURCES APPROPRIATE TO THE HUMANITIES 138
- CLASSROOM PARTICIPATION 138
- ASSESSMENT IN ENGLISH LANGUAGE ARTS 141

CHAPTER QUIZ — 144

FTCE PRACTICE TEST — 145

ANSWER KEY AND EXPLANATIONS — 170

ONLINE RESOURCES — 184

Introduction

Thank you for purchasing this resource! You have made the choice to prepare yourself for a test that could have a huge impact on your future, and this guide is designed to help you be fully ready for test day. Obviously, it's important to have a solid understanding of the test material, but you also need to be prepared for the unique environment and stressors of the test, so that you can perform to the best of your abilities.

For this purpose, the first section that appears in this guide is the **Secret Keys**. We've devoted countless hours to meticulously researching what works and what doesn't, and we've boiled down our findings to the five most impactful steps you can take to improve your performance on the test. We start at the beginning with study planning and move through the preparation process, all the way to the testing strategies that will help you get the most out of what you know when you're finally sitting in front of the test.

We recommend that you start preparing for your test as far in advance as possible. However, if you've bought this guide as a last-minute study resource and only have a few days before your test, we recommend that you skip over the first two Secret Keys since they address a long-term study plan.

If you struggle with **test anxiety**, we strongly encourage you to check out our recommendations for how you can overcome it. Test anxiety is a formidable foe, but it can be beaten, and we want to make sure you have the tools you need to defeat it.

Secret Key #1 – Plan Big, Study Small

There's a lot riding on your performance. If you want to ace this test, you're going to need to keep your skills sharp and the material fresh in your mind. You need a plan that lets you review everything you need to know while still fitting in your schedule. We'll break this strategy down into three categories.

Information Organization

Start with the information you already have: the official test outline. From this, you can make a complete list of all the concepts you need to cover before the test. Organize these concepts into groups that can be studied together, and create a list of any related vocabulary you need to learn so you can brush up on any difficult terms. You'll want to keep this vocabulary list handy once you actually start studying since you may need to add to it along the way.

Time Management

Once you have your set of study concepts, decide how to spread them out over the time you have left before the test. Break your study plan into small, clear goals so you have a manageable task for each day and know exactly what you're doing. Then just focus on one small step at a time. When you manage your time this way, you don't need to spend hours at a time studying. Studying a small block of content for a short period each day helps you retain information better and avoid stressing over how much you have left to do. You can relax knowing that you have a plan to cover everything in time. In order for this strategy to be effective though, you have to start studying early and stick to your schedule. Avoid the exhaustion and futility that comes from last-minute cramming!

Study Environment

The environment you study in has a big impact on your learning. Studying in a coffee shop, while probably more enjoyable, is not likely to be as fruitful as studying in a quiet room. It's important to keep distractions to a minimum. You're only planning to study for a short block of time, so make the most of it. Don't pause to check your phone or get up to find a snack. It's also important to **avoid multitasking**. Research has consistently shown that multitasking will make your studying dramatically less effective. Your study area should also be comfortable and well-lit so you don't have the distraction of straining your eyes or sitting on an uncomfortable chair.

The time of day you study is also important. You want to be rested and alert. Don't wait until just before bedtime. Study when you'll be most likely to comprehend and remember. Even better, if you know what time of day your test will be, set that time aside for study. That way your brain will be used to working on that subject at that specific time and you'll have a better chance of recalling information.

Finally, it can be helpful to team up with others who are studying for the same test. Your actual studying should be done in as isolated an environment as possible, but the work of organizing the information and setting up the study plan can be divided up. In between study sessions, you can discuss with your teammates the concepts that you're all studying and quiz each other on the details. Just be sure that your teammates are as serious about the test as you are. If you find that your study time is being replaced with social time, you might need to find a new team.

Secret Key #2 – Make Your Studying Count

You're devoting a lot of time and effort to preparing for this test, so you want to be absolutely certain it will pay off. This means doing more than just reading the content and hoping you can remember it on test day. It's important to make every minute of study count. There are two main areas you can focus on to make your studying count.

Retention

It doesn't matter how much time you study if you can't remember the material. You need to make sure you are retaining the concepts. To check your retention of the information you're learning, try recalling it at later times with minimal prompting. Try carrying around flashcards and glance at one or two from time to time or ask a friend who's also studying for the test to quiz you.

To enhance your retention, look for ways to put the information into practice so that you can apply it rather than simply recalling it. If you're using the information in practical ways, it will be much easier to remember. Similarly, it helps to solidify a concept in your mind if you're not only reading it to yourself but also explaining it to someone else. Ask a friend to let you teach them about a concept you're a little shaky on (or speak aloud to an imaginary audience if necessary). As you try to summarize, define, give examples, and answer your friend's questions, you'll understand the concepts better and they will stay with you longer. Finally, step back for a big picture view and ask yourself how each piece of information fits with the whole subject. When you link the different concepts together and see them working together as a whole, it's easier to remember the individual components.

Finally, practice showing your work on any multi-step problems, even if you're just studying. Writing out each step you take to solve a problem will help solidify the process in your mind, and you'll be more likely to remember it during the test.

Modality

Modality simply refers to the means or method by which you study. Choosing a study modality that fits your own individual learning style is crucial. No two people learn best in exactly the same way, so it's important to know your strengths and use them to your advantage.

For example, if you learn best by visualization, focus on visualizing a concept in your mind and draw an image or a diagram. Try color-coding your notes, illustrating them, or creating symbols that will trigger your mind to recall a learned concept. If you learn best by hearing or discussing information, find a study partner who learns the same way or read aloud to yourself. Think about how to put the information in your own words. Imagine that you are giving a lecture on the topic and record yourself so you can listen to it later.

For any learning style, flashcards can be helpful. Organize the information so you can take advantage of spare moments to review. Underline key words or phrases. Use different colors for different categories. Mnemonic devices (such as creating a short list in which every item starts with the same letter) can also help with retention. Find what works best for you and use it to store the information in your mind most effectively and easily.

Secret Key #3 – Practice the Right Way

Your success on test day depends not only on how many hours you put into preparing, but also on whether you prepared the right way. It's good to check along the way to see if your studying is paying off. One of the most effective ways to do this is by taking practice tests to evaluate your progress. Practice tests are useful because they show exactly where you need to improve. Every time you take a practice test, pay special attention to these three groups of questions:

- The questions you got wrong
- The questions you had to guess on, even if you guessed right
- The questions you found difficult or slow to work through

This will show you exactly what your weak areas are, and where you need to devote more study time. Ask yourself why each of these questions gave you trouble. Was it because you didn't understand the material? Was it because you didn't remember the vocabulary? Do you need more repetitions on this type of question to build speed and confidence? Dig into those questions and figure out how you can strengthen your weak areas as you go back to review the material.

Additionally, many practice tests have a section explaining the answer choices. It can be tempting to read the explanation and think that you now have a good understanding of the concept. However, an explanation likely only covers part of the question's broader context. Even if the explanation makes perfect sense, **go back and investigate** every concept related to the question until you're positive you have a thorough understanding.

As you go along, keep in mind that the practice test is just that: practice. Memorizing these questions and answers will not be very helpful on the actual test because it is unlikely to have any of the same exact questions. If you only know the right answers to the sample questions, you won't be prepared for the real thing. **Study the concepts** until you understand them fully, and then you'll be able to answer any question that shows up on the test.

It's important to wait on the practice tests until you're ready. If you take a test on your first day of study, you may be overwhelmed by the amount of material covered and how much you need to learn. Work up to it gradually.

On test day, you'll need to be prepared for answering questions, managing your time, and using the test-taking strategies you've learned. It's a lot to balance, like a mental marathon that will have a big impact on your future. Like training for a marathon, you'll need to start slowly and work your way up. When test day arrives, you'll be ready.

Start with the strategies you've read in the first two Secret Keys—plan your course and study in the way that works best for you. If you have time, consider using multiple study resources to get different approaches to the same concepts. It can be helpful to see difficult concepts from more than one angle. Then find a good source for practice tests. Many times, the test website will suggest potential study resources or provide sample tests.

Practice Test Strategy

If you're able to find at least three practice tests, we recommend this strategy:

Untimed and Open-Book Practice

Take the first test with no time constraints and with your notes and study guide handy. Take your time and focus on applying the strategies you've learned.

Timed and Open-Book Practice

Take the second practice test open-book as well, but set a timer and practice pacing yourself to finish in time.

Timed and Closed-Book Practice

Take any other practice tests as if it were test day. Set a timer and put away your study materials. Sit at a table or desk in a quiet room, imagine yourself at the testing center, and answer questions as quickly and accurately as possible.

Keep repeating timed and closed-book tests on a regular basis until you run out of practice tests or it's time for the actual test. Your mind will be ready for the schedule and stress of test day, and you'll be able to focus on recalling the material you've learned.

Secret Key #4 – Pace Yourself

Once you're fully prepared for the material on the test, your biggest challenge on test day will be managing your time. Just knowing that the clock is ticking can make you panic even if you have plenty of time left. Work on pacing yourself so you can build confidence against the time constraints of the exam. Pacing is a difficult skill to master, especially in a high-pressure environment, so **practice is vital**.

Set time expectations for your pace based on how much time is available. For example, if a section has 60 questions and the time limit is 30 minutes, you know you have to average 30 seconds or less per question in order to answer them all. Although 30 seconds is the hard limit, set 25 seconds per question as your goal, so you reserve extra time to spend on harder questions. When you budget extra time for the harder questions, you no longer have any reason to stress when those questions take longer to answer.

Don't let this time expectation distract you from working through the test at a calm, steady pace, but keep it in mind so you don't spend too much time on any one question. Recognize that taking extra time on one question you don't understand may keep you from answering two that you do understand later in the test. If your time limit for a question is up and you're still not sure of the answer, mark it and move on, and come back to it later if the time and the test format allow. If the testing format doesn't allow you to return to earlier questions, just make an educated guess; then put it out of your mind and move on.

On the easier questions, be careful not to rush. It may seem wise to hurry through them so you have more time for the challenging ones, but it's not worth missing one if you know the concept and just didn't take the time to read the question fully. Work efficiently but make sure you understand the question and have looked at all of the answer choices, since more than one may seem right at first.

Even if you're paying attention to the time, you may find yourself a little behind at some point. You should speed up to get back on track, but do so wisely. Don't panic; just take a few seconds less on each question until you're caught up. Don't guess without thinking, but do look through the answer choices and eliminate any you know are wrong. If you can get down to two choices, it is often worthwhile to guess from those. Once you've chosen an answer, move on and don't dwell on any that you skipped or had to hurry through. If a question was taking too long, chances are it was one of the harder ones, so you weren't as likely to get it right anyway.

On the other hand, if you find yourself getting ahead of schedule, it may be beneficial to slow down a little. The more quickly you work, the more likely you are to make a careless mistake that will affect your score. You've budgeted time for each question, so don't be afraid to spend that time. Practice an efficient but careful pace to get the most out of the time you have.

Secret Key #5 – Have a Plan for Guessing

When you're taking the test, you may find yourself stuck on a question. Some of the answer choices seem better than others, but you don't see the one answer choice that is obviously correct. What do you do?

The scenario described above is very common, yet most test takers have not effectively prepared for it. Developing and practicing a plan for guessing may be one of the single most effective uses of your time as you get ready for the exam.

In developing your plan for guessing, there are three questions to address:

- When should you start the guessing process?
- How should you narrow down the choices?
- Which answer should you choose?

When to Start the Guessing Process

Unless your plan for guessing is to select C every time (which, despite its merits, is not what we recommend), you need to leave yourself enough time to apply your answer elimination strategies. Since you have a limited amount of time for each question, that means that if you're going to give yourself the best shot at guessing correctly, you have to decide quickly whether or not you will guess.

Of course, the best-case scenario is that you don't have to guess at all, so first, see if you can answer the question based on your knowledge of the subject and basic reasoning skills. Focus on the key words in the question and try to jog your memory of related topics. Give yourself a chance to bring the knowledge to mind, but once you realize that you don't have (or you can't access) the knowledge you need to answer the question, it's time to start the guessing process.

It's almost always better to start the guessing process too early than too late. It only takes a few seconds to remember something and answer the question from knowledge. Carefully eliminating wrong answer choices takes longer. Plus, going through the process of eliminating answer choices can actually help jog your memory.

Summary: Start the guessing process as soon as you decide that you can't answer the question based on your knowledge.

How to Narrow Down the Choices

The next chapter in this book (**Test-Taking Strategies**) includes a wide range of strategies for how to approach questions and how to look for answer choices to eliminate. You will definitely want to read those carefully, practice them, and figure out which ones work best for you. Here though, we're going to address a mindset rather than a particular strategy.

Your odds of guessing an answer correctly depend on how many options you are choosing from.

Number of options left	5	4	3	2	1
Odds of guessing correctly	20%	25%	33%	50%	100%

You can see from this chart just how valuable it is to be able to eliminate incorrect answers and make an educated guess, but there are two things that many test takers do that cause them to miss out on the benefits of guessing:

- Accidentally eliminating the correct answer
- Selecting an answer based on an impression

We'll look at the first one here, and the second one in the next section.

To avoid accidentally eliminating the correct answer, we recommend a thought exercise called **the $5 challenge**. In this challenge, you only eliminate an answer choice from contention if you are willing to bet $5 on it being wrong. Why $5? Five dollars is a small but not insignificant amount of money. It's an amount you could afford to lose but wouldn't want to throw away. And while losing $5 once might not hurt too much, doing it twenty times will set you back $100. In the same way, each small decision you make—eliminating a choice here, guessing on a question there—won't by itself impact your score very much, but when you put them all together, they can make a big difference. By holding each answer choice elimination decision to a higher standard, you can reduce the risk of accidentally eliminating the correct answer.

The $5 challenge can also be applied in a positive sense: If you are willing to bet $5 that an answer choice *is* correct, go ahead and mark it as correct.

Summary: Only eliminate an answer choice if you are willing to bet $5 that it is wrong.

Which Answer to Choose

You're taking the test. You've run into a hard question and decided you'll have to guess. You've eliminated all the answer choices you're willing to bet $5 on. Now you have to pick an answer. Why do we even need to talk about this? Why can't you just pick whichever one you feel like when the time comes?

The answer to these questions is that if you don't come into the test with a plan, you'll rely on your impression to select an answer choice, and if you do that, you risk falling into a trap. The test writers know that everyone who takes their test will be guessing on some of the questions, so they intentionally write wrong answer choices to seem plausible. You still have to pick an answer though, and if the wrong answer choices are designed to look right, how can you ever be sure that you're not falling for their trap? The best solution we've found to this dilemma is to take the decision out of your hands entirely. Here is the process we recommend:

Once you've eliminated any choices that you are confident (willing to bet $5) are wrong, select the first remaining choice as your answer.

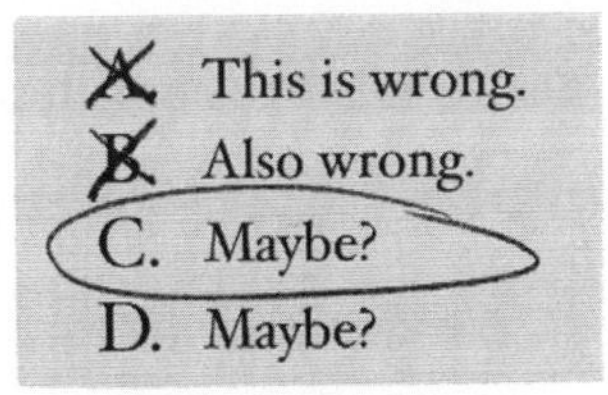

Whether you choose to select the first remaining choice, the second, or the last, the important thing is that you use some preselected standard. Using this approach guarantees that you will not be enticed into selecting an answer choice that looks right, because you are not basing your decision on how the answer choices look.

This is not meant to make you question your knowledge. Instead, it is to help you recognize the difference between your knowledge and your impressions. There's a huge difference between thinking an answer is right because of what you know, and thinking an answer is right because it looks or sounds like it should be right.

Summary: To ensure that your selection is appropriately random, make a predetermined selection from among all answer choices you have not eliminated.

Test-Taking Strategies

This section contains a list of test-taking strategies that you may find helpful as you work through the test. By taking what you know and applying logical thought, you can maximize your chances of answering any question correctly!

It is very important to realize that every question is different and every person is different: no single strategy will work on every question, and no single strategy will work for every person. That's why we've included all of them here, so you can try them out and determine which ones work best for different types of questions and which ones work best for you.

Question Strategies

✓ Read Carefully

Read the question and the answer choices carefully. Don't miss the question because you misread the terms. You have plenty of time to read each question thoroughly and make sure you understand what is being asked. Yet a happy medium must be attained, so don't waste too much time. You must read carefully and efficiently.

✓ Contextual Clues

Look for contextual clues. If the question includes a word you are not familiar with, look at the immediate context for some indication of what the word might mean. Contextual clues can often give you all the information you need to decipher the meaning of an unfamiliar word. Even if you can't determine the meaning, you may be able to narrow down the possibilities enough to make a solid guess at the answer to the question.

✓ Prefixes

If you're having trouble with a word in the question or answer choices, try dissecting it. Take advantage of every clue that the word might include. Prefixes can be a huge help. Usually, they allow you to determine a basic meaning. *Pre-* means before, *post-* means after, *pro-* is positive, *de-* is negative. From prefixes, you can get an idea of the general meaning of the word and try to put it into context.

✓ Hedge Words

Watch out for critical hedge words, such as *likely, may, can, often, almost, mostly, usually, generally, rarely,* and *sometimes.* Question writers insert these hedge phrases to cover every possibility. Often an answer choice will be wrong simply because it leaves no room for exception. Be on guard for answer choices that have definitive words such as *exactly* and *always.*

✓ Switchback Words

Stay alert for *switchbacks.* These are the words and phrases frequently used to alert you to shifts in thought. The most common switchback words are *but, although,* and *however.* Others include *nevertheless, on the other hand, even though, while, in spite of, despite,* and *regardless of.* Switchback words are important to catch because they can change the direction of the question or an answer choice.

✓ Face Value

When in doubt, use common sense. Accept the situation in the problem at face value. Don't read too much into it. These problems will not require you to make wild assumptions. If you have to go beyond creativity and warp time or space in order to have an answer choice fit the question, then you should move on and consider the other answer choices. These are normal problems rooted in reality. The applicable relationship or explanation may not be readily apparent, but it is there for you to figure out. Use your common sense to interpret anything that isn't clear.

Answer Choice Strategies

✓ Answer Selection

The most thorough way to pick an answer choice is to identify and eliminate wrong answers until only one is left, then confirm it is the correct answer. Sometimes an answer choice may immediately seem right, but be careful. The test writers will usually put more than one reasonable answer choice on each question, so take a second to read all of them and make sure that the other choices are not equally obvious. As long as you have time left, it is better to read every answer choice than to pick the first one that looks right without checking the others.

✓ Answer Choice Families

An answer choice family consists of two (in rare cases, three) answer choices that are very similar in construction and cannot all be true at the same time. If you see two answer choices that are direct opposites or parallels, one of them is usually the correct answer. For instance, if one answer choice says that quantity *x* increases and another either says that quantity *x* decreases (opposite) or says that quantity *y* increases (parallel), then those answer choices would fall into the same family. An answer choice that doesn't match the construction of the answer choice family is more likely to be incorrect. Most questions will not have answer choice families, but when they do appear, you should be prepared to recognize them.

✓ Eliminate Answers

Eliminate answer choices as soon as you realize they are wrong, but make sure you consider all possibilities. If you are eliminating answer choices and realize that the last one you are left with is also wrong, don't panic. Start over and consider each choice again. There may be something you missed the first time that you will realize on the second pass.

✓ Avoid Fact Traps

Don't be distracted by an answer choice that is factually true but doesn't answer the question. You are looking for the choice that answers the question. Stay focused on what the question is asking for so you don't accidentally pick an answer that is true but incorrect. Always go back to the question and make sure the answer choice you've selected actually answers the question and is not merely a true statement.

✓ Extreme Statements

In general, you should avoid answers that put forth extreme actions as standard practice or proclaim controversial ideas as established fact. An answer choice that states the "process should be used in certain situations, if..." is much more likely to be correct than one that states the "process should be discontinued completely." The first is a calm rational statement and doesn't even make a definitive, uncompromising stance, using a hedge word *if* to provide wiggle room, whereas the second choice is far more extreme.

✓ Benchmark

As you read through the answer choices and you come across one that seems to answer the question well, mentally select that answer choice. This is not your final answer, but it's the one that will help you evaluate the other answer choices. The one that you selected is your benchmark or standard for judging each of the other answer choices. Every other answer choice must be compared to your benchmark. That choice is correct until proven otherwise by another answer choice beating it. If you find a better answer, then that one becomes your new benchmark. Once you've decided that no other choice answers the question as well as your benchmark, you have your final answer.

✓ PREDICT THE ANSWER

Before you even start looking at the answer choices, it is often best to try to predict the answer. When you come up with the answer on your own, it is easier to avoid distractions and traps because you will know exactly what to look for. The right answer choice is unlikely to be word-for-word what you came up with, but it should be a close match. Even if you are confident that you have the right answer, you should still take the time to read each option before moving on.

General Strategies

✓ TOUGH QUESTIONS

If you are stumped on a problem or it appears too hard or too difficult, don't waste time. Move on! Remember though, if you can quickly check for obviously incorrect answer choices, your chances of guessing correctly are greatly improved. Before you completely give up, at least try to knock out a couple of possible answers. Eliminate what you can and then guess at the remaining answer choices before moving on.

✓ CHECK YOUR WORK

Since you will probably not know every term listed and the answer to every question, it is important that you get credit for the ones that you do know. Don't miss any questions through careless mistakes. If at all possible, try to take a second to look back over your answer selection and make sure you've selected the correct answer choice and haven't made a costly careless mistake (such as marking an answer choice that you didn't mean to mark). This quick double check should more than pay for itself in caught mistakes for the time it costs.

✓ PACE YOURSELF

It's easy to be overwhelmed when you're looking at a page full of questions; your mind is confused and full of random thoughts, and the clock is ticking down faster than you would like. Calm down and maintain the pace that you have set for yourself. Especially as you get down to the last few minutes of the test, don't let the small numbers on the clock make you panic. As long as you are on track by monitoring your pace, you are guaranteed to have time for each question.

✓ DON'T RUSH

It is very easy to make errors when you are in a hurry. Maintaining a fast pace in answering questions is pointless if it makes you miss questions that you would have gotten right otherwise. Test writers like to include distracting information and wrong answers that seem right. Taking a little extra time to avoid careless mistakes can make all the difference in your test score. Find a pace that allows you to be confident in the answers that you select.

✓ KEEP MOVING

Panicking will not help you pass the test, so do your best to stay calm and keep moving. Taking deep breaths and going through the answer elimination steps you practiced can help to break through a stress barrier and keep your pace.

Final Notes

The combination of a solid foundation of content knowledge and the confidence that comes from practicing your plan for applying that knowledge is the key to maximizing your performance on test day. As your foundation of content knowledge is built up and strengthened, you'll find that the strategies included in this chapter become more and more effective in helping you quickly sift through the distractions and traps of the test to isolate the correct answer.

Now that you're preparing to move forward into the test content chapters of this book, be sure to keep your goal in mind. As you read, think about how you will be able to apply this information on the test. If you've already seen sample questions for the test and you have an idea of the question format and style, try to come up with questions of your own that you can answer based on what you're reading. This will give you valuable practice applying your knowledge in the same ways you can expect to on test day.

Good luck and good studying!

Vocabulary and Concepts Basic to the Humanities

Music History and Literature

Characteristics of Music in the Medieval Era

Music of the Middle Ages (~500–1400 AD) was dominated by vocal music that could be separated into two separate genres. **Sacred music** included Gregorian chant and masses, and **secular music** included music for dance and entertainment, such as that of the troubadours and trouvères. **Gregorian chant** had melodies that were free flowing with no distinct meter, melismatic, and largely monophonic, sung by unaccompanied voice or choir. The sacred music of the Middle Ages evolved with the development of organum, an early form of polyphony in which voices were sung in parallel motion. Masses were also an important religious ritual and featured non-imitative polyphony. The most important form of Medieval polyphony was the **motet**, which was introduced in the 13th century and spanned both sacred and secular genres. By the end of the Middle Ages, secular music became the driving force of musical development, and the music of troubadours and trouvères saw drone accompaniment and had regular meter, syncopations, polyphony, and harmony.

Musical Importance of the Mass

As one of the most important services of the Roman Catholic Church, the **mass** was a driving force of musical development in the Medieval and Renaissance eras. **The liturgy of the Ordinary** was most often set to music, and musical advancements were applied to the composition of the mass. By the Renaissance era (~1400–1600 AD), polyphony was common, musical notation had been refined, and complete masses were written by a single composer. The first mass by a known composer was the *Messe de Notre Dame* written by Guillaume de Machaut in the 1360s. As a large-scale form, the mass continued to appear in the oeuvres of many composers, including that of Dufay, Josquin, Palestrina, Haydn, Mozart, Beethoven, Schubert, Weber, Berlioz, Verdi, Wagner, Fauré, and others. Although the genre declined through the 20th century, composers continue to set the mass to new musical settings (Hindemith, Stravinsky, Bernstein, etc.) The Ordinary includes six sections and is outlined as follows: Kyrie, Gloria, Credo, Sanctus, Benedictus, and Agnus Dei.

Medieval Motet vs. Renaissance Motet

The motet was a major musical form of the Medieval and Renaissance periods that emerged from medieval organum and clausulae. The **Medieval motet** featured a tenor line derived from plainchant with one or more upper voices in French or Latin. The tenor vocal line usually had a short, repeated rhythmic pattern, while the upper voices had contrasting, lively melodic lines. The texts of the upper voices were sometimes independent and in a different language from the tenor line. The **Renaissance motet**, in contrast, referred more to a genre of music than to a certain form or structure. By the mid-15th century, the motet was known as a polyphonic setting of any sacred Latin text, not restricted to the liturgy. Composers of the Renaissance introduced imitation, homophony, and four-part harmony to the motet.

Polyphony, Homophony, and Monophony

The terms polyphony, homophony, and monophony all refer to a certain texture of music. **Polyphony** refers to a texture of music in which all voices or parts hold similar musical prominence or interest. This can be thought of as several distinct melodic lines occurring at the same time. The rhythm of each line in polyphonic music moves independently of each other line. **Homophony** also has several voices or parts, but melodic interest is reduced to a single voice or part. All other voices or parts support the main melody as accompaniment and move together in rhythmic likeness. In this way, homophony can be thought of as any form of melody and accompaniment texture. **Monophony** also centers on a single melodic line; however, unlike homophony, it does not have supplemental accompaniment parts. A prime example of monophony is plainchant in which a single line of melody embodies the entire work itself.

Critiques of Baroque Music by Classical Composers

In the **Baroque** era (~1600–1750 AD), music was stylistically ornate and heavily ornamented. During this period, tonality was established, counterpoint was invented, and the size, range, and complexity of orchestrations were expanded. By the end of the Baroque era, music innovations became so complex that a new aesthetic was formed in reaction against the overly embellished Baroque aesthetic. Homophony replaced polyphony, simplicity replaced complexity, and gentler sentiment replaced strong passion. With the prominence of homophony, music of the **Classical** era (~1750–1830 AD) featured a slower harmonic rhythm than the ornate Baroque music, which normally featured a linear bass line. Classical composers emphasized a natural melody above textural complexity and wrote music with a clear phrase and period structure. Instead of keeping a musical piece in one affect as in the Baroque period, Classical composers introduced stylistic contrasts within a piece.

Nationalism

The Nationalist movement was a facet of the Romantic era during the late 19th and early 20th centuries in which music evoked the national or regional character of a place. Composers used folk music in their compositions either as a direct quote or as a framework for the composition of melodies and rhythms that resemble folk music of the area. Nationalistic composers who represented Russia include Glinka, Borodin, Balakirev, Mussorgsky, and Rimsky-Korsakov. Nationalistic composers who represented Czechoslovakia include Smetana, Dvořák, and Janáček. Composers who famously represented Norway and Finland, respectively, are Grieg and Sibelius. Composers who represented England include Elgar, Vaughan Williams, and Holst. Composers who represented Spain include Albéniz, Granados, and de Falla. Composers who represented Hungary include Bartók and Kodály. Nationalistic composers who represented the United States include Ives, Harris, Gershwin, and Copland.

Nineteenth-Century Debate Over Program Music and Absolute Music

In the 19th century, music philosophers debated the value of program music versus absolute music. **Programmatic music**, or music that represented non-musical images or ideas, flourished in the Romantic era with program symphonies, symphonic poems, and character pieces with descriptive titles. Examples of Romantic-period program music include *Don Quixote* by Richard Strauss, *Danse Macabre* by Camille Saint-Saëns, *Symphonie Fantastique* by Hector Berlioz, and *The Sorcerer's Apprentice* by Paul Dukas. **Absolute music** was defined by opponents of program music as instrumental music that existed apart from extra-musical references, able to move audiences solely on the purity of the music itself. Proponents of programmatic music argued that music alone could not express anything and that music needed associations for audiences to fully grasp musical expression. Recent scholars acknowledge that the divide over program music and absolute music is not as distinct as once believed, and is open to interpretation.

Impact of Valved Horns and Trumpets

Before the 19th century, horns had a range limited to the notes of the overtone series and to crooks or hand-stopping techniques that changed the pitch of the instrument. Although the hand-stopping technique added a wider range to the horn, tone and volume were highly variable. The trumpets of the Classical era were more limited than the horns; although they also had a range limited to the notes of the overtone series, hand-stopping techniques could not be used to add a wider range because of the length of the early trumpet. The invention of the **valved horn and keys** for the modern trumpet in 1814 allowed players to play chromatically throughout their entire range. Composers began to incorporate more brass into their orchestral writing and, as a result, brass instruments became essential instruments in any orchestra with leading parts and solos. The orchestral sound of the 19th century increased substantially in power and capacity, and composers such as Wagner, Strauss, Stravinsky, and Mahler became known for their tremendously large orchestrations and vast scope of sound.

Impressionist Movement

The Impressionist movement (~1890–1920 AD) in music was influenced by the synonymous movement in visual arts by painters such as Monet, Cézanne, Degas, Manet, and Renoir, in which subtle brushstrokes obscured any sharp lines to give a general "impression" of a scene without precise details. French composer Claude Debussy (1862–1918) developed a musical equivalent in which sound defied strict harmonic rules and soft instrumental colors focused on constant movement without distinct sectional borders, giving the audience a similar effect as in Impressionist art of a general experience rather than one that draws attention to specific details. Melodies tended to center around a single pitch without much climax, similar to the individual brushstrokes utilized by Impressionist painters of the time. Debussy was a key Impressionist composer; other composers who have worked in the Impressionist aesthetic include Maurice Ravel, Béla Bartók, Olivier Messiaen, György Ligeti, and George Crumb.

Schoenberg

Arnold Schoenberg (1874–1951) was an Austrian theorist and painter, and one of the most influential composers of his time. Schoenberg developed the **12-tone technique** of music in which all 12 pitches of the chromatic scale are treated as equal, rejecting the conventions of traditional tonality. The 12 pitches are ordered into a series that becomes the basic structure for the composition. The pitches can be in any range or duration, but they must be introduced in the composition in that order. Schoenberg's revolutionary system of composition broke away from the traditional tonality of the 20th century and abandoned any hint of a tonal center. The impact of Schoenberg's 12-tone system of composition continued in the music of Milton Babbitt, Pierre Boulez, Charles Wuorinen, Anton Webern, Karlheinz Stockhausen, Alban Berg, Luigi Nono, Roger Sessions, and multiple other composers.

Neoclassical Movement

At the end of the 19th century, Romantic music reached the height of expressive emotionalism with the large-scale works of program music by composers such as Tchaikovsky, Liszt, and Mahler. The beginning of the 20th century brought about **Modernism** and the rejection of tonality by experimental composers such as Schoenberg, Boulez, Berg, and Webern. **Neoclassicism** was a trend of the 20th century that emerged as a reaction to the emotionalism of the late Romantic era and the abandonment of tonality in the early-20th century. Composers of the neoclassical movement sought a return to the order, restraint, clarity, and formal balance of the music of the 18th century. Neoclassical music usually featured restraint, lighter texture, objectivity, a transparent melodic line, and a call to music of the past. Prominent composers of the neoclassical movement include Paul Hindemith, Igor Stravinsky, Richard Strauss, Sergei Prokofiev, Manuel de Falla, and Aaron Copland.

Minimalist Movement

Minimalism began as a compositional movement in the late 1960s, as a reaction to the traditional goal-oriented, narrative, and representational music of the previous centuries. As an extension of experimental music, **minimalist music** often features compositional techniques that emphasize the process of music rather than motion toward a goal. Minimalist composers sought to create music that uses a minimal amount of notes, minimal instruments, and minimal focal points, so that the music could become more a wall of sound than a goal-oriented mission. Minimalist music tends to have a consonant harmony, perpetually repeated patterns or drones, interlocking rhythmic phrases and rhythms, and gradual transformation. In minimalist music, the form tends to be continuous without well-defined separate sections; notes may be added to a repeating pattern slowly so that the resulting effect of the music becomes somewhat hypnotic. Representative minimalist composers include Steve Reich, Terry Riley, Philip Glass, John Adams, and La Monte Young.

Latin Jazz

Latin jazz is a style of jazz that originated in the late 1940s when musicians merged the rhythms and instruments of Afro-Latin music with American jazz music. The two prominent sub-genres of Latin jazz are Afro-Cuban jazz and Afro-Brazilian jazz. **Afro-Cuban jazz** incorporated Cuban rhythms such as the mambo and the habanera with elements of bebop. Afro-Cuban bass lines featured distinctive syncopated rhythms labeled as either a 2–3 clave or 3–2 clave. **Afro-Brazilian jazz** incorporated rhythms of the samba with music of Europe and America. A new style of samba known as bossa nova featured a laid-back singing style, increased textural complexity, and a distinctive rhythmic pattern known as the bossa nova clave. Famous Latin jazz musicians include Mario Bauzá, Luciano Pozo, Machito (Frank Grillo), W. C. Handy, Dizzy Gillespie, Antônio Carlos Jobim, and João Gilberto, among others.

Bossa Nova Movement

The bossa nova movement originated in Rio de Janeiro, Brazil, in the late 1950s and combined elements of the popular Brazilian samba with elements of American jazz. It soon became popular in the United States and then became an international sensation. **Bossa nova** is characterized by a laid-back singing style, complex harmonies, and a distinctive rhythmic pattern known as the **bossa nova clave**. The music of bossa nova often features acoustic guitar as a principal instrument and also includes bass, drums, voice, and piano. The bossa nova rhythm, often notated in duple meter, starts with a downbeat but is otherwise syncopated to give a swaying feeling rather than a strong, measured pulse. Central figures of the bossa nova movement include Antônio Carlos Jobim, João Gilberto, Vinícius de Moraes, Sérgio Mendes, Roberto Menescal, and Nara Leão. Famous tunes include "Chega de Saudade," "Girl from Ipanema," "Desafinado," "Corcovado," "Águas de Março," and "Mas Que Nada."

Blues

Music of the blues originated through African work songs that were brought over to the United States in the 19th and early-20th centuries. The rise of the **blues** occurred approximately around the time of the emancipation of slaves in the US, especially in the Mississippi delta and east Texas. Elements such as the call and response format, the unaccompanied voice, and accompaniment styles all have roots in traditional African music. By the mid-20th century, the blues had a standard 12-bar harmonic progression: I-I-I-I-IV-IV-I-I-V-IV-I-I. The blues also utilizes the **blues scale** that features a lowered third and a dominant seventh, called the "blue notes." Music usually centers on a melancholy emotion, with instrumental and vocal techniques such as moans, growls, and cries to express that emotion. Famous blues musicians include Blind Lemon Jefferson, Charley Patton, Blind Blake, Blind Willie McTell, Lead Belly, Bukka White, Big Bill Broonzy, Muddy Waters, B. B. King, and T-Bone Walker.

Leitmotif

The term leitmotif is used to identify a reoccurring motivic fragment that musically represents some part of a musical drama, usually a person, place, or idea. The **leitmotif** must be clearly recognizable by its melody, harmonic progression, or rhythm. In the context of an opera, the leitmotif becomes a useful tool for composers as a means of character development and the unfolding of the story. In a musical drama, the leitmotif can reinforce the action taking place onstage, as well as recall an event or person from a previous scene. The leitmotif can also be modified through **thematic transformation** and even combined with other leitmotifs to suggest a change in the narrative and the characters' relationships. The term is most often associated with Wagner's later operatic works, although he preferred the terms *Grundthema* and *Hauptmotiv* instead.

Evolution of Harmonic Language

Harmonic language before Wagner (1813–1883) was dominated by the rules of diatonicism and straightforward voice leading. By the middle of the 19th century, composers started to explore ideas of chromaticism and common tone relationships rather than strong root progressions. The arrival of Wagner's *Tristan und Isolde* in 1865 brought a major change to the harmonic language of the past and signaled a new era of modern compositional techniques. In the four-hour opera, chromaticism plays a prominent role in the dissolution of typical harmonic expectation. Now known as the **Tristan chord**, the leitmotif of the main character reveals a functionally ambiguous tritone chord (f-b-d#'-g#'), which, instead of resolving, progresses to another equally chromatic and dissonant tritone chord. Wagner's use of harmonic suspension, full chromaticism, polyphony, and range of colors in *Tristan und Isolde* paved the way to the modern collapse of traditional tonal writing and to the advent of experimental, atonal compositions of the 20th century such as those of Bruckner, Mahler, and Schoenberg.

Organum

Organum is considered to be one of the earliest forms of polyphony and appeared in the Medieval period in the 9th century. **Organum** was based on a cantus firmus and began as improvised voices that duplicated the original melody. Organum types included parallel voices at the octave and parallel voices at the fifth below. Composers adjusted the lines to avoid tritones as necessary. Organum expanded to include contrary and oblique motion, as well as free or florid organum in which the tenor chant held notes and upper voices decorated the tenor with phrases of varying length. In the 12th century, the development of the **discant** in organum moved the compositional techniques further toward polyphony as voices became increasingly complex and independent. By the 13th century, the motet had replaced organum as a major polyphonic genre.

Classic Greek Tragedy

Ancient Greek tragedies hold an important influence on the modern opera and theatre of today. Many of the initial developments of modern opera and theatre were based on this classic form that arose in the 6th century BC. The elements of a classic tragedy include plot, character, thought, diction, melody, and spectacle. In a classic Greek tragedy, the hero often has a goal but encounters limits through human frailty, the gods, or nature, and usually encounters suffering. The characters of a tragedy must show **essential qualities** or morals that remain consistent throughout the plot. **Thought** is often displayed through a Greek tragedy to drive the plot line and to reveal key plot elements. **Diction** must be clear and serve the lines of the tragedy as one of the most important elements of tragedy. **Melody** is subservient to words and should only be used to accessorize the plot. **Spectacle** refers to the setting of the drama and, like melody, should be used as an accessory.

Opera Seria vs. Opera Buffa

By the end of the 17th century, opera as a musical form had been widely accepted. Two genres appeared as the philosophical focus as the new century turned its attention to the Enlightenment. Thinkers and composers of the Enlightenment held that opera should reflect ancient Greek values such as clarity and unity, structure, and propriety; the **opera seria** that arose during this time focused on tragic and serious subjects that were historical rather than mythical. The structure, number of singers, and plot line were organized so that the action usually took place in three acts with alternating arias and recitatives, and the number of characters usually numbered six or seven, with two to four main characters. **Opera buffa**, in contrast, focused on humorous and light-hearted elements. There was often a wide range of characters, and spoken dialogue replaced recitative. The form was less structured and often featured prominent orchestral and instrumental parts. Music tended to be faster and helped portray comic elements of the plot line, such as laughter and sneezing.

Authentic Musical Modes

The authentic musical modes are commonly used in modern times and have origins in the Medieval musical tradition as well as the Greek musical tradition. The most commonly known authentic musical modes are Ionian, Dorian, Phrygian, Lydian, Mixolydian, Aeolian, and Locrian. The **Ionian** mode is also known as the major scale in modern musical theory. **Dorian** is similar to the natural minor scale, but has a raised sixth scale degree. **Phrygian** is similar to the natural minor scale, but has a lowered second scale degree. **Lydian** is similar to the major scale, but has a raised fourth scale degree. **Mixolydian** is similar to the major scale, but has a lowered seventh scale degree. **Aeolian** is also known as the natural minor scale in modern musical theory. **Locrian** is similar to the natural minor scale, but has a lowered second scale degree and a lowered fifth scale degree.

Classical Sonata Form

The sonata form has been a key compositional structure since the Classical era in the mid- to late-18th century. Usually referring to a convention within a single movement of a sonata or symphony, the **sonata form** features three main sections: the exposition, development, and recapitulation. The melodic and harmonic themes of the movement are usually introduced in the **exposition**. The initial first subject is introduced in the tonic key, while the second subject is usually in the dominant or relative minor key. In a typical sonata form, a bridge or a short transition connects the first and second subjects. In the **development** section, the thematic material from the exposition is altered, modified, and transformed through mood, key, and modulations. The development section of a sonata form introduces tension that demands resolution; tension builds until the beginning of the **recapitulation**, in which tonal balance is reinstated with a shortened version of the initial subject and the second subject, this time in the tonic key instead of the dominant or relative minor. A coda may round out the sonata at the end.

Classical Symphonic Form

The symphony was a major compositional form in the Classical era (~1750–1820 AD) and refers to a large musical work usually for orchestra or another combination of instruments in four movements. The **classical symphonic form** has a fast first movement, a slow second movement, a dance form in the third movement, and a fast fourth movement. The first movement is usually in sonata allegro form, which contains an exposition, development, and recapitulation. The second slow movement is usually in a gentle, lyrical ABA pattern or a theme and variations. The third movement is typically in a dance form such as the Minuet and Trio or the Scherzo. The fourth movement is typically in Rondo form, or Sonata Rondo form, in which a principal theme in the tonic key alternates with new episodes: ABACADA...etc.

Operas vs. Oratorios

Opera began as an art form in the late-16th century and consisted of a staged dramatic work with singers and orchestra. **Oratorios** began as an art form in the 17th century and became popular in part because of the success of opera and because of religious bans on secular operas during Lent. Both opera and oratorio are large-scale musical works that feature dramatic, musical, and narrative elements. The two forms both utilize solo vocalists, chorus, ensembles, and orchestras. However, opera is usually theatrically staged, while oratorio is not. Also, oratorio usually centers on a religious or ethical subject, while opera usually centers on historical, mythological, or other secular plot lines. Famous operas include Jacopo Peri's *Dafne*, Gioachino Rossini's *Barber of Seville*, Giacomo Puccini's *Madame Butterfly*, W.A. Mozart's *The Marriage of Figaro*, Giuseppe Verdi's *La Traviata*, and Georges Bizet's *Carmen*. Famous oratorios include G.F. Handel's *Messiah*, Joseph Haydn's *Creation*, and Felix Mendelssohn's *Elijah*.

Waltz Form

The waltz is a dance form that has been popular since the late-18th century and features triple meter in a lively tempo. The term literally means "to turn about," and musical aspects of the **waltz** help dancers feel the refined and fluid motion of the turn. In waltz time, emphasis is on the downbeat, while the other two beats create a sense of floating, as on the dance floor. Early forms of the waltz featured two simple repeated phrases of about eight measures. As the dance evolved, the waltz became longer in form and more complex, with introductory material as well as a coda. The ballroom dance achieved popularity across all of Europe and reached its height of fashion with the **Viennese waltz**. Representative composers of the Viennese waltz include Joseph Lanner, Johann Strauss, Franz Schubert, Frédéric Chopin, Franz Liszt, Johannes Brahms, and Pyotr Tchaikovsky.

Changes Giving Rise to the Renaissance Movement

The period of 1400–1600 AD was a time of major change not only in Western musical history, but also in Western history in general. The 1400s marked the end of the Hundred Years' War, the fall of the

Byzantine Empire, and the end of the Great Schism. During the **Renaissance**, religious conflicts emerged through the Reformation, European colonialism expanded, and a middle class grew in many European nations. As a result of the Ottoman Turks' victory in 1453, displaced Byzantine scholars brought ancient Greek writings with them to other European countries, and the Western world had access to the plays and histories of ancient Greece for the first time. Renaissance art featured classical Greek and Roman ideals of humanism, clarity, and clean form. As a result, music of the Renaissance featured Greek modes, clarity of vocal lines, harmonic consonance, imitative counterpoint, and expressivity. The **printing press** was also invented during this time around 1440, so music became widely available to the expanding middle class.

Baroque Music

Music of the Baroque era (~1600–1750 AD), was influenced by the rise of rationalism in the philosophy of the time. Composers sought to portray emotions through objectivity rather than subjectivity, and the expression of any one piece or movement was limited to a single affect. Thoroughbass was prominent during the Baroque era, and a Baroque ensemble would typically read music and improvise on the figured bass, also known as continuo. **Ornamentation** was used heavily in the Baroque period and consisted of embellished notes of a musical line. These included trills, mordents, and grace notes that were rarely written out but instead were improvised by the performers. Famous composers of the Baroque era include Claudio Monteverdi, Girolamo Frescobaldi, Arcangelo Corelli, Antonio Vivaldi, Domenico Scarlatti, François Couperin, Jean-Philippe Rameau, Georg Philipp Telemann, G.F. Handel, J.S. Bach, and Henry Purcell.

Influence of African Song and Dance on Latin American Music

The historically large African population found in the Caribbean region near South America has had a substantial influence on the development of Latin American music. Common features of African music include call and response singing, repeated and improvised musical figures, polyrhythm, and the use of African instruments such as congas, rattles, thumb pianos, claves, and drum ensembles. **Calypso** music, originally developed in Trinidad in the early 19th century, is a popular song and dance form in the Caribbean. Typically played with a steel drum band, calypso music is witty, lively, and humorous. The **rumba**, originating in the late 19th century, is another African song and dance form now popular in Cuba that uses conga drums and sticks. The rumba has a three-part form with fast polyrhythms, and includes improvised verses and repetitive call and response sections. The **merengue**, becoming prominent in both the Dominican Republic and Haiti in the middle of the 19th century, is a popular song and dance style in a swift duple meter. Instruments with some African influences include the double-headed tambora drum and the metal guayo scraper.

Pre-Columbian Indigenous Musical Culture of South America

Most of the Pre-Columbian indigenous musical culture of South America studied today is drawn from the Inca of Peru and the Aztecs of central Mexico. The Spanish conquerors of the 16th century recorded the role of music in these highly developed civilizations. The Inca and Aztecs produced public ceremonies, professional musicians, and musician-specific educational institutions. Aztec and Inca rulers employed musicians who were responsible for new compositions and performances of large repertoires. Standards of performance were held high, and a mistake in a ceremonial performance or dance could mean death. Since no evidence has been found of a Pre-Columbian musical notation, little is known about the actual sound and style of their music. However, evidence from Aztec and Inca sites reveals instruments such as the huehuetl and teponaztli types of drums, gourd rattles, flutes and panpipes, clay jingles, wood and conch shell trumpets, bone rasps, and ocarinas.

Mambo

The mambo is a song and dance genre of music that stems from the Afro-Cuban movement of the 1940s. The form developed in Cuba with influences from Mexico and the USA, as well as those from European dances and African rhythms. The genre soon became popular in Latin America and crossed over to the

United States, where the mambo dance became a ballroom staple, especially in New York City. **Mambo** is performed by an ensemble that usually consists of double bass, bongo, tumbadora, trumpets, guitar, and voices. The mambo rhythms are moderate to fast and feature distinctive riffs for the rhythm section and brass instruments. Cowbells often play strong syncopations over the second beat in a mambo ostinato, while the conga drum varies struck tones through unaccented strokes, strongly accented strokes, and open tones.

Early Broadway Songwriters and American Musical Theater

The first Broadway songwriters of the 1920s included Irving Berlin, Jerome Kern, the Gershwins, Harold Arlen, Oscar Hammerstein, Richard Rodgers, and Cole Porter. American musical theater of the early 20th century was intricately tied to the New York music industry called **Tin Pan Alley**, a geographical location where musicians and composers came together to create popular new songs for the working class as a reaction against upper-class parlor music. The style borrowed heavily from the jazz scene as well as African-American sounds and themes. The success of Tin Pan Alley songs depended on large-scale production and stage shows on Broadway, and the first Broadway shows were loosely related singing, dancing, and vaudeville music from Tin Pan Alley. Historians mark ***Show Boat*** (1927) by Kern and Hammerstein as the first full-fledged Broadway musical with a complete beginning-to-end plot.

Review Video: Musicals vs Plays
Visit mometrix.com/academy and enter code: 537548

Appalachian Music

Appalachian music refers to the folk traditions of the Eastern US, specifically the Appalachian mountain range. The music is heavily influenced by the Irish, Scottish, and English emigrants of the 18th century and features musical traditions such as English and Scottish ballads, dance tunes, and fiddle songs. African-American musical traditions also contributed to the development of **Appalachian music**, and conventional aspects of the genre, such as the banjo, strong rhythmic drive, harmonic blue notes, and group singing, all originate from African-American slaves of the time. Appalachian music features heavy ornamentation, improvisation, rhythmic and melodic focus, and an upbeat tempo. Typical instruments used in the genre include the banjo, mandolin, guitar, autoharp, American fiddle, fretted dulcimer, dobro, and dulcimer.

Early Jazz Music

Early jazz music originated from a wide variety of cultural, social, and instrumental influences from the 1890s through the 1910s. **New Orleans jazz** was one of the earliest forms of jazz music and borrowed from the music of black and creole musicians; it featured frequent interplay between instruments, improvisations, and syncopated march rhythms. Early jazz music, as well as blues music, was heavily influenced by the black church through improvisation, storytelling, call and response, vocal inflections, and the blues progression. Early jazz music also borrowed features of American marching band music and ragtime, such as strong stride rhythms and multi-thematic material. Pianistic harmonies of composers such as Debussy and Ravel also contributed to early jazz music, and jazz composers also incorporated the claves and syncopations of Latin song and dance forms.

Waltz vs. Mazurka

Both the waltz and the mazurka were important European dances of the Romantic era and became popular compositional forms in the 1800s. The waltz originated in southern Germany and Austria in the 13th century, while the **mazurka** originated in the province of Mazovia in Poland in the 16th century. Both dances feature triple time; however, the waltz places emphasis on the downbeat while the mazurka places emphasis on either the second or third beats. Both dances usually consisted of two or four repeated eight-measure sections; however, the waltz eventually evolved to become a longer complex work within art music and included an introduction as well as a coda. The waltz usually held a faster tempo with an elegant style, but stylistic variation among mazurkas was common. **Obertas** were livelier and more jovial versions; **kujawiak** were slower and more melancholic forms of the mazurka, while the conventional mazurka typically featured an intense, militant aesthetic.

Importance of Arab Culture in the Development of North African Music

The region of North Africa received considerable cultural influence from the bordering Arabic countries, and the music of North Africa reflects that cultural diversity. The North African region that includes present-day Morocco, Libya, Tunisia, and Algeria is also known by the Arabic term **Maghreb** ("west"). Although Egypt is geographically included on the African continent, it holds its own unique cultural, musical, and sociopolitical place within North Africa. Arabic-Islamists ruled the Maghreb from approximately the 7th century to the 16th century. Beginning in the eleventh century, Jewish and Muslim refugees from the al-Andalus region of the Iberian Peninsula brought with them the Arab-Andalusian music traditions that originated in Baghdad. Elements of Arabic influence in North African music include the Quranic chant, poetry/harp/lute playing, and instruments such as the gimbri, drums, and metal castanets.

West African Musical Traditions

West Africa holds several local musical traditions such as those used in praise singing, various ceremonies, work activities, and national identities. Historically, court musicians were responsible for continuing the **oral tradition** through singing and performing several instruments such as the lute, long trumpet, fiddle, and drum. Drum ensembles in south Ghana frequently use bell patterns, but those in Senegal, Niger, and other parts of Ghana use the talking drum, one of the oldest instruments in West Africa, dating back to the 7th century. Music plays an important role in birth, adulthood initiations, marriages, and death through singing, drumming, and dancing. During ceremonies, professional musicians perform special music to induce trance, possession, or direct communication with spirits. **Praise singing** emerged in the 20th century through the Ghanaian musical genre called highlife, which incorporates guitar playing with traditional Akan music.

Djembe

The djembe is a rope-tuned, skin-covered drum dating back to the Mali Empire around 1230 AD that can produce a variety of pitches through different hand-striking techniques and drum positions. Typically made of hollowed-out wood, the **djembe** yields a large sound relative to its size and has been used for speech-like communication. Up until the 1950s, the djembe was only known in its local West African ethnic groups, but it has since become popular in Western culture as well. In a traditional African ensemble, multiple drums are used, including a lead djembe and other dunun. Drummers repeat various rhythmic figures, resulting in polyrhythms, while the lead djembe accentuates dancers' movements and improvises over the rest of the drumming ensemble. Musicians and singers typically form a circle with the dancers on the inside.

Use of Dialogue in African Musical Form and Rhythm

Dialogue, also known as call and response, is an important and unique feature of African musical expression. Within musical aesthetics, **dialogue** occurs when a musical line "responds" to a previous musical line; this response can come from a different musician, instrument, group, or register within a solo performer. A vocal or instrumental leader might make a call, and another musician or group of musicians might respond with a musical interjection so that phrases are exchanged between the two groups. Solo performers can also have a musical dialogue through musical or extra-musical interjections such as whistles, percussive sounds, or other alternating musical phrases. The call and response form has been an influential African musical element that can be seen in the genres of blues, jazz, hip-hop, rock, and gospel.

Traditional African Music

Although the continent of Africa holds a great variety of musical expressions, traditions, and instruments among its different regions, certain musical elements remain uniquely African. The **call and response**

form that has so heavily influenced other modern musical genres has been a central feature of African music for centuries. Also distinctive is the use of polyrhythms, syncopation, and offbeat phrasing in rhythmic patterns of the area. Much of African music uses a **cyclic form** in which various phrases with a set number of beats can be continued as long as the performers want; musicians can begin at any part of the cycle and frequently improvise over the form. Instruments that jingle, buzz, or rattle are also popular in African cultures; examples include the mbira, the dagbamba, and xylophones, lutes, and harps that have been manipulated to buzz, jingle, or rattle when played.

Kabuki

Kabuki is a Japanese theater form stemming from the Edo period of the 1600s that was originally performed by females, but is now performed by males as well. Kesho, the kabuki makeup, is a hallmark of the art form in which a white Oshiroi base is decorated with boldly colored kumadori to produce exaggerated and dramatic masks. There are three types of kabuki: **jidaimono** are historical plays; **sewamono** are domestic theater dramas; and **shosagoto** are dance pieces. The form of a kabuki play generally contains four parts: the first part called the deha includes two sections that introduce the mood and the characters (oki and michiyuki). The second part called the chuha includes two sections that build the plot emotionally and climactically (kudoki and monogatari). The third part called the odoriji is a dance component. The fourth part called the iriha includes both the musical finale and the end of the plot (chirashi and dangire).

Middle Eastern Maqam System of Melodic Organization

The maqam system of melodic organization used in Middle Eastern music most resembles the Western mode but is distinctively confined to the lower tetrachord. There are more than 30 different maqamat, and each defines the melodic contour, pitches, and hierarchical development of the scale. The Middle Eastern maqam, which came into use in the 9th century, is not even-tempered as in Western music, as fifth notes are tuned based on the third harmonic; additionally, each of the remaining notes may be tuned differently depending on which maqam is being used. Scalar intervals may include approximations of quartertones, semitones, and even microtones. Musicians frequently compose and improvise over a single maqam but may also modulate to others before returning. Since the nature of the Middle Eastern maqam contains numerous subtle microtonal variations, music of the region is mostly melodic and is rarely ever harmonic.

Traditional Chinese Musical Instruments

The **pipa** is a pear-shaped Chinese plucked lute traditionally made with silk thread that has four strings and a bent neck. The pipa has been an important and popular instrument of Chinese culture since the 7th century and is often played as a solo instrument in performance. The standard tuning for the pipa, A-d-c-a, allows the full chromatic scale to be played. The **erhu** is another traditional Chinese lute often featured as a solo instrument and has two strings with a bow that sits in between the strings. The traditional instrument is typically made with snakeskin on the sound box and horsehair for the bow. The **yangqin** is a trapezoidal, hammered dulcimer that is often played solo as well as in ensembles. The **dizi** is a transverse flute that plays an important role in Chinese folk, operatic, and orchestral music. The instrument includes a special hole in addition to the blowing and finger holes that, when applied, gives the resulting sounds a nasal and buzzing quality.

Australian Aboriginal Music

Australian Aboriginal Musical Instruments

Australian Aboriginal musical instruments include the didgeridoo, the bull-roarer, and the gum leaf. The **didgeridoo**, most well-known of the Aboriginal instruments, has been used for at least 1500 years and consists of a simple wooden tube that is slightly flared at the end. Didgeridoo musicians buzz their lips similarly to trumpet players but without a mouthpiece. The sound produced by the didgeridoo is likened to a low-pitched drone and is often used to accompany songs or traditional stories. The **bull-roarer** consists of a simple wooden slat connected to the end of a length of cord. Sound is produced when the cord is wound and the bull-roarer is whirled in a circular motion. The aerodynamics of this instrument creates a pulsing, low-pitched roar. The **gum leaf** is a more primitive Aboriginal instrument, yet still plays an important role in the culture and tradition of native Australians. Musicians use the leaf of the Eucalyptus tree, held taut against the lip, as a simple wind valve for the mouth. Skilled players can easily play tunes using the same techniques as in whistling.

Role of Music in Australian Aboriginal Culture

Music played a key role in Australian Aboriginal culture through storytelling, preserving history, and leading ceremonies. Since there was no formal system of writing, the Aborigines held a strong **oral tradition**; records were passed down through generations via song and dance. The Aborigines believed that all music comes from the spiritual realm, and new songs were discovered through visions and dreams. Music played an integral role in Aboriginal daily life, and children were encouraged at an early age to sing and dance while doing everyday tasks. The Aborigines had songs that recorded family histories, geographies of the land, rules, and customs. The Aborigines also had secular gossip songs about controversies and relationships. Ceremonial music played an important role in the various spiritual ceremonies, whether to invoke ancestral beings or to purify items of the deceased.

Polynesian Nose Flute

The **nose flute** is a widely important wind instrument throughout the Pacific, except for Australia and New Zealand. Commonly made out of bamboo, the nose flute is played through a single nostril, while the other nostril is held shut. Since the nose flute produces a soft and gentle sound, it played an important role in many Polynesian musical traditions. The nose flute was popular during courtship and lovemaking; the timbre and tone of the nose flute had an enticing sound, and as a quiet instrument, encouraged intimacy and privacy for current and prospective lovers. In Tonga, the nose flute was also used as a respectful way to gently awaken the chief of a tribe. Some cultures believed that nose flutes were also instruments that could evoke magical and spiritual qualities.

Contributions of Women to Music Composition

While most of the historical record is made up of male composers, women have always had a place in composition throughout history. Below is a brief record of female composers throughout the ages.

- **Hildegard von Bingen (1098–1179)** - 12th century German abbess, composer, and writer.
- **Fanny Mendelssohn (1805–1847)** - Early 19th century composer, writing many of her works under the name of her brother, Felix Mendelssohn.
- **Clara Schumann (1819–1896)** - 19th century composer and pianist, known for influencing Romantic music with her piano compositions.
- **Amy Beach (1867–1944)** - Late 19th and early 20th century composer.
- **Lili Boulanger (1893–1918)** - Early 20th century French composer known for choral and orchestral works. She was the first female to win the Prix de Rome, a major scholarship by the French government, enabling artists to travel to Rome to study.
- **Florence Price (1887–1953)** - Early to mid-20th century African-American composer. She was the first black woman to have her work performed by a major US orchestra (Chicago Symphony Orchestra, 1933).
- **Ma Rainey (1886–1939)** - Early 20th century blues singer.
- **Bessie Smith (1894–1937)** - Blues singer primarily active in the 1920s and 1930s.
- **Sister Rosetta Tharpe (1915–1973)** - Gospel and blues musician in the 1930s to the 1960s. Her work went on to heavily influence developing rock and roll music.
- **Astrud Gilberto (1940–2023)** - Brazilian Bossa Nova singer and songwriter popular in the 1960s.

Costumes and Makeup

Costume Designing

The costume designer's role is very important in helping to achieve the director's vision. The costumes should contribute to the tone and style of a production and the time period in which the play is set must be taken into account. It is important to consider the many facets of a character's personality and lifestyle, including their job and social status. The costumes also serve to differentiate or unify certain characters. For example, a play in which the characters are divided between servants and the aristocracy should involve two distinct costuming groups. Costumes must also be practical for the actors, allowing them to move freely and change quickly. It is important for costume designers to consult with the director in order to ensure that the costume designs will be consistent with the theme of the production.

Functions of Costumes in Theatrical Productions

Costumes serve many functions in a production, including the formation of a character, clarity of time and place, and the creation of an immersive environment. Costume pieces come together to create a visual for the actors and the audience. Many actors say they can't fully be in character until their costume is on. Part of the rationale for this is that the costumes help create the setting of the show, and may make the transition into a role smoother. Costuming provides clarity for the time and place of the show, because the visuals are already there rather than having to be imagined. For example, if a show is set in 1920, one could imagine a setting fairly well due to pop culture depictions. However, a show set in 1750 might be a bit more challenging to accurately imagine. Costuming can help take the guesswork out and provide concrete details for the audience and actors.

Construction Techniques for Creating Costumes

Prior to beginning costume construction, it is critical to fully understand the costume needs of the project. This will first begin by understanding the setting of the production. Period pieces will likely require more effort in costume sourcing than productions set in the current time-period. The costume designer should then thoroughly read the script and take note of costume needs. For example, if a scene requires an actor to remove an article of clothing, such as a coat or gloves, the designer will need to ensure these pieces are part of the costume design. Following the script read, measurements need to be taken of the actors to ensure costume pieces will fit. With all the aforementioned information, the designer can begin plotting costumes. This includes sketching costumes, creating vision boards, and obtaining sample pieces. Once a final vision has been established, the designer will begin to make, buy, or rent costume pieces. These decisions are typically made based on cost and availability. For modern productions, it is usually easiest to purchase most pieces while productions set in different eras will likely require more pieces be made. For elaborate or expensive articles of clothing, renting is a more cost and time effective option than buying or making.

Obtaining Costumes

Costumes are obtained in four main ways: buying new costume pieces, renting from a store or neighboring company, constructing pieces, or thrifting pieces. Buying new costume pieces is often the easiest, but most expensive, method. Teachers who choose this route can get appropriate measurements from their cast members and purchase clothes that exactly fit these measurements. Sometimes stores carry rentable costumes, and while this may be cheaper than buying new, it may be harder to find exactly what teachers are looking for.

1. On occasion, a neighboring school or company might have a costume shop they are willing to rent from, but this is far from a sure solution.
2. Constructing costume pieces is a creative solution, but one that takes a lot of time and energy. For this option to work, teachers must have seamstress and perhaps even millinery experience, or they must be willing to learn.

3. Teachers that have a section of Technical Theatre students may be able to teach their students some basic sewing skills to help shoulder the burden, but this is also not a perfect solution.
4. The final strategy for sourcing costumes is thrifting. This can be accomplished by going to local garage sales, secondhand clothing shops, thrift stores, or even using social media to post what a teacher is in need of to see if any friends or colleagues have something similar in their closets.

Most programs use some combination of the four of these techniques.

Types of Stage Makeup

There are many types of stage makeup, but they can be broken down into the following groups: alcohol-based, cream-based, powder-based, wax-based, and water-based. The cost and ease of use vary by type. Alcohol-based makeup must be activated with 99% alcohol, and is formulated to be long-lasting. Cream-based makeup, also known as "grease-paint," is typically oil-based and is very long lasting. This type of makeup is frequently packaged in stick form, and must be set with powder in order to stay on under hot lights. Powder-based makeup, also known as "cake" or "pancake" makeup, can be applied wet or dry, and is typically full-coverage. Wax-based makeup is buildable, and hypoallergenic. Water-based makeup must be activated with water, and is applied to the skin much like watercolor paint.

Suggesting Character and Communicating the Concept of the Production

Stage makeup is intended to combat the effects of the harsh stage lighting and distance from the stage for audience members, but must also be tailored to each individual actor or actress. When applying **stage makeup**, teachers must keep in mind what characteristics should be accentuated based on the role the student is playing. For example, if a character is a female villain, the teacher might choose to apply darker eyeshadow, a darker shade of lipstick, and more accentuated cheekbones. For a male villain, darker eyeliner, shadowy contouring, and a dark brown lip would be appropriate.

Techniques Used in Costume Construction

Constructing a costume will require a variety of skills that vary in difficulty, the most common being sewing. Sewing may be completed by hand or machine. There are several different types of stitches used in sewing to meet different needs. The most common is the **running stitch** in which two pieces of fabric are joined by the thread passing between them. When constructing a garment from scratch, the designer will select a fabric that meets their needs based on stretch and texture, the drape of the fabric, durability, and care requirements. The designer will also have to consider fastener needs. **Fasteners** include items like buttons, hooks and eyes, snaps, buckles, magnets, and pins that join parts of clothing. The type of fastener used will be determined by the way that pieces will be used. If it is an article that requires quick removal, the designer should go with an easy-to-use fastener like magnets or snaps over buttons or hooks and eyes. **Care** for costumes after they are worn and between uses will vary based on the delicacy of the item and fabric as well as the soil level of the individual articles. Delicate or heavily soiled pieces may need professional cleaning while other items can be washed in a standard washing machine.

Purpose of Cutting and Dying Fabric

Designing costumes from scratch requires a designer to select fabrics that meet their needs. In almost all cases, the fabric will need to be cut and in many it will require dying. When using existing articles of clothing, it may be necessary to alter the clothing to fit an actor or dye it to fit the needs of the production. A costume designer will use **fabric shears**, sharp scissors intended for cutting fabrics, as well as a **fabric cutter**, a rotary blade on a handle, for cutting fabric. When using those tools to cut pieces with a pattern, a designer may also use **textile weights** which help ensure there is no movement of the fabric or pattern. When dying fabrics, there are two general choices for the type of dye used: natural or synthetic. As the names suggest, **natural dyes** are made from natural resources like plants and minerals while **synthetic dyes** are made of chemicals. Both dyes work by saturating the fabric and creating a bond between the molecules in the dye and the fibers in the fabric.

PRINCIPLES OF MAKEUP APPLICATION WHEN UTILIZING SIMPLE PROSTHETICS

The use of simple **prosthetics** such as bald caps, false noses, and ear tips is common in stage productions. Prior to applying prosthetics teachers should check the dates on all of their products to ensure they are still usable. Teachers should ensure that none of their students are allergic to latex. If a latex allergy is present, the severity of the allergy should be confirmed with parents. Latex alternatives include white glue, makeup wax, and silicon rubber. Silicon rubber is very difficult to work with, so the teacher should practice before attempting with a student. Teachers should ensure that they have plenty of gloves, spirit gum, non-latex sponges, makeup in the skin tones of all students, cotton balls, applicators, and makeup wipes. Students must be taught about appropriate removal methods so they don't over-exfoliate their skin. After use, reusable prosthetic pieces should be washed in warm soapy water, carefully dried, and stored away from extreme temperatures.

SAFE USE AND CARE OF COSTUMES AND MAKEUP

All costumes should be properly laundered after each show, and should comfortably fit the student. If a costume becomes ill-fitting for any reason, it should be altered or replaced. It's important to check hem length, as well as how shoes are fitting. Depending on the age of the student, their shoe size may change fairly rapidly. Any student, cast member, or adult applying makeup needs to be trained in infection control procedures. Appropriate application materials (single use sponges, wands, foam applicators, etc.) must be provided and sanitized (makeup brushes for powders, implements such as tweezers, etc.) when necessary. All makeup should be selected by the teacher, as some makeup materials contain dangerous chemicals and additives. Students should not share makeup with one another, or use their personal makeup from home.

CREATING THEATRICAL ENVIRONMENT WITH COSTUME SELECTION AND MAKEUP

Costumes and makeup work together to create theatrical environments, particularly by influencing perception. The way a person dresses in real life causes them to be perceived in a certain way, and the same is true on the stage. Since audience members and fellow actors are interacting with the show in a visual way, the way things look influences the way they feel. For example, a character dressed simply with a clean appearance is likely to be more trustworthy than a character dressed in dirty or unkempt clothing with a grungy appearance. Each individual's costume and makeup comes together to form a general impression of the show, including setting, that creates an immersive environment.

Stages and Set Design

STAGES

Most simply, a stage is the space where a dramatic production takes place. There are currently three major types of stages in use:

1. Theatre in the round or the arena stage allows the audience to surround the stage, which provides a much different dramatic experience for both players and audiences alike. Originally, this form of stage was used in classical theatre in Greece and Rome, and is widely used today in smaller experimental theaters around the world.
2. The apron or thrust stage seats audiences on the sides of a platform. Less commonly used today, Shakespeare's Globe Theatre was an early form of the apron stage.
3. The most common stage in current use is the proscenium stage where the audience sits in front of a stage framed by the acting space. This form is very common in drama, opera, and musical presentations.

The type of stage used affects the action of the dramatic work, and each offers a unique experience to the audience.

STAGE AREAS:

↔BACKSTAGE AREA↔

Stage Right	Up Stage Center	Stage Left
Center Stage Right	Center Stage	Center Stage Left
Down Stage Right	Down Stage Center	Down Stage Left

↔AUDIENCE SEATING↔

SET DESIGN

TOOLS FOR MODELING

Modern set designers are able to utilize a variety of modeling software to create set designs and layouts, but design software can be costly and difficult to learn. More primitive methods that are still very common include renderings. A rendering is a free-hand drawing of a set based on the first impressions of the designer or director. The renderings rarely ever represent a complete idea and are changed throughout preproduction. Designers may also create a set using a ground plan, which is a drawing of the set design from above the stage looking directly down. This allows the designer to gauge the space between items on the stage. Set designers may also use three-dimensional models and thumbnail sketches. Scale drawings of the set are called elevations and are commonly used in set design.

MISE-EN-SCENE

Mise-en-scene is a French term that translates as "put in the scene." The term refers to everything that is placed upon a stage to be filmed or shown as part of a performance. The term can refer to actors, scenery, lighting and costumes. It can refer to the manner in which the performance space is utilized or to the movements of the actors in relation to the scenery. It is a very all-encompassing term. Scholars agree that the term can take on various meanings and some feel that mise-en-scene is better defined as the emotional tone of a film.

TERMS RELATING TO THE THEATER, STAGE, AND AUDIENCE

- The **acting area** is the space on a stage or in another performance space in which an actor can move while remaining in full view of the audience.
- **Apron**: the section of a stage that projects into the auditorium.
- **Black box**: a studio theatre, usually surrounded by black curtains, in which the audience and actors share space.
- **Curtain line**: either the imaginary line across the stage where the curtain would be if it were closed or to the final spoken line in a play.
- **Dark**: term used when referring to a venue that has been closed either permanently or temporarily between productions.
- **FOH**: front of house.
- **Forestage**: part of a stage that projects outward into the auditorium.

- **Found space**: a theatre space suitable for performances but not originally designed to be a theatre.
- **House**: can refer to the theatre auditorium or to the audience in the theatre.
- **House manager**: member of the theatre staff who is responsible for ensuring the health and safety of audience members during a performance.
- **In the round**: a theatre layout in which the acting stage is entirely encircled by audience seating.
- **Opening the house**: when stage management alerts the FOH staff that the stage is set and the audience can begin taking their seats.
- **Papering the house**: a marketing technique in which tickets are given away to make a show seem to be selling better than it actually is.
- **Pass door**: door that is located in the wall of the proscenium arch, which acts as a passage between the auditorium and stage.
- **Passarelle**: walkway that allows actors to get close to audience via a path beyond the proscenium arch into the orchestra pit.
- **Pit**: refers to the area of a theatre in which the orchestra is seated.
- **Pit net**: net placed over the pit area of the theatre to prevent actors and objects from falling into the area where the orchestra is be located.
- **Platform stage**: usually refers to an acting stage that is lifted from the floor in a space that was not created as a theatre.
- **Promenade**: a theatrical arrangement in which the audience moves around the acting area to see the performance from multiple locations.
- **Prompt**: side-generally refers to the left side of the stage or whichever side the prompt corner is located.
- **Proscenium arch**: refers to the frame through which the audience sees a performance; usually the wall opening between the stage and auditorium.
- **Raked auditorium**: refers to audience seating that is arranged in a forward sloping manner.
- **Raked stage**: refers to a stage that slopes upwards towards the upstage or back end.
- **Receiving house**: venue that hosts incoming touring companies.
- **Scene shop**: section of the theatre where technicians and designers construct scenery.
- **Sightlines**: lines that are drawn on plans and diagrams to identify the areas of the stage that are visible to the extreme seating areas of the audience.
- **Stage door keeper**: a member of the theatrical crew, positioned inside the stage door whose role is to know each actor and member of the technical staff, know fire safety procedures for the theatre, greet visitors and press, and pass messages between any parties.
- **Stalls**: refers to the audience's seating that is just below stage level.
- **Thrust**: refers to a stage that reaches forward into the auditorium and has audience seating on at least two sides; also called a theatre in the round.
- **Tormentors**: screens or curtains that are usually set up at right angles to the proscenium arch to keep the audience from seeing activity occurring off-stage.
- **Traverse**: theatre set-up in which the audience is seated on either side of the acting area.
- **Trap**: an opening built into the stage floor.
- **Grave trap**: a rectangular drop-down, resembling a grave, built into a stage floor.
- **Cauldron trap**: a trap built into a stage floor to facilitate placing items into a prop (such as a cauldron) from beneath the stage.
- **Star trap**: refers to a trap that has multiple triangular hinged doors through which an actor can enter the stage from below.
- **Trap room**: the room directly under the trap door of a stage.
- **Treads**: refers to stairs or steps connected to a stage area.
- **Upper circle**: usually raked seating in a theatre, located at the highest level in the auditorium.

- **Upstage**: refers to the part of the acting stage that is farthest away from the audience seating; may also be used to refer to the undesirable movement of one actor while on stage that causes another actor to turn their back towards the audience.
- **Ushers**: theatre staff members who lead audience to their seats; ushers are often seated in the auditorium during performances in case of an emergency.
- **Vomitory**: entrance to the auditorium located in the banked seating areas.
- **Wings**: the sides of the stage that are not in the audience's line of sight; may also refer to scenery that is set up at the point where the acting area meets the technical area.

Staging a Play

Staging a play is the process of determining where actors should physically be located at various points in the play. The aim of this exercise is to ensure that the position of the actors achieves the desired visual focus. The actors, props, set and lighting need to all work together to focus the audience's attention to the right place at the right time. Staging a play also involves blocking, which is pinpointing where the actors should be situated on stage. Staging a play also involves coordinating stage business, which is any activity that takes place on stage during a performance. For example, an actor may answer a telephone as part of a scene.

Stage Positions

Actors and directors should be familiar with the various stage positions that best achieve visual focus. It is important for the stage to be set up in an appropriate manner so that the audience can focus on the action occurring on stage. Actors can use body positions to gain the audience's attention. A full front position or center stage automatically warrants the audience's attention. On stages that have multiple levels built into the set, an actor who stands at the highest level will hold the most visual focus. On a flat stage, the actor who stands farthest downstage, which is closest to the audience, will hold the most visual focus. If multiple actors are on stage they can be arranged in a triangular pattern with the actor at the apex of the triangle receiving the most visual focus. Actors can also be separated from the group by contrast. For example, if one actor on stage is standing while the rest are seated, the standing actor receives the visual focus.

Review Video: Understanding Action and Stage Directions
Visit mometrix.com/academy and enter code: 539974

Body Positions

Full front is a position in which the actor faces the audience exposing the entire front of the body. It is an open position that allows the actor to be fully seen and heard by the audience. Open positions are those in which the actor's face, at the very least is facing the audience. Quarter (¼) right and left positions are those in which the actor stands facing slightly left or right of the audience. Quarter positions are open positions. Quarter positions allow two actors to be on stage interacting with each other naturally while still allowing the audience to hear and see them. Left and right profiles are positions in which the actor exposes only one side of their face and body to the audience. Profiles are not open positions and drastically reduce the visibility of the actor to the audience. In between the profile and quarter positions are the three-quarter (¾) right and left positions. These are not quite profiles. Opposite of full front is the full back position. In full back position the actor faces away from the audience.

Staging Terms

A cross is a stage direction given by the director. It means the actor needs to move from one point on stage to another. For example, a director may instruct the actor to cross stage right. In a script, instructions to cross the stage are often shown by the letter "x." A direction to counter-cross is given in order to compensate for the cross of another actor. In order to retain a visual balance in a scene, the director may instruct one actor to cross stage right while instructing another actor to counter cross in order to avoid being blocked from view by the crosser. In general, if there are two actors on stage, each is of equal importance. If one actor steps farther away from the audience (or upstage), it causes an awkward interaction between the actors. The actor who has been upstaged must then turn his back to the audience in order to look as though he is naturally communicating with the other actor; however, this means the audience will not be able to hear the actor speaking. Upstaging should be avoided.

PREPARING THE UNIT SET

Prior to using the unit set, each piece should be inspected for damage or instability. The pieces should be checked frequently for any signs of wear or damage, such as exposed nails, torn canvas, holes in the fabric, or exposed wood which might splinter. At the end of each show, any set pieces which were stood upon should be wiped down to avoid damage. Students must be taught that the unit set is extremely expensive and valuable, and should not be allowed to horseplay or jump on the set pieces (with the exception of blocked stage movements where applicable).

SAFELY SETTING THE STAGE

Setting a stage is the process of constructing the scene that will take place, this includes moving props, changing lighting, moving and adjusting curtains, and making any changes that impact the appearance of the stage as needed in a scene. This begins with planning sets and drawing detailed scenes to scale, these drawings provide all crew with a detailed outline and better understanding of the needed outcome. To meet some settings needs, it may be necessary to build props which may require the use of cutting, fastening, clamping, and measuring tools. As such, wearing proper safety gear, like safety glasses and gloves, and appropriate attire, like close toed shoes and tying back long hair, is the first step in ensuring safety. Every power tool should have its own set of instructions and safety features that crew members need to familiarize themselves with before using. Because a stage is set multiple times during a production, there are some considerations to take regarding safety. Props, specifically furniture and large pieces, should be kept light where that is an option. When that is not an option, crew members need to be taught proper, safe lifting and moving techniques as they will be frequently and quickly moving these pieces between scenes.

SAFELY STRIKING THE STAGE

Striking is the deconstruction process of a set and occurs following the final performance. It is considered the most dangerous part of a production as the physical demands of this process carry an inherent risk, so it is crucial to follow safety procedures. Striking begins with the creation of a **strike plan** that outlines where and what type of deconstruction needs to occur and how many crew members it will require. After the plan has been created but before the strike occurs, a **strike training** will take place. The plan is shared and all safety information is reviewed during training. Personal protection equipment, like glasses, helmets, and gloves, need to be provided to the crew before beginning the strike. Understanding stage terminology will also ensure safety. **"Heads-up"** alerts crew members that something above them is moving or falling while **"clear"** alerts members that an object in the area is falling and they need to move. These cumulative actions help to ensure the safety of crew members as they strike the set and return the stage back to its original condition.

Backstage Procedures and Production Crews

BACKSTAGE ETIQUETTE AND SAFETY

Backstage, particularly when the lights are off, is the place where stage accidents or injuries are most likely to happen. Safety procedures such as using glow-in-the-dark gaff tape around designated prop areas can help actors and crew members avoid dangerous areas when the lights are out. All cast and crew should be taught backstage etiquette such as not running, avoiding horseplay, team carrying heavier items, and whispering when a show is in progress. Depending on the age of students, clear guidelines for not utilizing backstage spaces inappropriately must be discussed. Many high school programs choose to keep their curtains open and backstage lights on during rehearsals to avoid giving students dark and secluded areas for extended periods of time.

PROPERLY PREPARING THE SET AND LIGHTING CREW FOR PERFORMANCES

Preparing lighting begins with a thorough reading of the script to determine production needs. The type and style of lighting to be used is determined by the setting and desired ambiance. While reading the script, a **cue list** is created. The cue list tells the crew what type of lighting to use, when to use it, and what effect it will create if applicable. This information will also be used to prepare a **lighting plan** to properly set the stage. The lighting plan lays out where the light sources need to come from, what type of lights to use, and how to use them to meet the needs outlined in the cue list. Using that plan, the crew will begin to construct the **lighting rigs**. This portion of set up requires the lights to be physically installed and manipulated, so it carries the risk of injury; therefore, it is vital to review safety precautions with the crew before beginning. Once the lights are set, the set designer continues the creative process to finalize the use of lights. Preparing the crew for curtain and fly rail operation use follows a similar process. **Curtain cues** are pulled from the script and tell the crew how and when to open and draw curtains. **Rail cues** signify when the fly rail system should be used to remove or place props from or onto the stage.

STAGE MANAGER, PRODUCTION MANAGER, TECHNICAL DIRECTOR, AND PRODUCTION CREW

- **Stage Manager:** The stage manager is responsible for the people involved in a production. Some of the responsibilities include coordinating cast and crew schedules, scheduling rehearsals, coordinating and communicating between parties involved in the production, calling cues, and overseeing the show when performed live.
- **Production Manager:** Production managers work in a more typical managerial capacity. This can include budgeting, safety procedures, and general problem solving to prevent any issues that interfere with the production and a timely opening.
- **Technical Director:** Technical directors work to oversee all of the technical work done in a production. This includes lighting, sound, construction, carpentry, and general maintenance.
- **Production Crew:** The production crew is responsible for setting and striking the stage. They prepare and maintain equipment needed for performances. They oversee any moving components of the production, such as curtains, lights, props, or special effects.

SAFETY PRACTICES AND PROCEDURES RELATED TO TECHNICAL THEATRE

Technical theatre is the components of a production that establish a setting and mood. It is also called **stagecraft**. Much of the preparation of technical theatre is physically involved, such as building sets, rigging lights, operating curtains, and moving large scene pieces. As such, safety practices and procedures should be established and reviewed with the crew to keep them safe. Most common safety practices include wearing personal protection equipment, such as goggles, gloves, and closed-toe shoes, and ensuring no clothing or hair is loose as it may get caught in equipment. Ensuring exits are clear and easy to access at all times is necessary for the safety of all individuals. For large and heavy set pieces, the crew needs to ensure they are properly lifting using safe techniques and implementing assistive devices for moving. Individual tools, set pieces, and various pieces of equipment may have their own sets of instructions and safety procedures. These need to be reviewed by crew members and physical copies should be easy to access for anyone using them. Reminding the crew to stay alert at all times will help prevent injury by ensuring they remain aware of the risks that surround them.

ASSEMBLING A PRODUCTION CREW

Assembling a production crew starts with establishing the needs of the production and creating roles that will fulfill those needs. This will include things like building set pieces, working lighting and curtains, and costume design. Those roles and expectations are then communicated with any interested parties, typically through theatre class periods, postings within the school building, or email blasts. Roles will vary in the level of time commitment required and if any prior theatre experience is necessary. With this information, the theatre teacher should begin connecting with students enrolled in the theatre class or interviewing interested students. During this time, the teacher should be as clear and direct as possible in outlining expectations. This will ensure that the students are aware of their commitments and the teacher will find someone ready to fill the role. Once students are selected for their roles, the crew can begin meeting as a whole to prepare for the production.

Teaching Proper Etiquette, Safety, and Backstage Techniques

Theatre crew plays a massive role in ensuring a production runs smoothly and is enjoyable for the audience as well as for the cast. As such, it is vital to ensure they have an understanding of proper etiquette, safety, and backstage techniques. Theatre etiquette encompasses the behaviors expected from the crew, such as speaking to one another and making requests respectfully, arriving on-time to rehearsals, adhering to deadlines, and general respect for all other parties involved in the production. The etiquette expectations should be clearly communicated to the crew as should consequences of not meeting these expectations. Having **"crew only" rehearsal** opportunities allow for intense crew training as well as time for the teacher to build rapport with the crew. These rehearsals serve as a time to ensure proper safety procedures are taught as well as an ample amount of time to practice any backstage techniques, like handling props, making changes and adjustments between scenes, and adjusting lighting and sounds. This again serves as an opportunity to outline what is expected and what happens if those expectations are not met. By working with crew only, the teacher also opens lines of communication that will make things run more smoothly.

Craft and Comprehension

Examples of Themes and Plots in Literature

Themes in Literature

When we read parables, their themes are the lessons they aim to teach. When we read fables, the moral of each story is its theme. When we read fictional works, the authors' perspectives regarding life and human behavior are their themes. Unlike in parables and fables, themes in literary fiction are usually not meant to preach or teach the readers a lesson. Hence, themes in fiction are not as explicit as they are in parables or fables. Instead, they are implicit, and the reader only infers them. By analyzing the fictional characters through thinking about their actions and behavior, understanding the setting of the story, and reflecting on how its plot develops, the reader comes to infer the main theme of the work. When writers succeed, they communicate with their readers such that common ground is established between author and audience. While a reader's individual experience may differ in its details from the author's written story, both may share universal underlying truths which allow author and audience to connect.

Determining Theme

In well-crafted literature, theme, structure, and plot are interdependent and inextricable: each element informs and reflects the others. The structure of a work is how it is organized. The theme is the central idea or meaning found in it. The plot is what happens in the story. Titles can also inform us of a work's theme. For instance, the title of Edgar Allan Poe's "The Tell-Tale Heart" informs readers of the story's theme of guilt before they even read about the repeated heartbeat the protagonist hears immediately before and constantly after committing and hiding a murder. Repetitive patterns of events or behaviors also give clues to themes. The same is true of symbols. For example, in F. Scott Fitzgerald's *The Great Gatsby,* for Jay Gatsby the green light at the end of the dock symbolizes Daisy Buchanan and his own dreams for the future. More generally, it is also understood as a symbol of the American Dream, and narrator Nick Carraway explicitly compares it to early settlers' sight of America rising from the ocean.

Thematic Development

Theme in The Great Gatsby

In *The Great Gatsby*, F. Scott Fitzgerald portrayed 1920s America as greedy, cynical, and rife with moral decay. Jay Gatsby's lavish weekly parties symbolize the reckless excesses of the Jazz Age. The growth of bootlegging and organized crime in reaction to Prohibition is symbolized by the character of Meyer Wolfsheim and by Gatsby's own ill-gotten wealth. Fitzgerald symbolized social divisions using geography. The "old money" aristocrats like the Buchanans lived on East Egg, while the "new money" bourgeois like Gatsby lived on West Egg. Fitzgerald also used weather, as many authors have, to reinforce narrative and emotional tones in the novel. Just as in *Romeo and Juliet*, where William Shakespeare set the confrontation of Tybalt and Mercutio and its deadly consequences on the hottest summer day under a burning sun, in *The Great Gatsby*, Fitzgerald did the same with Tom Wilson's deadly confrontation with Gatsby. Both works are ostensible love stories carrying socially critical themes about the destructiveness of pointless and misguided behaviors—family feuds in the former, pursuit of money in the latter.

Review Video: Thematic Development
Visit mometrix.com/academy and enter code: 576507

Theme in Les Misérables

In Victor Hugo's novel *Les Misérables*, the overall metamorphosis of protagonist Jean Valjean from a cynical ex-convict into a noble benefactor demonstrates Hugo's theme of the importance of love and compassion for others. Hugo also reflects this in more specific plot events. For example, Valjean's love for Cosette sustains him through many difficult periods and trying events. Hugo illustrates how love and compassion for others beget the same in them: Bishop Myriel's kindness to Valjean eventually inspires him to become honest. Years later, Valjean, as M. Madeleine, has rescued Fauchelevent from under a fallen carriage, Fauchelevent returns the compassionate act by giving Valjean sanctuary in the convent. M. Myriel's kindness also ultimately enables Valjean to rescue Cosette from the Thénardiers. Receiving Valjean's father-like love enables Cosette to fall in love with and marry Marius, and the love between Cosette and Marius enables the couple to forgive Valjean for his past crimes when they are revealed.

Theme in "The Tell-Tale Heart"

In one of his shortest stories, "The Tell-Tale Heart," Poe used economy of language to emphasize the murderer-narrator's obsessive focus on bare details like the victim's cataract-milky eye, the sound of a heartbeat, and insistence he is sane. The narrator begins by denying he is crazy, even citing his extreme agitation as proof of sanity. Contradiction is then extended: the narrator loves the old man, yet kills him. His motives are irrational—not greed or revenge, but to relieve the victim of his "evil eye." Because "eye" and "I" are homonyms, readers may infer that eye/I symbolizes the old man's identity, contradicting the killer's delusion that he can separate them. The narrator distances himself from the old man by perceiving his eye as separate, and dismembering his dead body. This backfires when he imagines the victim's heartbeat, which is really his own, just before he kills him and frequently afterward. Guilty and paranoid, he gives himself away. Poe predated Freud in exploring the paradox of killing those we love and the concept of projecting our own processes onto others.

Theme in the Works of William Faulkner and Charles Dickens

William Faulkner contrasts the traditions of the antebellum South with the rapid changes of post-Civil War industrialization in his short story "A Rose for Emily." Living inside the isolated world of her house, Emily Grierson denies the reality of modern progress. Contradictorily, she is both a testament to time-honored history and a mysterious, eccentric, unfathomable burden. Faulkner portrays her with deathlike imagery even in life, comparing her to a drowned woman and referring to her skeleton. Emily symbolizes the Old South; as her social status is degraded, so is the antebellum social order. Like Miss Havisham in Charles Dickens' *Great Expectations,* Emily preserves her bridal bedroom, denying change and time's passage. Emily tries to control death through denial, shown in her necrophilia with her father's corpse and her killing of Homer Barron to stop him from leaving her, then also denying his death. Faulkner uses the motif of dust throughout to represent not only the decay of Emily, her house, and Old Southern traditions, but also how her secrets are obscured from others.

Theme in Moby-Dick

The great White Whale in *Moby-Dick* plays various roles to different characters. In Captain Ahab's obsessive, monomaniacal quest to kill it, the whale represents all evil, and Ahab believes it his duty and destiny to rid the world of it. Ishmael attempts through multiple scientific disciplines to understand the whale objectively, but fails—it is hidden underwater and mysterious to humans—reinforcing Melville's theme that humans can never know everything; here the whale represents the unknowable. Melville reverses white's usual connotation of purity in Ishmael's dread of white, associated with crashing waves, polar animals, albinos—all frightening and unnatural. White is often viewed as an absence of color, yet white light is the sum total of all colors in the spectrum. In the same way, white can signify both absence of meaning, and totality of meaning incomprehensible to humans. As a creature of nature, the whale also symbolizes how 19th-century white men's exploitative expansionistic actions were destroying the natural environment.

Theme in The Old Man and the Sea

Because of the old fisherman Santiago's struggle to capture a giant marlin, some people characterize Ernest Hemingway's *The Old Man and the Sea* as telling of man against nature. However, it can more properly be interpreted as telling of man's role as part of nature. Both man and fish are portrayed as brave, proud, and honorable. In Hemingway's world, all creatures, including humans, must either kill or be killed. Santiago reflects, "man can be destroyed but not defeated," following this principle in his life. As heroes are often created through their own deaths, Hemingway seems to believe that while being destroyed is inevitable, destruction enables living beings to transcend it by fighting bravely with honor and dignity. Hemingway echoes Romantic poet John Keats' contention that only immediately before death can we understand beauty as it is about to be destroyed. He also echoes ancient Greek and Roman myths and the Old Testament with the tragic flaw of overweening pride or overreaching. Like Icarus, Prometheus, and Adam and Eve, the old man "went out too far."

Universal Themes

The Old Testament book of Genesis, the Quran, and the Epic of Gilgamesh all contain flood stories. Versions differ somewhat, yet marketed similarities also exist. Genesis describes a worldwide flood, attributing it to God's decision that mankind, his creation, had become incontrovertibly wicked in spirit and must be destroyed for the world to start anew. The Quran describes the flood as regional, caused by Allah after sending Nuh (notice the similarity in name to Noah) as a messenger to his people to cease their evil. The Quran stipulates that Allah only destroys those who deny or ignore messages from his messengers. In the Gilgamesh poems Utnapishtim, like Noah, is instructed to build a ship to survive the flood. Both men also send out birds afterward as tests, using doves and a raven, though with different outcomes. Many historians and archeologists believe a Middle Eastern tidal wave was a real basis for these stories. However, their universal themes remain the same: the flood was seen as God's way of wiping out humans whose behavior had become ungodly.

Theme of Overreaching

A popular theme throughout literature is the human trait of **reaching too far** or **presuming too much**. In Greek mythology, Daedalus constructed wings of feathers and wax that men might fly like birds. He permitted his son Icarus to try them, but cautioned the boy not to fly too close to the sun. The impetuous youth (in what psychologist David Elkind later named adolescence's myth of invincibility) ignored this, flying too close to the sun. The wax melted, the wings disintegrated, and Icarus fell into the sea and perished. In the Old Testament, God warned Adam and Eve not to eat fruit from the tree of knowledge of good and evil. Because they ignored this command, they were banished from Eden's eternal perfection, condemning them to mortality and suffering. The Romans were themselves examples of overreaching in their conquest and assimilation of most of the then-known world and their ultimate demise. In Christopher Marlowe's *Dr. Faustus* and Johann Wolfgang von Goethe's *Faust*, the protagonist sells his soul to the Devil for unlimited knowledge and success, ultimately leading to his own tragic end.

Story Vs. Discourse

In terms of plot, "story" is the characters, places, and events originating in the author's mind, while "discourse" is how the author arranges and sequences events—which may be chronological or not. Story is imaginary; discourse is words on the page. Discourse allows a story to be told in different ways. One element of plot structure is relating events differently from the order in which they occurred. This is easily done with cause-and-effect; for example, in the sentence, "He died following a long illness," we know the illness preceded the death, but the death precedes the illness in words. In Kate Chopin's short story "The Story of an Hour" (1894), she tells some of the events out of chronological order, which has the effect of amplifying the surprise of the ending for the reader. Another element of plot structure is selection. Chopin omits some details, such as Mr. Mallard's trip home; this allows readers to be as surprised at his arrival as Mrs. Mallard is.

Plot and Meaning

Novelist E. M. Forster has made the distinction between story as relating a series of events, such as a king dying and then his queen dying, versus plot as establishing motivations for actions and causes for events, such as a king dying and then his queen dying from grief over his death. Thus, plot fulfills the function of helping readers understand cause-and-effect in events and underlying motivations in characters' actions, which in turn helps them understand life. This affects a work's meaning by supporting its ability to explain why things happen, why people do things, and ultimately the meaning of life. Some authors find that while story events convey meaning, they do not tell readers there is any one meaning in life or way of living, but rather are mental experiments with various meanings, enabling readers to explore. Hence stories may not necessarily be constructed to impose one definitive meaning, but rather to find some shape, direction, and meaning within otherwise random events.

Classic Analysis of Plot Structure

In *Poetics*, Aristotle defined plot as "the arrangement of the incidents." He meant not the story, but how it is structured for presentation. In tragedies, Aristotle found results driven by chains of cause and effect preferable to those driven by the protagonist's personality or character. He identified "unity of action" as necessary for a plot's wholeness, meaning its events must be internally connected, not episodic or relying on *deus ex machina* or other external intervention. A plot must have a beginning, middle, and end. Gustav Freytag adapted Aristotle's ideas into his Pyramid (1863). The beginning, today called the exposition, incentive, or inciting moment, emphasizes causes and de-emphasizes effects. Aristotle called the ensuing cause and effect *desis*, or tying up, today called complications which occur during the rising action. These culminate in a crisis or climax, Aristotle's *peripateia.* This occurs at the plot's middle, where cause and effect are both emphasized. The falling action, which Aristotle called the *lusis* or unraveling, is today called the dénouement. The resolution comes at the catastrophe, outcome, or end, when causes are emphasized and effects de-emphasized.

Review Video: Plot Line
Visit mometrix.com/academy and enter code: 944011

Analysis of Plot Structures Through Recurring Patterns

Authors of fiction select characters, places, and events from their imaginations and arrange them to create a story that will affect their readers. One way to analyze plot structure is to compare and contrast different events in a story. For example, in Kate Chopin's "The Story of an Hour," a very simple but key pattern of repetition is the husband's leaving and then returning. Such patterns fulfill the symmetrical aspect that Aristotle said was required of sound plot structure. In James Baldwin's short story, "Sonny's Blues," the narrator is Sonny's brother. In an encounter with one of Sonny's old friends early in the story, the brother initially disregards his communication. In a subsequent flashback, Baldwin informs us that this was the same way he had treated Sonny. In Nathaniel Hawthorne's "Young Goodman Brown," a pattern is created by the protagonist's recurrent efforts not to go farther into the wood. In Herman Melville's "Bartleby the Scrivener" and in William Faulkner's "Barn Burning," patterns are also created by repetition such as Bartleby's repeated refusals and the history of barn-burning episodes, respectively.

LITERARY ANALYSIS

ANALYZING LITERARY TEXTS

The best literary analysis shows special insight into at least one important aspect of a text. When **analyzing literary texts**, it can be difficult to find a starting place. Many texts can be analyzed several different ways, often leaving an overwhelming number of options for writers to consider. However, narrowing the focus to a particular element of literature can be helpful when preparing to analyze a text. Symbolism, themes, and motifs are common starting points for literary analysis. These three methods of analysis can lead to a holistic analysis of a text, since they involve elements that are often distributed throughout the text. However, not all texts feature these elements in a way that facilitates a strong analysis, if they are present at all. It is also common to focus on character or plot development for analysis. These elements are compatible with theme, symbolism, and allusion. Setting and imagery, figurative language, and any external contexts can also contribute to analysis or complement one of these other elements. The application of a critical, or literary, theory to a text can also provide a thorough and strong analysis.

LITERARY THEORIES AND CRITICISM AND INTERPRETATION

Literary theory includes ideas that guide readers through the process of interpreting literature. Literary theory, as a subject, encompasses several specific, focused theories that lead readers to interpret or analyze literature through the context of the theory using the subjects and elements it involves. Some commonly used and discussed literary theories include **postcolonial theory**, **gender and feminist theory**, **structuralism**, **new historicism**, **reader-response theory**, and **sociological criticism**.

- **Postcolonial theory** involves the historical and geographical context of a work and leads readers to consider how colonization informs the plot, characters, setting, and other elements in the work.
- **Gender and feminist theory** invites readers to interpret a text by looking at its treatment of and suggestions about women and a culture's treatment of women. As with most literary theories, this information can be clearly stated or strongly implied in a work, but it may also be gleaned through looking closely at symbols, characters, and plot elements in a work.
- **Structuralism** uses the structure and organization of a work and the foundations of language to examine how and what a text conveys about the human experience and how those findings connect to common human experiences.
- **New historicism** heavily relies on the cultural and historical context of a work, including when it was written, where the author lives or lived, the culture and history of that location, and other works from the same culture. New historical readings seek to examine these details to expose the ideologies of the location and culture that influenced the work.
- **Reader-response theory** uses the individual reader's response to the text and experience while reading the text to examine the meaning of the reader's relationship with the text and what that relationship suggests about the reader or the factors impacting their experience.
- **Sociological criticism** considers the societies that are relevant to a text. The author's society and any reader's society are important to the text, as sociological criticism seeks to uncover what the text implies or reveals about those societies. This method of criticism can also involve studying the presentation of a society within the text and applying it to the author's society or their other writings.

LANGUAGE AND DIALECT

DIVERSITY AND SITUATIONAL NATURE OF LANGUAGE

Language is a diverse tool that allows people to communicate. However, language is often impacted and molded by the culture that uses it. This can make it difficult to learn and use a new language, since not all native speakers of the language will use it or interpret it the same way. For example, English is spoken all over America, but Americans in various regions of the country speak using different **dialects**. Other differences in speech include **accents** and **rhythm of speech**. Language is also manipulated by situations. Some terms and phrases have multiple meanings. A word's meaning often depends on the **context** in which the word or phrase is used, meaning that non-native speakers must learn to interpret situations to understand messages.

FACTORS OF LANGUAGE AND COMMUNICATION

INFLUENCES ON LANGUAGE

While dialect and diction are heavily influenced by an individual's culture and the location and history of the place they live, other personal factors can also impact language. A person's ethnicity, religious beliefs or background, and gender can influence the way they use and understand language. **Ethnicity** impacts language by incorporating a group's communication norms into an individual's speech and behavior. These norms may affect a speaker's tone, volume, or pace. These factors may lead others outside of that group to misinterpret the speaker's message, depending on their understanding of how those factors are used in speech. A person's **religious beliefs** can also affect their use of language. Religious beliefs and practices may lead an individual to abstain from using certain terms and may change the context in which a speaker uses specific words, or change their understanding of the word's usage. Additionally, a person may use language differently depending on their gender. **Gender's** influence on communication varies by region and industry. A region or industry's treatment of gender roles often impacts language use among its members. This can lead members of one gender group to be more assertive or submissive or to use different terms and phrases.

CULTURE AND COMMUNICATION

Individuals from different countries and cultures communicate differently. Not only do many people speak different languages, but they also speak using different inflections, volumes, tones, and dialects. These factors can have a significant impact on communication, even if the communicators speak the same language. In different cultures, certain behaviors are associated with different meanings and implications. When communicators from different cultures have a conversation, these expectations and associations may lead to misunderstanding. For example, Americans are considered to be louder and more demonstrative than people from other countries. Someone from a country where people speak more quietly who is not aware of this characterization may perceive an American's volume or large gestures as an indication of anger, when in reality, the American speaker is calm. The American may similarly perceive the other person as sad or shy due to their quiet voice, when the speaker is actually happy and comfortable in the conversation. Awareness of these factors and effects promotes respect for others and helps speakers understand the reasons for differences in communication, rather than allowing these differences to create division or conflict.

LANGUAGE VS. DIALECT

Languages are distinct and structured forms of verbal communication. Languages have cohesive sets of rules and words that are shared between the majority of that language's users. The main identifier of a language is that members of one language group are incapable of communicating fluently with members of another language group. New languages are formed as different dialects grow further apart until the members of each dialect can no longer innately communicate with each other.

Dialects are subsets of languages that do not violate the rules of the language as a whole, but which vary from other dialects in vocabulary usage, grammar forms, pronunciation, and spelling. Two major groupings of dialects are American and British English. Most American English and British English speakers can communicate with relative ease with one another, though the pronunciation, vocabulary (torch vs. flashlight; trunk vs. boot), spelling (meter vs. metre; color vs. colour), and grammar (in American English, collective nouns are always considered singular, but can be singular or plural in British English).

Development of Dialects over Time

Dialects are formed primarily through the influences of location and time, but can be the result of other elements of **social stratification** as well (economic, ethnic, religious, etc.). As one group of a language's speakers is separated from another, in British and American English speakers for example, the language develops in isolated locations at the same time, resulting in distinct dialects. Language changes continuously over time as new words and phrases are adopted and others are phased out. Eventually, these small changes result culminate into enough grammar and vocabulary changes that the speakers of the distinct dialects cannot easily communicate with one another. The dialects can then be recognized as distinct languages.

Use of Dialect in Media

Literary authors often use dialect when writing dialogue to illustrate the social and geographical backgrounds of specific characters, which supports character development. For example, in *The Adventures of Huckleberry Finn* (1885), Mark Twain's novel is written in the dialect of a young, uneducated, white, Southern character, opening with this sentence: "You don't know about me without you have read a book by the name of The Adventures of Tom Sawyer, but that ain't no matter." Twain uses a different and exaggerated dialect to represent the speech of the African-American slave Jim: "We's safe, Huck, we's safe! Jump up and crack yo' heels. Dat's de good ole Cairo at las', I jis knows it."

In *To Kill a Mockingbird,* author Harper Lee used dialect in the characters' dialogue to portray an uneducated boy in the American South: "Reckon I have. Almost died the first year I come to school and et them pecans—folks say he pizened 'em." Lee also uses many Southern regional expressions, such as "right stove up," "What in the sam holy hill?", "sit a spell," "fess" (meaning "confess"), "jim-dandy," and "hush your fussing." These contribute to Lee's characterization of the people she describes, who live in a small town in Alabama circa the 1930s. In *Wuthering Heights* (1847), Emily Bronte reproduces Britain's 18th–19th-century Yorkshire dialect in the speech of servant Joseph: "Running after t'lads, as usuald!... If I war yah, maister, I'd just slam t'boards i' their faces all on 'em, gentle and simple! Never a day ut yah're off, but yon cat o' Linton comes sneaking hither; and Miss Nelly, shoo's a fine lass!"

Dialect vs. Diction

When written as characters' dialogue in literary works, dialect represents the particular pronunciation, grammar, and figurative expressions used by certain groups of people based on their geographic region, social class, and cultural background. For example, when a character says, "There's gold up in them thar hills," the author is using dialect to add to the characterization of that individual. Diction is more related to individual characters than to groups of people. The way in which a specific character speaks, including his or her choice of words, manner of expressing himself or herself, and use of grammar all represent individual types of diction. For example, two characters in the same novel might describe the same action or event using different diction: One says "I'm heading uptown for the evening," and the other says "I'm going out for a night on the town." These convey the same literal meaning, but due to their variations in diction, the speakers are expressing themselves in slightly different ways.

Influences on Regional Dialect

Linguistic researchers have identified regional variations in vocabulary choices, which have evolved because of differences in local climates and how they influence human behaviors. For example, in the Southern United States, the Linguistic Atlas of the Gulf States (LAGS) Project by Dr. Lee Pederson of Emory University discovered and documented that people living in the northern or Upland section of the Piedmont plateau region call the fungal infection commonly known as athlete's foot "toe itch," but people living in the southern or Lowland section call it "ground itch." The explanation for this difference is that in the north, temperatures are cooler and people wear shoes accordingly, so they associate the itching with the feet in their description, but in the south, temperatures are hotter and people often went barefoot, so they associated the itching with the ground that presumably transmitted the infection.

USING DIALECT IN WRITING

Dialect is most appropriate for informal or creative writing. Using dialectal writing when communicating casually or informally, such as in a text message or a quick email to a peer, is acceptable. However, in academic and professional contexts, writing using indications of dialect is inappropriate and often unacceptable. If the audience includes individuals who have a higher rank than the author, or authority over the author, it is best not to write in a way that suggests a dialect.

Elements of Story

PLOT AND STORY STRUCTURE

PLOT AND STORY STRUCTURE

The **plot** includes the events that happen in a story and the order in which they are told to the reader. There are several types of plot structures, as stories can be told in many ways. The most common plot structure is the chronological plot, which presents the events to the reader in the same order they occur for the characters in the story. Chronological plots usually have five main parts, the **exposition**, **rising action**, the **climax**, **falling action**, and the **resolution**. This type of plot structure guides the reader through the story's events as the characters experience them and is the easiest structure to understand and identify. While this is the most common plot structure, many stories are nonlinear, which means the plot does not sequence events in the same order the characters experience them. Such stories might include elements like flashbacks that cause the story to be nonlinear.

Review Video: How to Make a Story Map
Visit mometrix.com/academy and enter code: 261719

EXPOSITION

The **exposition** is at the beginning of the story and generally takes place before the rising action begins. The purpose of the exposition is to give the reader context for the story, which the author may do by introducing one or more characters, describing the setting or world, or explaining the events leading up to the point where the story begins. The exposition may still include events that contribute to the plot, but the **rising action** and main conflict of the story are not part of the exposition. Some narratives skip the exposition and begin the story with the beginning of the rising action, which causes the reader to learn the context as the story intensifies.

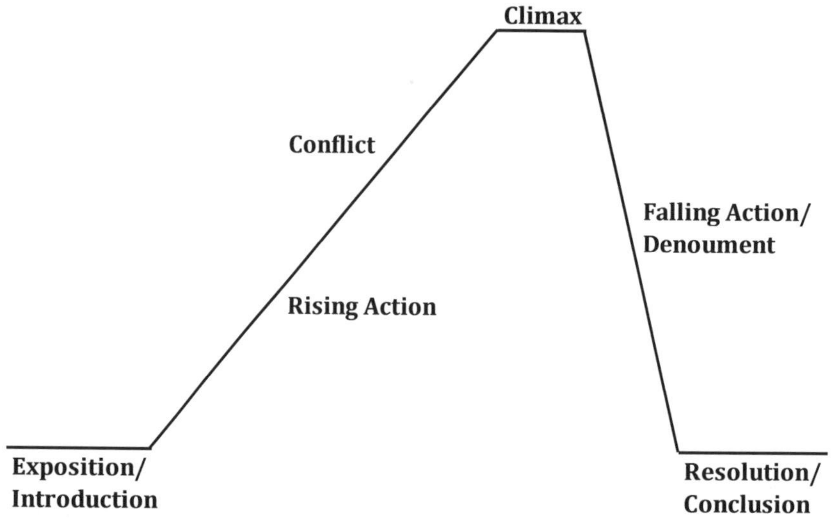

Review Video: Plot Line
Visit mometrix.com/academy and enter code: 944011

CONFLICT

A **conflict** is a problem to be solved. Literary plots typically include one conflict or more. Characters' attempts to resolve conflicts drive the narrative's forward movement. **Conflict resolution** is often the protagonist's primary occupation. Physical conflicts like exploring, wars, and escapes tend to make plots most suspenseful and exciting. Emotional, mental, or moral conflicts tend to make stories more personally gratifying or rewarding for many audiences. Conflicts can be external or internal. A major type of internal conflict is some inner personal battle, or **man versus self**. Major types of external conflicts include **man versus nature**, **man versus man**, and **man versus society**. Readers can identify conflicts in literary plots by identifying the protagonist and antagonist and asking why they conflict, what events develop the conflict, where the climax occurs, and how they identify with the characters.

Read the following paragraph and discuss the type of conflict present:

> Timothy was shocked out of sleep by the appearance of a bear just outside his tent. After panicking for a moment, he remembered some advice he had read in preparation for this trip: he should make noise so the bear would not be startled. As Timothy started to hum and sing, the bear wandered away.

There are three main types of conflict in literature: **man versus man**, **man versus nature**, and **man versus self**. This paragraph is an example of man versus nature. Timothy is in conflict with the bear. Even though no physical conflict like an attack exists, Timothy is pitted against the bear. Timothy uses his knowledge to "defeat" the bear and keep himself safe. The solution to the conflict is that Timothy makes noise, the bear wanders away, and Timothy is safe.

Review Video: Conflict
Visit mometrix.com/academy and enter code: 559550

Review Video: Determining Relationships in a Story
Visit mometrix.com/academy and enter code: 929925

Rising Action

The **rising action** is the part of the story where conflict **intensifies**. The rising action begins with an event that prompts the main conflict of the story. This may also be called the **inciting incident**. The main conflict generally occurs between the protagonist and an antagonist, but this is not the only type of conflict that may occur in a narrative. After this event, the protagonist works to resolve the main conflict by preparing for an altercation, pursuing a goal, fleeing an antagonist, or doing some other action that will end the conflict. The rising action is composed of several additional events that increase the story's tension. Most often, other developments will occur alongside the growth of the main conflict, such as character development or the development of minor conflicts. The rising action ends with the **climax**, which is the point of highest tension in the story.

Climax

The **climax** is the event in the narrative that marks the height of the story's conflict or tension. The event that takes place at the story's climax will end the rising action and bring about the results of the main conflict. If the conflict was between a good protagonist and an evil antagonist, the climax may be a final battle between the two characters. If the conflict is an adventurer looking for heavily guarded treasure, the climax may be the adventurer's encounter with the final obstacle that protects the treasure. The climax may be made of multiple scenes, but can usually be summarized as one event. Once the conflict and climax are complete, the **falling action** begins.

Falling Action

The **falling action** shows what happens in the story between the climax and the resolution. The falling action often composes a much smaller portion of the story than the rising action does. While the climax includes the end of the main conflict, the falling action may show the results of any minor conflicts in the story. For example, if the protagonist encountered a troll on the way to find some treasure, and the troll demanded the protagonist share the treasure after retrieving it, the falling action would include the protagonist returning to share the treasure with the troll. Similarly, any unexplained major events are usually made clear during the falling action. Once all significant elements of the story are resolved or addressed, the story's resolution will occur. The **resolution** is the end of the story, which shows the final result of the plot's events and shows what life is like for the main characters once they are no longer experiencing the story's conflicts.

Resolution

The way the conflict is **resolved** depends on the type of conflict. The plot of any book starts with the lead up to the conflict, then the conflict itself, and finally the solution, or **resolution**, to the conflict. In **man versus man** conflicts, the conflict is often resolved by two parties coming to some sort of agreement or by one party triumphing over the other party. In **man versus nature** conflicts, the conflict is often resolved by man coming to some realization about some aspect of nature. In **man versus self** conflicts, the conflict is often resolved by the character growing or coming to an understanding about part of himself.

Theme

A **theme** is a central idea demonstrated by a passage. Often, a theme is a lesson or moral contained in the text, but it does not have to be. It also is a unifying idea that is used throughout the text; it can take the form of a common setting, idea, symbol, design, or recurring event. A passage can have two or more themes that convey its overall idea. The theme or themes of a passage are often based on **universal themes**. They can frequently be expressed using well-known sayings about life, society, or human nature, such as "Hard work pays off" or "Good triumphs over evil." Themes are not usually stated **explicitly**. The reader must figure them out by carefully reading the passage. Themes are created through descriptive language or events in the plot. The events of a story help shape the themes of a passage.

EXAMPLE

Explain why "if you care about something, you need to take care of it" accurately describes the theme of the following excerpt.

> Luca collected baseball cards, but he wasn't very careful with them. He left them around the house. His dog liked to chew. One day, Luca and his friend Bart were looking at his collection. Then they went outside. When Luca got home, he saw his dog chewing on his cards. They were ruined.

This excerpt tells the story of a boy who is careless with his baseball cards and leaves them lying around. His dog ends up chewing them and ruining them. The lesson is that if you care about something, you need to take care of it. This is the theme, or point, of the story. Some stories have more than one theme, but this is not really true of this excerpt. The reader needs to figure out the theme based on what happens in the story. Sometimes, as in the case of fables, the theme is stated directly in the text. However, this is not usually the case.

Review Video: Themes in Literature
Visit mometrix.com/academy and enter code: 732074

NARRATOR'S POINT OF VIEW

POINT OF VIEW

Another element that impacts a text is the author's point of view. The **point of view** of a text is the perspective from which a passage is told. An author will always have a point of view about a story before he or she draws up a plot line. The author will know what events they want to take place, how they want the characters to interact, and how they want the story to resolve. An author will also have an opinion on the topic or series of events which is presented in the story that is based on their prior experience and beliefs.

The two main points of view that authors use, especially in a work of fiction, are first person and third person. If the narrator of the story is also the main character, or *protagonist*, the text is written in first-person point of view. In first person, the author writes from the perspective of *I*. Third-person point of view is probably the most common that authors use in their passages. Using third person, authors refer to each character by using *he* or *she*. In third-person omniscient, the narrator is not a character in the story and tells the story of all of the characters at the same time.

Review Video: Point of View
Visit mometrix.com/academy and enter code: 383336

FIRST-PERSON NARRATION

First-person narratives let narrators express inner feelings and thoughts, especially when the narrator is the protagonist as Lemuel Gulliver is in Jonathan Swift's *Gulliver's Travels*. The narrator may be a close friend of the protagonist, like Dr. Watson in Sir Arthur Conan Doyle's *Sherlock Holmes*. Or, the narrator can be less involved with the main characters and plot, like Nick Carraway in F. Scott Fitzgerald's *The Great Gatsby*. When a narrator reports others' narratives, she or he is a "**frame narrator**," like the nameless narrator of Joseph Conrad's *Heart of Darkness* or Mr. Lockwood in Emily Brontë's *Wuthering Heights*. **First-person plural** is unusual but can be effective. Isaac Asimov's *I, Robot*, William Faulkner's *A Rose for Emily*, Maxim Gorky's *Twenty-Six Men and a Girl*, and Jeffrey Eugenides' *The Virgin Suicides* all use first-person plural narration. Author Kurt Vonnegut is the first-person narrator in his semi-autobiographical novel *Timequake*. Also unusual, but effective, is a **first-person omniscient** (rather than the more common third-person omniscient) narrator, like Death in Markus Zusak's *The Book Thief* and the ghost in Alice Sebold's *The Lovely Bones*.

Second-Person Narration

While **second-person** address is very commonplace in popular song lyrics, it is the least used form of narrative voice in literary works. Popular serial books of the 1980s like *Fighting Fantasy* or *Choose Your Own Adventure* employed second-person narratives. In some cases, a narrative combines both second-person and first-person voices, using the pronouns *you* and *I*. This can draw readers into the story, and it can also enable the authors to compare directly "your" and "my" feelings, thoughts, and actions. When the narrator is also a character in the story, as in Edgar Allan Poe's short story "The Tell-Tale Heart" or Jay McInerney's novel *Bright Lights, Big City,* the narrative is better defined as first-person despite it also addressing "you."

Third-Person Narration

Narration in the third person is the most prevalent type, as it allows authors the most flexibility. It is so common that readers simply assume without needing to be informed that the narrator is not a character in the story, or involved in its events. **Third-person singular** is used more frequently than **third-person plural**, though some authors have also effectively used plural. However, both singular and plural are most often included in stories according to which characters are being described. The third-person narrator may be either objective or subjective, and either omniscient or limited. **Objective third-person** narration does not include what the characters described are thinking or feeling, while **subjective third-person** narration does. The **third-person omniscient** narrator knows everything about all characters, including their thoughts and emotions, and all related places, times, and events. However, the **third-person limited** narrator may know everything about a particular character, but is limited to that character. In other words, the narrator cannot speak about anything that character does not know.

Alternating-Person Narration

Although authors more commonly write stories from one point of view, there are also instances wherein they alternate the narrative voice within the same book. For example, they may sometimes use an omniscient third-person narrator and a more intimate first-person narrator at other times. In J. K. Rowling's series of *Harry Potter* novels, she often writes in a third-person limited narrative, but sometimes changes to narration by characters other than the protagonist. George R. R. Martin's series *A Song of Ice and Fire* changes the point of view to coincide with divisions between chapters. The same technique is used by Erin Hunter (a pseudonym for several authors of the *Warriors, Seekers,* and *Survivors* book series). Authors using first-person narrative sometimes switch to third-person to describe significant action scenes, especially those where the narrator was absent or uninvolved, as Barbara Kingsolver does in her novel *The Poisonwood Bible.*

Review Video: The Narrator of a Story
Visit mometrix.com/academy and enter code: 742528

Setting, Mood, and Tone

Setting and Time Frame

A literary text has both a setting and time frame. A **setting** is the place in which the story as a whole is set. The **time frame** is the period in which the story is set. This may refer to the historical period the story takes place in or if the story takes place over a single day. Both setting and time frame are relevant to a text's meaning because they help the reader place the story in time and space. An author uses setting and time frame to anchor a text, create a mood, and enhance its meaning. This helps a reader understand why a character acts the way he does, or why certain events in the story are important. The setting impacts the **plot** and character **motivations**, while the time frame helps place the story in **chronological context**.

EXAMPLE

Read the following excerpt from The Adventures of Huckleberry Finn by Mark Twain and analyze the relevance of setting to the text's meaning:

> We said there warn't no home like a raft, after all. Other places do seem so cramped up and smothery, but a raft don't. You feel mighty free and easy and comfortable on a raft.

This excerpt from *The Adventures of Huckleberry Finn* by Mark Twain reveals information about the **setting** of the book. By understanding that the main character, Huckleberry Finn, lives on a raft, the reader can place the story on a river, in this case, the Mississippi River in the South before the Civil War. The information about the setting also gives the reader clues about the **character** of Huck Finn: he clearly values independence and freedom, and he likes the outdoors. The information about the setting in the quote helps the reader to better understand the rest of the text.

SYNTAX AND WORD CHOICE

Authors use words and **syntax**, or sentence structure, to make their texts unique, convey their own writing style, and sometimes to make a point or emphasis. They know that word choice and syntax contribute to the reader's understanding of the text as well as to the tone and mood of a text.

Review Video: Syntax
Visit mometrix.com/academy and enter code: 242280

MOOD AND TONE

Mood is a story's atmosphere, or the feelings the reader gets from reading it. The way authors set the mood in writing is comparable to the way filmmakers use music to set the mood in movies. Instead of music, though, writers judiciously select descriptive words to evoke certain **moods**. The mood of a work may convey joy, anger, bitterness, hope, gloom, fear, apprehension, or any other emotion the author wants the reader to feel. In addition to vocabulary choices, authors also use figurative expressions, particular sentence structures, and choices of diction that project and reinforce the moods they want to create. Whereas mood is the reader's emotions evoked by reading what is written, **tone** is the emotions and attitudes of the writer that she or he expresses in the writing. Authors use the same literary techniques to establish tone as they do to establish mood. An author may use a humorous tone, an angry or sad tone, a sentimental or unsentimental tone, or something else entirely.

MOOD AND TONE IN THE GREAT GATSBY

To understand the difference between mood and tone, look at this excerpt from F. Scott Fitzgerald's *The Great Gatsby*. In this passage, Nick Caraway, the novel's narrator, is describing his affordable house, which sits in a neighborhood full of expensive mansions.

> "I lived at West Egg, the—well the less fashionable of the two, though this is a most superficial tag to express the bizarre and not a little sinister contrast between them. My house was at the very tip of the egg, only fifty yard from the Sound, and squeezed between two huge places that rented for twelve or fifteen thousand a season ... My own house was an eyesore, but it was a small eyesore, and it had been overlooked, so I had a view of the water, a partial view of my neighbor's lawn, and the consoling proximity of millionaires—all for eighty dollars a month."

In this description, the mood created for the reader does not match the tone created through the narrator. The mood in this passage is one of dissatisfaction and inferiority. Nick compares his home to his neighbors', saying he lives in the "less fashionable" neighborhood and that his house is "overlooked," an "eyesore," and "squeezed between two huge" mansions. He also adds that his placement allows him the "consoling proximity of millionaires." A literal reading of these details leads the reader to have negative feelings toward Nick's house and his economic inferiority to his neighbors, creating the mood.

However, Fitzgerald also conveys an opposing attitude, or tone, through Nick's description. Nick calls the distinction between the neighborhoods "superficial," showing a suspicion of the value suggested by the neighborhoods' titles, properties, and residents. Nick also undermines his critique of his own home by calling it "a small eyesore" and claiming it has "been overlooked." However, he follows these statements with a description of his surroundings, claiming that he has "a view of the water" and can see some of his wealthy neighbor's property from his home, and a comparison between the properties' rent. While the mental image created for the reader depicts a small house shoved between looming mansions, the tone suggests that Nick enjoys these qualities about his home, or at least finds it charming. He acknowledges its shortcomings, but includes the benefits of his home's unassuming appearance.

Review Video: Style, Tone, and Mood
Visit mometrix.com/academy and enter code: 416961

Historical and Social Context

Fiction that is heavily influenced by a historical or social context cannot be comprehended as the author intended if the reader does not keep this context in mind. Many important elements of the text will be influenced by any context, including symbols, allusions, settings, and plot events. These contexts, as well as the identity of the work's author, can help to inform the reader about the author's concerns and intended meanings. For example, George Orwell published his novel *1984* in the year 1949, soon after the end of World War II. At that time, following the defeat of the Nazis, the Cold War began between the Western Allied nations and the Eastern Soviet Communists. People were therefore concerned about the conflict between the freedoms afforded by Western democracies versus the oppression represented by Communism. Orwell had also previously fought in the Spanish Civil War against a Spanish regime that he and his fellows viewed as oppressive. From this information, readers can infer that Orwell was concerned about oppression by totalitarian governments. This informs *1984*'s story of Winston Smith's rebellion against the oppressive "Big Brother" government, of the fictional dictatorial state of Oceania, and his capture, torture, and ultimate conversion by that government. Some literary theories also seek to use historical and social contexts to reveal deeper meanings and implications in a text.

Character Development and Dialogue

Character Development

When depicting characters or figures in a written text, authors generally use actions, dialogue, and descriptions as characterization techniques. Characterization can occur in both fiction and nonfiction and is used to show a character or figure's personality, demeanor, and thoughts. This helps create a more engaging experience for the reader by providing a more concrete picture of a character or figure's tendencies and features. Characterizations also gives authors the opportunity to integrate elements such as dialects, activities, attire, and attitudes into their writing.

To understand the meaning of a story, it is vital to understand the characters as the author describes them. We can look for contradictions in what a character thinks, says, and does. We can notice whether the author's observations about a character differ from what other characters in the story say about that character. A character may be dynamic, meaning they change significantly during the story, or static, meaning they remain the same from beginning to end. Characters may be two-dimensional, not fully developed, or may be well developed with characteristics that stand out vividly. Characters may also symbolize universal properties. Additionally, readers can compare and contrast characters to analyze how each one developed.

A well-known example of character development can be found in Charles Dickens's *Great Expectations*. The novel's main character, Pip, is introduced as a young boy, and he is depicted as innocent, kind, and humble. However, as Pip grows up and is confronted with the social hierarchy of Victorian England, he becomes arrogant and rejects his loved ones in pursuit of his own social advancement. Once he achieves his social goals, he realizes the merits of his former lifestyle, and lives with the wisdom he gained in both environments and life stages. Dickens shows Pip's ever-changing character through his interactions with others and his inner thoughts, which evolve as his personal values and personality shift.

Dialogue

Effectively written dialogue serves at least one, but usually several, purposes. It advances the story and moves the plot, develops the characters, sheds light on the work's theme or meaning, and can, often subtly, account for the passage of time not otherwise indicated. It can alter the direction that the plot is taking, typically by introducing some new conflict or changing existing ones. **Dialogue** can establish a work's narrative voice and the characters' voices and set the tone of the story or of particular characters. When fictional characters display enlightenment or realization, dialogue can give readers an understanding of what those characters have discovered and how. Dialogue can illuminate the motivations and wishes of the story's characters. By using consistent thoughts and syntax, dialogue can support character development. Skillfully created, it can also represent real-life speech rhythms in written form. Via conflicts and ensuing action, dialogue also provides drama.

Dialogue in Fiction

In fictional works, effectively written dialogue does more than just break up or interrupt sections of narrative. While **dialogue** may supply exposition for readers, it must nonetheless be believable. Dialogue should be dynamic, not static, and it should not resemble regular prose. Authors should not use dialogue to write clever similes or metaphors, or to inject their own opinions. Nor should they use dialogue at all when narrative would be better. Most importantly, dialogue should not slow the plot movement. Dialogue must seem natural, which means careful construction of phrases rather than actually duplicating natural speech, which does not necessarily translate well to the written word. Finally, all dialogue must be pertinent to the story, rather than just added conversation.

Figurative Language

Literal and Figurative Meaning

When language is used **literally**, the words mean exactly what they say and nothing more. When language is used **figuratively**, the words mean something beyond their literal meaning. For example, "The weeping willow tree has long, trailing branches and leaves" is a literal description. But "The weeping willow tree looks as if it is bending over and crying" is a figurative description—specifically, a **simile** or stated comparison. Another figurative language form is **metaphor**, or an implied comparison. A good example is the metaphor of a city, state, or city-state as a ship, and its governance as sailing that ship. Ancient Greek lyrical poet Alcaeus is credited with first using this metaphor, and ancient Greek tragedian Aeschylus then used it in *Seven Against Thebes*, and then Plato used it in the *Republic.*

Figures of Speech

A **figure of speech** is a verbal expression whose meaning is figurative rather than literal. For example, the phrase "butterflies in the stomach" does not refer to actual butterflies in a person's stomach. It is a metaphor representing the fluttery feelings experienced when a person is nervous or excited—or when one "falls in love," which does not mean physically falling. "Hitting a sales target" does not mean physically hitting a target with arrows as in archery; it is a metaphor for meeting a sales quota. "Climbing the ladder of success" metaphorically likens advancing in one's career to ascending ladder rungs. Similes, such as "light as a feather" (meaning very light, not a feather's actual weight), and hyperbole, like "I'm starving/freezing/roasting," are also figures of speech. Figures of speech are often used and crafted for emphasis, freshness of expression, or clarity.

Review Video: Figures of Speech
Visit mometrix.com/academy and enter code: 111295

FIGURATIVE LANGUAGE

Figurative language extends past the literal meanings of words. It offers readers new insight into the people, things, events, and subjects covered in a work of literature. Figurative language also enables readers to feel they are sharing the authors' experiences. It can stimulate the reader's senses, make comparisons that readers find intriguing or even startling, and enable readers to view the world in different ways. When looking for figurative language, it is important to consider the context of the sentence or situation. Phrases that appear out of place or make little sense when read literally are likely instances of figurative language. Once figurative language has been recognized, context is also important to determining the type of figurative language being used and its function. For example, when a comparison is being made, a metaphor or simile is likely being used. This means the comparison may emphasize or create irony through the things being compared. Seven specific types of figurative language include: alliteration, onomatopoeia, personification, imagery, similes, metaphors, and hyperbole.

Review Video: Figurative Language
Visit mometrix.com/academy and enter code: 584902

ALLITERATION AND ONOMATOPOEIA

Alliteration describes a series of words beginning with the same sounds. **Onomatopoeia** uses words imitating the sounds of things they name or describe. For example, in his poem "Come Down, O Maid," Alfred Tennyson writes of "The moan of doves in immemorial elms, / And murmuring of innumerable bees." The word "moan" sounds like some sounds doves make, "murmuring" represents the sounds of bees buzzing. Onomatopoeia also includes words that are simply meant to represent sounds, such as "meow," "kaboom," and "whoosh."

Review Video: Alliteration in Everyday Expressions
Visit mometrix.com/academy and enter code: 462837

PERSONIFICATION

Another type of figurative language is **personification**. This is describing a non-human thing, like an animal or an object, as if it were human. The general intent of personification is to describe things in a manner that will be comprehensible to readers. When an author states that a tree *groans* in the wind, he or she does not mean that the tree is emitting a low, pained sound from a mouth. Instead, the author means that the tree is making a noise similar to a human groan. Of course, this personification establishes a tone of sadness or suffering. A different tone would be established if the author said that the tree was *swaying* or *dancing*. Alfred Tennyson's poem "The Eagle" uses all of these types of figurative language: "He clasps the crag with crooked hands." Tennyson used alliteration, repeating /k/ and /kr/ sounds. These hard-sounding consonants reinforce the imagery, giving visual and tactile impressions of the eagle.

Review Video: Personification
Visit mometrix.com/academy and enter code: 260066

SIMILES AND METAPHORS

Similes are stated comparisons using "like" or "as." Similes can be used to stimulate readers' imaginations and appeal to their senses. Because a simile includes *like* or *as,* the device creates more space between the description and the thing being described than a metaphor does. If an author says that *a house was like a shoebox,* then the tone is different than the author saying that the house *was* a shoebox. Authors will choose between a metaphor and a simile depending on their intended tone.

Similes also help compare fictional characters to well-known objects or experiences, so the reader can better relate to them. William Wordsworth's poem about "Daffodils" begins, "I wandered lonely as a cloud." This simile compares his loneliness to that of a cloud. It is also personification, giving a cloud the human quality loneliness. In his novel *Lord Jim* (1900), Joseph Conrad writes in Chapter 33, "I would have given anything for the power to soothe her frail soul, tormenting itself in its invincible ignorance like a small bird beating about the cruel wires of a cage." Conrad uses the word "like" to compare the girl's soul to a small bird. His description of the bird beating at the cage shows the similar helplessness of the girl's soul to gain freedom.

Review Video: Similes
Visit mometrix.com/academy and enter code: 642949

A **metaphor** is a type of figurative language in which the writer equates something with another thing that is not particularly similar, instead of using *like* or *as*. For instance, *the bird was an arrow arcing through the sky*. In this sentence, the arrow is serving as a metaphor for the bird. The point of a metaphor is to encourage the reader to consider the item being described in a *different way*. Let's continue with this metaphor for a flying bird. You are asked to envision the bird's flight as being similar to the arc of an arrow. So, you imagine the flight to be swift and bending. Metaphors are a way for the author to describe an item *without being direct and obvious*. This literary device is a lyrical and suggestive way of providing information. Note that the reference for a metaphor will not always be mentioned explicitly by the author. Consider the following description of a forest in winter: *Swaying skeletons reached for the sky and groaned as the wind blew through them.* In this example, the author is using *skeletons* as a metaphor for leafless trees. This metaphor creates a spooky tone while inspiring the reader's imagination.

Literary Examples of Metaphor

A **metaphor** is an implied comparison, i.e., it compares something to something else without using "like", "as", or other comparative words. For example, in "The Tyger" (1794), William Blake writes, "Tyger Tyger, burning bright, / In the forests of the night." Blake compares the tiger to a flame not by saying it is like a fire, but by simply describing it as "burning." Henry Wadsworth Longfellow's poem "O Ship of State" (1850) uses an extended metaphor by referring consistently throughout the entire poem to the state, union, or republic as a seagoing vessel, referring to its keel, mast, sail, rope, anchors, and to its braving waves, rocks, gale, tempest, and "false lights on the shore." Within the extended metaphor, Wordsworth uses a specific metaphor: "the anchors of thy hope!"

Ted Hughes' Animal Metaphors

Ted Hughes frequently used animal metaphors in his poetry. In "The Thought Fox," a model of concise, structured beauty, Hughes characterizes the poet's creative process with succinct, striking imagery of an idea entering his head like a wild fox. Repeating "loneliness" in the first two stanzas emphasizes the poet's lonely work: "Something else is alive / Beside the clock's loneliness." He treats an idea's arrival as separate from himself. Three stanzas detail in vivid images a fox's approach from the outside winter forest at starless midnight—its nose, "Cold, delicately" touching twigs and leaves; "neat" paw prints in snow; "bold" body; brilliant green eyes; and self-contained, focused progress—"Till, with a sudden sharp hot stink of fox," he metaphorically depicts poetic inspiration as the fox's physical entry into "the dark hole of the head." Hughes ends by summarizing his vision of a poet as an interior, passive idea recipient, with the outside world unchanged: "The window is starless still; the clock ticks, / The page is printed."

Review Video: Metaphors in Writing
Visit mometrix.com/academy and enter code: 133295

Metonymy

Metonymy is naming one thing with words or phrases of a closely related thing. This is similar to metaphor. However, the comparison has a close connection, unlike metaphor. An example of metonymy is to call the news media *the press*. Of course, *the press* is the machine that prints newspapers. Metonymy is a way of naming something without using the same name constantly.

SYNECDOCHE

Synecdoche points to the whole by naming one of the parts. An example of synecdoche would be calling a construction worker a *hard hat*. Like metonymy, synecdoche is an easy way of naming something without having to overuse a name. The device allows writers to highlight pieces of the thing being described. For example, referring to businessmen as *suits* suggests professionalism and unity.

Review Video: Metonymy and Synecdoche
Visit mometrix.com/academy and enter code: 900306

HYPERBOLE

Hyperbole is excessive exaggeration used for humor or emphasis rather than for literal meaning. For example, in *To Kill a Mockingbird*, Harper Lee wrote, "People moved slowly then. There was no hurry, for there was nowhere to go, nothing to buy and no money to buy it with, nothing to see outside the boundaries of Maycomb County." This was not literally true; Lee exaggerates the scarcity of these things for emphasis. In "Old Times on the Mississippi," Mark Twain wrote, "I... could have hung my hat on my eyes, they stuck out so far." This is not literal, but makes his description vivid and funny. In his poem "As I Walked Out One Evening", W. H. Auden wrote, "I'll love you, dear, I'll love you / Till China and Africa meet, / And the river jumps over the mountain / And the salmon sing in the street." He used things not literally possible to emphasize the duration of his love.

UNDERSTATEMENT

Understatement is the opposite of hyperbole. This device discounts or downplays something. Think about someone who climbs Mount Everest. Then, they say that the journey was *a little stroll*. As with other types of figurative language, understatement has a range of uses. The device may show self-defeat or modesty as in the Mount Everest example. However, some may think of understatement as false modesty (i.e., an attempt to bring attention to you or a situation). For example, a woman is praised on her diamond engagement ring. The woman says, *Oh, this little thing?* Her understatement might be heard as stuck-up or unfeeling.

Review Video: Hyperbole and Understatement
Visit mometrix.com/academy and enter code: 308470

LITERARY DEVICES

LITERARY IRONY

In literature, irony demonstrates the opposite of what is said or done. The three types of irony are **verbal irony**, **situational irony**, and **dramatic irony**. Verbal irony uses words opposite to the meaning. Sarcasm may use verbal irony. One common example is describing something that is confusing as "clear as mud." For example, in his 1986 movie *Hannah and Her Sisters*, author, director, and actor Woody Allen says to his character's date, "I had a great evening; it was like the Nuremburg Trials." Notice these employ similes. In situational irony, what happens contrasts with what was expected. O. Henry's short story *The Gift of the Magi* uses situational irony: a husband and wife each sacrifice their most prized possession to buy each other a Christmas present. The irony is that she sells her long hair to buy him a watch fob, while he sells his heirloom pocket-watch to buy her the jeweled combs for her hair she had long wanted; in the end, neither of them can use their gifts. In dramatic irony, narrative informs audiences of more than its characters know. For example, in *Romeo and Juliet*, the audience is made aware that Juliet is only asleep, while Romeo believes her to be dead, which then leads to Romeo's death.

Review Video: Irony
Visit mometrix.com/academy and enter code: 374204

IDIOMS

Idioms create comparisons, and often take the form of similes or metaphors. Idioms are always phrases and are understood to have a meaning that is different from its individual words' literal meaning. For example, "break a leg" is a common idiom that is used to wish someone luck or tell them to perform well. Literally, the phrase "break a leg" means to injure a person's leg, but the phrase takes on a different meaning when used as an idiom. Another example is "call it a day," which means to temporarily stop working on a task, or find a stopping point, rather than literally referring to something as "a day." Many idioms are associated with a region or group. For example, an idiom commonly used in the American South is "'til the cows come home." This phrase is often used to indicate that something will take or may last for a very long time, but not that it will literally last until the cows return to where they reside.

ALLUSION

An allusion is an uncited but recognizable reference to something else. Authors use language to make allusions to places, events, artwork, and other books in order to make their own text richer. For example, an author may allude to a very important text in order to make his own text seem more important. Martin Luther King, Jr. started his "I Have a Dream" speech by saying "Five score years ago..." This is a clear allusion to President Abraham Lincoln's "Gettysburg Address" and served to remind people of the significance of the event. An author may allude to a place to ground his text or make a cultural reference to make readers feel included. There are many reasons that authors make allusions.

Review Video: Allusions
Visit mometrix.com/academy and enter code: 294065

COMIC RELIEF

Comic relief is the use of comedy by an author to break up a dramatic or tragic scene and infuse it with a bit of **lightheartedness**. In William Shakespeare's *Hamlet*, two gravediggers digging the grave for Ophelia share a joke while they work. The death and burial of Ophelia are tragic moments that directly follow each other. Shakespeare uses an instance of comedy to break up the tragedy and give his audience a bit of a break from the tragic drama. Authors sometimes use comic relief so that their work will be less depressing; other times they use it to create irony or contrast between the darkness of the situation and the lightness of the joke. Often, authors will use comedy to parallel what is happening in the tragic scenes.

Review Video: Comic Relief
Visit mometrix.com/academy and enter code: 779604

FORESHADOWING

Foreshadowing is a device authors use to give readers **hints** about events that will take place later in a story. Foreshadowing most often takes place through a character's dialogue or actions. Sometimes the character will know what is going to happen and will purposefully allude to future events. For example, consider a protagonist who is about to embark on a journey through the woods. Just before the protagonist begins the trip, another character says, "Be careful, you never know what could be out in those woods!" This alerts the reader that the woods may be dangerous and prompts the reader to expect something to attack the protagonist in the woods. This is an example of foreshadowing through warning. Alternatively, a character may unknowingly foreshadow later events. For example, consider a story where a brother and sister run through their house and knock over a vase and break it. The brother says, "Don't worry, we'll clean it up! Mom will never know!" However, the reader knows that their mother will most likely find out what they have done, so the reader expects the siblings to later get in trouble for running, breaking the vase, and hiding it from their mother.

SYMBOLISM

Symbolism describes an author's use of a **symbol**, an element of the story that **represents** something else. Symbols can impact stories in many ways, including deepening the meaning of a story or its elements, comparing a story to another work, or foreshadowing later events in a story. Symbols can be objects, characters, colors, numbers, or anything else the author establishes as a symbol. Symbols can be clearly established through direct comparison or repetition, but they can also be established subtly or gradually over a large portion of the story. Another form of symbolism is **allusion**, which is when something in a story is used to prompt the reader to think about another work. Many well-known works use **Biblical allusions**, which are allusions to events or details in the Bible that inform a work or an element within it.

Chapter Quiz

Ready to see how well you retained what you just read? Scan the QR code to go directly to the chapter quiz interface for this study guide. If you're using a computer, simply visit the online resources page at **mometrix.com/resources719/ftcehumank-12** and click the Chapter Quizzes link.

Historical Periods, Styles, and Movements and Prominent Aesthetic Principles

Architecture

African Architecture and Its Purpose

The **architecture in Africa** is diverse, and its structure and materials depend on the region. Architecture in North Africa is largely influenced by Islamic architecture, with intricate tilework, domes, and courtyards. West African architecture is earthen, using sunbaked mud bricks and plaster. East Africa has a blend of influences like Persian, Indian, and Arab shown in the Swahili architecture along its coast. The architecture of central Africa is not as well documented but is known to use local materials like bamboo, thatch, and wood. In southern Africa, architecture is often made of stone.

Buildings are designed to stand up to local conditions, such as insects, heavy rains, or intense sun. Many African structures have repetitive patterns and geometric designs. They are designed with aesthetics in mind as well as the cultural identity expressed by the unique ethnic groups. Many societies live in communal compounds with extended families, where the architecture supports interaction. Houses are made to be cool in hot climates and to guard against cold temperatures. Religious buildings like churches, mosques, and spiritual huts serve as points for community gatherings. Marketplaces and town halls are central areas for trading and holding meetings.

Examples of African Architecture

The **Great Mosque of Djenne** in Mali was built in 1907 on the Bani River's floodplain. It is made of adobe and was the second mosque to be built. The first was constructed around the 13th century and was found to have fallen into ruin by a French explorer in 1828. It is built on a raised platform to prevent flooding. It is the main worship site in the city and the biggest mud and brick building in the world.

The **Kasubi Tombs,** built in 13th century Uganda, are a burial site for four Bugandan kings and their families. It's an important political and religious site for the community and is known for its plant-based construction materials. The site includes a main building with surrounding smaller buildings. Some buildings were destroyed by a fire in 2010, but the remains are still intact.

The **Pyramids of Meroe** in Sudan are a group of steeply sloped Nubian pyramids that served as burial sites for Kushite monarchs, royal family members, and officials. There are three cemetery groups. While there are around 1,000 total graves, around 150 of the gravesites are pyramids. They were constructed from the third century BC to the fourth century AD and are the best relics remaining of the Kush kingdom.

Asian/Eastern Architecture and Purpose

Eastern and Asian architecture includes a wide range of styles and purposes depending on the region. Some architecture has a religious or spiritual purpose, like Hindu temples in India, Buddhist temples throughout East and Southeast Asia, mosques in the Middle East, and Shinto shrines in Japan. Other architecture has a political purpose, like Imperial palaces in China and Japan or some of the fortresses throughout India and other regions. Some notable examples of Eastern architecture include the Great Wall of China, which is a defensive wall; the Taj Mahal, which is a mausoleum in India; and Angkor Wat, which is a temple complex in Cambodia.

Asian architecture often includes decorative elements that are intricately ornamented and contain symbolic meaning. Islamic architecture uses calligraphy and geometric patterns to show the infinite nature of Allah. Hindu and Buddhist structures contain statues and carvings of deities and myths. Colors are often symbolic as well. Chinese architecture often includes red and gold, which are associated with prosperity and luck.

Mesoamerican Architecture and Purpose

Mesoamerican architecture was created from 1500 BC to the early 16th century AD by pre-Columbian civilizations like the Aztec, Maya, Olmec, and Teotihuacan cultures. They commonly created pyramid-shaped structures out of stone with flat tops for altars or temples. They also made large, open plazas, elaborate palaces, and ball courts for playing a sport.

The architecture had a variety of purposes. The pyramids and temples were built for religious and ceremonial use. They made sacrifices and astronomical observations. Palaces were centers for political power, where rulers lived and governed. They symbolized the power of the ruler's authority. Ball courts were used for playing a ritualistic ball game. Plazas and markets served as a hub for both social and economic dealings. The Teotihuacan culture created the Pyramid of the Sun and the Pyramid of the Moon, which were massive religious centers. The Mayan civilization made the Tikal, which is a complex of 3,000 structures that includes pyramids and palaces. The Aztecs constructed Tenochtitlan, a capital city with a major religious temple.

Examples of Mesoamerican Pyramids

El Castillo is the best-known pyramid located at the Chichen Itza archaeological site. Chichen Itza was a large city built by the Mayans between the 8th and 12th centuries AD. This step pyramid in the center of the ancient city is a set of square terraces with steps going up the center of each side. With 91 steps on each side, plus another step at the top, there is a total of 365 steps, which is the same as the number of days in a solar year. There is a temple on top of the pyramid. The building was constructed as a temple to Kukulcan, the Mayan feathered serpent deity.

Teotihuacan is an ancient Mesoamerican city in Mexico that is the site of several prominent pyramids. The Pyramid of the Sun was constructed around 200 AD, and the Pyramid of the Moon was constructed around 250 AD. The pyramids were built on top of earlier structures. They served as the focal point of the city. The Pyramid of the Sun was the largest structure built in Mesoamerica at the time. A tunnel-like cave has been found under the Pyramid of the Sun, and the chambers at the end were used for rituals. Since the temple on top of the pyramid has been destroyed, it is unknown what the purpose of the pyramid was. The temple at the top of the Pyramid of the Moon was built to honor the Goddess of Teotihuacan, who was the goddess of fertility, water, and the Earth.

Egyptian Architecture and Context

Ancient Egyptian architecture was mainly created along the Nile. It was designed to reflect the world's perfection at its moment of creation, as well as reflecting the relationship between the king, humankind, and the gods. Art and architecture in ancient Egypt were not meant to show the artistic creativity of individuals. Iconic examples of ancient Egyptian architecture include the pyramids and the Sphinx.

The **Giza Necropolis** is a complex of pyramids consisting of three main and several smaller pyramids. These were constructed during the Fourth Dynasty, between 2613 and 2494 BC, and served as grave sites for pharaohs. They show the great power of the pharaohs as well as the incredible engineering skills of the Egyptians. The Great Pyramid of Giza is the oldest and largest pyramid in the world. It is the only monument left standing of the Seven Wonders of the Ancient World.

The **Great Sphinx of Giza** is a monument of a mythical creature reclining near the Giza Necropolis. It was built during the Old Kingdom of Egypt between 2575–2150 BC. It was created for the builder of the Khafre pyramid, one of the three large pyramids at Giza. This monolith was carved from bedrock, which also served as material for the pyramids.

Classical Architecture

Classical architecture includes buildings that employ the principles and aesthetics of Greek and Roman architecture. This style includes a post and beam system with columns bearing the load. The pediment (shown) is the triangular part of a building above the columns. It might include elaborate sculptures within. Greek architects used the golden mean, or golden ratio, to create their ideal proportions for some of their buildings.

Columns were units of measurement in human scale, and several styles, orders, were developed over time. Caryatids were stone carvings of females, used as support pillars, which functioned as columns in Greek architecture. Greek architecture often used marble and stone, but the Roman discovery of concrete enabled the construction of arches, domes, and vaults, as used in the Pantheon in Rome. Whereas Greek temples were invariably oriented east to west, Romans would orient their temples with respect to the other surrounding buildings.

Greek and Roman Column Orders

Ancient Greek architecture has three distinct column orders. These styles are distinguished by their proportions and their unique characteristics. The Doric order is the simplest design, with a flat and unadorned design for the top and bottom of the column. This order is four to eight times its diameter. The Ionic order consists of spiral scrolls, or twin volutes, at the tops of the columns. This column's height is nine times its bottom diameter. The Corinthian order is much more ornate, embellished with floral designs. This column is taller, at 10 times its diameter.

The Romans adopted all of these column styles, and they later added two of their own. Their Tuscan order is very plain, and it is a simplified version of the Doric order. The composite order is a blend of the Ionic and Corinthian orders, using the scrolls of the Ionic order and the floral motifs of the Corinthian order.

Byzantine Architecture

Byzantine architecture is the architecture of the Byzantine, or later Eastern Roman Empire. This style was highly influenced by Greek and Roman architecture. Buildings became more complex, geometrically; in addition to stone, bricks and plaster were used in some instances. Mosaics were used in place of carved stone decorations, and many domes were used at this time. The architects used pendentives to support a circular dome over a square space, or they used an elliptical dome over a rectangular space. Prior to this, domes were used over circular spaces. Most of the surviving examples of Byzantine architecture are sacred in nature.

The greatest surviving example of Byzantine architecture is the Hagia Sophia in Constantinople (shown). A huge dome was constructed over a square space. The interior of the church included colored marble and other stones, and the vaults and domes were covered with elaborate mosaics.

Romanesque Architecture

Romanesque architecture is a style of medieval Europe beginning around the 11th century. This style is characterized by semicircular arches for doors and windows, and barrel or groin vaults. Many castles and churches were built in this style. Romanesque churches had large, thick walls and piers with few windows, a large tower where the nave and transept cross, and smaller towers at the western end of the church. An arcade, or row of columns, was constructed in the center of larger churches, separating the nave from the aisles. These buildings, both secular and sacred, give a feeling of solidity and strength by their massive size, thick walls, and masonry construction. Instead of relying on columns for support as in Greek and Roman architecture, this style, like the Byzantine style, relies more on walls. This example shows the few small arched windows that exemplify the Romanesque style.

Gothic Architecture

The **Gothic architecture** style in Europe spanned from the mid-12th to the 16th century. Architects sought to solve problems created by simple, dark, damp buildings from previous styles and instead create light, airy, beautiful structures. Gothic architecture is characterized by grand tall designs with upward visual movement. New building techniques allowed builders to create taller towers. The flying buttress is a defining element of this style, and it helped to allow these new heights. The pointed arch is another characteristic of medieval architecture, along with the advent of vaulted ceilings and gargoyles. Gargoyles serve a practical purpose as a drainage spout, but they also serve as decorations with evil or menacing features. The medieval style is known for being ornate, as seen in this example of the Amiens Cathedral in France. Beauty and aesthetic considerations are shown in the designs for these highly decorative buildings.

Balustrade, Pediment, and Flying Buttress

A **balustrade** is a series of pillars, or balusters, that support a rail to form a low wall or barrier. This could also be used for an ornamental parapet or balcony.

A **pediment** is the triangular gable used in classical Greek temples, as well as Renaissance and neoclassical architecture. It is found under the roof of the building and above the entablature. This would usually be on top of a portico or columns. The triangular area within the pediment is called a tympanum, and this was usually decorated with relief sculptures.

A **flying buttress** (shown) is a masonry support that transmits the thrust of a vault or a roof into the outer support. This is usually an inclined bar on a partial arch that extends, or flies out, from the wall and carries the weight of the vault or roof. This architectural element developed in Gothic architecture, from prior hidden supports in previous styles. This helped architects create the high ceilings characteristic of Gothic-style churches.

Spire, Facade, Caryatid, and Entablature

A **spire** is a tapering structure that comes to a point at the top of a building. These are often found on skyscrapers and church towers. A spire can function as a symbol of the power of religion, giving a sense of strength and reaching toward heaven.

The architectural term **facade** comes from a French word meaning "face." The facade of a building is its front or face, and this is often the most important design aspect when planning a building.

A **caryatid** is a stone carving of a female figure, draped in clothing, used to support an entablature. This caryatid, as shown, was used in place of a column in a Greek building. The entablature is the upper section of a classical order, and this is divided into the architrave, frieze, and cornice. The architrave is the lowest section of the entablature, which rests on the columns. The frieze is the middle section, in which relief sculpture might be found. The cornice is the crowning molding that will be found directly under the pediment.

Basilica, Apse, Nave, and Transept

A **basilica** was originally a type of Roman building, but this later became the basis for the design of the Christian church. In ancient Rome, a basilica was a public building in which courts were held, and other public functions were held there as well. The basilica would be centrally located in town, near the main forum. It is a rectangular building divided by rows of columns, or colonnades, into three aisles. The center aisle is called the nave. The nave runs from the entrance or vestibule of the church to the apse. The apse, or chancel, is the vaulted semicircular structure at the end of the center aisle. This is where the altar would be located. The transept is part of the church that lies across the main body and forms the cross shape. In this illustration, it is just before the apse.

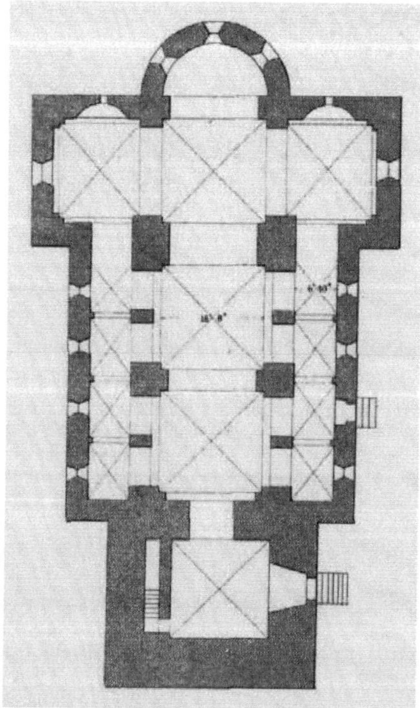

Obelisk, Oculus, Pilaster, and Rotunda

An **obelisk** is a tall, four-sided structure that is freestanding and tapers to a pyramidal point. These were often found at the entrances to Egyptian temples, and they continue to be used in Western architecture. One well-known example is the Washington Monument in Washington, D.C.

Oculus is the Latin word for "eye." In architecture, it is a circular opening in the center of a dome, and it is a feature in Roman, Byzantine, or neoclassical buildings. An oculus can also be found in a wall. The oculus in the Roman Pantheon is open and allows rain in, which leaves the building through drains in the floor.

A rotunda is a building that is round inside and out and is topped with a dome. A rotunda can also be a large interior space topped with a dome.

A pilaster (shown) is a flat, upright architectural element that projects from a wall, giving the appearance of a column inset in the wall. A pilaster only functions as decoration, not as support.

Renaissance Architecture

Renaissance architecture occurred in Europe between the 14th and 17th centuries. This style followed Gothic architecture, and was itself followed by the Baroque style. The Renaissance style emphasized proportion, geometry, and symmetry, and it included orderly composition of the columns and pilasters they used. These architects used semicircular arches, as well as hemispherical domes. The building plans are square and symmetrical, and facades are symmetrical as well. Church facades would usually be topped by a pediment, as shown in this example of St. Peter's Basilica. Renaissance architecture used the Greek and Roman orders of columns, either as structural objects or as purely decorative pilasters. The dome was used often as a large external feature or as a structural internal dome. Doors would have square lintels, and openings without doors would have arches with a decorative keystone. The keystone is the top center stone in an arch that carries the load of the arch structure. Moldings and decorative details were created with great attention to detail because they found it critical to master the techniques of the ancient Romans.

Baroque Architecture

Baroque architecture originated in Italy in the late 16th century, and it was prevalent in areas including Germany and South America until the 18th century. The baroque style is characterized by complex architectural plans often based on an oval design, with broader naves in an oval shape. Other characteristics include purposely fragmented elements, dramatic lighting and contrast, large frescoes on the ceiling, trompe l'oeil paintings, sumptuous colors and decorations, pear-shaped domes, and marble or faux finishing in the interior. The interior might also include bronze gilding, sculpted angels, and twisting columns. Baroque architects sought to explore new forms and styles as well as methods of lighting. They were using this architectural style to express the wealth and power of the Catholic Church during the time of the Counter-Reformation, a movement in response to the Protestant Reformation.

Rococo Architecture

The **rococo** style of architecture began in Paris in the early 18th century. It then spread throughout France and other countries. The rococo style first developed in interior design and decorative arts; then it expanded to architecture and other arts. This architectural style is characterized by pastel colors, serpentine lines, and excessive, elaborate ornamentation. The exterior of a rococo building will be simple, and the interior is filled with ornament and decoration, with the intent to wow the viewer. Floor plans of churches were complex, sometimes with interlocking oval shapes, and the stairways of palaces became ornate, central focuses. This style was meant to be highly theatrical and have something for a visitor to see at every turn. One example of rococo architecture is St. Andrew's Church in Kiev, Ukraine (shown). This facade shows a simplicity with a pastel blue and some ornamentation, but in keeping with the style, the interior is much grander and more elaborate.

Neoclassical Architecture

Classical architecture of ancient Greece and Rome was revived later with neoclassical architecture in the mid-18th century. This style began as a reaction to the excessive ornamentation of the rococo style. This international movement was characterized by a return to the clarity, restraint, and balance, as well as subjects and motifs, of classical styles. Neoclassical architecture used columns, especially the Doric order, and it showed a desire for blank walls rather than decorations. The roof would be flat, sometimes with a pediment, and the facade would be flat and long, with a wall of columns across. No domes or towers were used in this style. Examples of this style include the National Mall and the Lincoln Memorial in Washington, D.C. (shown). The Lincoln Memorial exemplifies the long, flat facade with a row of columns and the flat roof used in this style of architecture.

Art Nouveau Architecture

The **art nouveau style of architecture** was popular in the United States and Europe beginning in the 1880s, and it declined around 1910. Architects using this style sought to express modern ideas and use nontraditional forms in their buildings. This is sometimes referred to as the first modern architectural style. It is characterized by curved, graceful lines and decorations influenced by nature including leaves, vines, peacocks, and dragonflies. Ironwork and glass were used as sculptural elements as architects tried to embrace what was then possible because of the industrial revolution. These buildings also might contain mosaics, stained glass, and Japanese motifs. The architectural detail was often colorful and decorative, helping bring in the new, modern era.

This example, the Casa Batlló in Barcelona Spain, was remodeled and redesigned by Antoni Gaudi in 1904. It has the irregular shapes and flowing stone sculptural work that is characteristic of the art nouveau style. The facade is decorated with a mosaic made from broken tiles, and the roof is arched and rounded.

Beaux Arts Architecture

The **beaux arts architectural style** was taught from the 1830s to the end of the 19th century at the École des Beaux-Arts in Paris. From there, it strongly influenced architecture in the United States. Beaux arts architecture drew from Greek and Roman styling and included arched and pedimented doors, arched windows, flat roofs, columns, and symmetry. Beaux arts may also include sculptural details as well as classical details such pilasters, garlands, and balustrades. Interiors often have grand stairways and marble floors, with arched doorways and large rooms. Government buildings may have domes and high, vaulted ceilings.

The San Francisco Opera House (shown), built in 1932, is an example of the beaux arts style in the United States. The bottom floor is rusticated, with rough-cut stones. The top floor features columns and archways, as well as a low-pitched roof.

Neo-Gothic Architecture

Neo-Gothic architecture, also known as Gothic Revival or Victorian Gothic, is a style that occurred in the late 18th century in England. The use of this style increased in the early 19th century as architects sought to revive the Gothic architecture style. This style follows the original Gothic architectural style, with pointed arches for doors and windows; steeply pitched roofs; decorative ornamental patterns; spires; leaded glass, quatrefoil, or clover-shaped windows; pinnacles; grouped chimneys; stone carvings of gargoyles, leaves, and birds; and sometimes patterned brick or multicolored stone. A Gothic Revival building will emphasize vertical elements, leading the eye up to the sky. The style was often used in church architecture and also in the construction of colleges.

This example is the Salt Lake Temple in Utah, and it exhibits many of the Gothic architecture characteristics, including the emphasis on vertical elements. The spires are also reminiscent of the Gothic style.

Art Deco Architecture

The **art deco style of architecture** began in Paris in 1903. This style was applied to apartment buildings and public structures, but rarely to private homes. Art deco architecture used rectangular, block-like forms, arranged geometrically, with these elements broken up by ornamental and curved decorative motifs. This style was sleek and linear, with a modern feel. Buildings were embellished with repetitive designs, such as chevrons or geometric shapes, and these decorations might be machine made rather than hand-crafted. Art deco emphasized the horizontal rather than the vertical, and for practicality, a simple geometric box-shaped building could be embellished in this style to create a modern fashionable design on a budget. Materials used in art deco architecture were smooth stone, terra-cotta, stucco, steel, aluminum, and glass blocks.

The Chrysler Building, built in New York City in 1928, is an example of this architectural style. It includes ornaments protruding from the corners, as well as contrasting brickwork and emphasis on horizontal elements.

Bauhaus Architecture

Bauhaus architecture developed from the Bauhaus School of Art and Design in Germany beginning in 1927. The Bauhaus School sought to connect art with design and technology. The director of this school was Walter Gropius, who was a German architect known as a pioneer of modern architecture. The architectural style is simple and straightforward, following the Bauhaus minimalist and industrial aesthetic. Bauhaus architects sought unadorned functionality rather than aesthetics, and they often used a limited palette of neutral colors. This style favored function over form. Gropius designed door handles that became a well-known component of Bauhaus architecture and design.

The Bauhaus Building in Dessau, Germany (shown), built in 1926, is attributed to Gropius and embodies the Bauhaus style. The building is simple, with a clean design and geometric styling, and it uses a limited palette other than the red doors. This building is an example of Bauhaus architecture valuing function over aesthetics.

The Prairie School Movement

The Prairie School was a style of architecture prevalent in the Midwestern United States in the late 19th and early 20th centuries. Most architects associated with this movement were employed by Frank Lloyd Wright or Louis Sullivan, but Sullivan himself is not considered an architect of this style. The Prairie School style was used on some public buildings, but it is mostly known for home design. Common features include an emphasis on horizontal lines, overhanging eaves, low pitched or flat roofs, an open floor plan, clean lines, strings of windows in a row, built-in cabinetry, and the use of natural materials such as stone and wood. Wright favored geometric shapes as decorative designs in his buildings, whereas some other Prairie School architects used floral and circular geometric decorations. This example, Wright's Frederick C. Robie House in Chicago, Illinois, shows the clean lines, horizontal emphasis, overhanging eaves, and emphasis on geometric shapes prevalent in this style.

Skyscrapers

Architect Louis Sullivan is known as the "father of skyscrapers" and is considered the originator of the modern skyscraper. The name skyscraper was first used in the 1880s as the first skyscrapers were built in the United States. Originally this referred to buildings containing 10 or 20 stories, but later it came to describe buildings higher than 40 or 50 stories tall. After the first safe passenger elevator was created in 1857 and a need for more business space arose in cities, it became desirable to build buildings more vertically than horizontally. The refinement of the steel process in the 1860s also allowed for taller buildings to be constructed. These buildings had a steel skeleton rather than load-bearing walls, and this steel construction allowed these skyscrapers to rise to greater heights. This load-bearing steel frame was developed by architect William Jenney. Sullivan's Wainwright Building (shown), built in 1891, was the first building with a steel frame and vertical bands to emphasize its height. It is considered the first skyscraper.

The International Style of Architecture

The **International style of architecture** developed after World War I in the 1920s and 1930s, and it emphasized modern design. This was the dominant style of architecture until the 1970s, and it was influenced by the de Stijl and Bauhaus movements. This style is characterized by industrial materials, linear or geometric forms, and an absence of ornamentation. Glass, steel, and reinforced concrete were the main building materials. The style grew from a desire to get away from eclectic and mixed architectural styles and decorations, the development of new construction technologies, and a growing need for office buildings and other industrial structures. These architects took advantage of the inexpensive mass-produced iron and steel, and sheathed the buildings in glass, creating a new, modern look for the era. Prominent architects of this style include Walter Gropius, Ludwig Mies van der Rohe, Le

Corbusier, and Philip Johnson. A notable example (shown) is van der Rohe's Seagram Building in New York, built in 1958.

Grotesque, Plinth, Keystone, and Stringcourse

- A **grotesque** is a carved mythical creature that is used for decoration on a building. Grotesques look similar to gargoyles, but gargoyles have a functional purpose as a water spout that carries water away from the side of a building.
- A **plinth** is the square slab at the bottom of a column. This term can also refer to a flat block at the base of a door, or a projecting course of brick or stone at the base of a wall.
- A **keystone** is the wedge-shaped stone at the top of an arch. This stone locks the arch pieces in place; it is the last piece placed in the arch to give stability to the structure.
- A **stringcourse** is a projecting horizontal course, or band, of bricks or stonework on a building. It can be thin and undecorated or larger and ornate. This stringcourse, above the window, runs along the building horizontally and has a decorative pattern.

The Principles of Form and Function

The principle "form follows function" is associated with modernist architecture and design. It suggests that the design of a building should be led by its function, or purpose. This quote is attributed to American architect Louis Sullivan, who is known as the "father of skyscrapers," as well as America's first modern architect. Sullivan saw the purpose of the building as determining the form, reflecting the activities that will happen inside, instead beginning with a design and fitting the function to it. This became a maxim of modernist architects in the 1930s, who thought that decorative elements were inessential and should not be used in the design of modern buildings. Sullivan, however, continued to use some decorative art nouveau and Celtic elements in his designs, including green ironwork that became a recognizable hallmark of his work. Sullivan was a mentor of Frank Lloyd Wright, who later altered the saying to "form and function are one."

Art from Around the World

Prehistoric Art

Prehistoric art is art that was produced in preliterate times, prior to writing or recordkeeping. The first known art is from the Paleolithic era, and it consisted of petroglyphs, cave paintings, and sculptures and carvings in bone. Humans were making art to express ideas and to represent their beliefs and surroundings visually. One of the earliest representational artworks from prehistory is the *Venus of Willendorf* (shown), from roughly 28,000 BC.

In China and Japan, prehistoric pottery has been found, as well as bronze figures. In Europe, cave paintings were found in Lascaux and Chauvet, France, and in parts of Spain. Aboriginal painted rock art has been found in Australia, and engravings and paintings on stone and walls have been found in African caves. A large percentage of known prehistoric art is attributed to hunters and foragers. Repeated motifs include animals, humans, tools, maps, and symbols. Portable objects, such as rocks and bones, and stationary surfaces, such as cave walls, were used for art creation.

Characteristics and Purpose

Whereas some think that cave art was purely decorative, others think it was created for other reasons. Some of the cave walls used were remote and inaccessible, so it is thought that they were used for religious ceremonies, perhaps to summon better hunting conditions. Animals and other figures were generally depicted from a simplified side view. Artists painted and drew animals, hunting scenes, landscapes, maps, and many different symbols.

Petroglyphs have also been found, which are prehistoric rock carvings created by removing parts of the rock. Some show real subjects, whereas others are abstract. They might have been used to convey information or for religious purposes. Some might even be a form of prewriting, or a way to map the stars.

The Venus figurines from prehistory are women with exaggerated features, and they are thought to be fertility idols, good luck statues, or a symbol of a mother goddess. The *Venus of Willendorf* is one of the earliest examples of a female nude.

MATERIALS

Paleolithic artists used five main colors: black, white, yellow, red, and brown, as shown in this example from the Lascaux cave art in France. Color pigments were used for body and face decoration long before creating artwork. Some would mix earth or charcoal with animal fat for blacks and browns, and many paintings like this most likely vanished over time. Later rock art that has been discovered used materials such as iron oxide, kaolin, hematite, and manganese. Crayons were developed from solid pieces of pigment, and brushes were formed from animal hairs. Artists would also apply paint with their fingers or a pad made from lichen or moss.

Later in the Stone Age, artists used ochre for yellows, browns, and reds and used manganese or charcoal for black. White was ground calcite or kaolin. The artist would grind the pigment into a powder and mix it with water, blood, animal fat, juice, or other materials to help the pigment stick to cave walls or other surfaces.

EXAMPLES OF PREHISTORIC ART

There are several notable examples of cave paintings from prehistory. The **Lascaux** cave paintings in France date back to 15,000 BC. These Paleolithic paintings include detailed depictions of horses, bison, and deer. The large animals depicted in the paintings are ones that were native to the area. Although reindeer were a source of food, they are not depicted in the art. Among the more than 6,000 figures painted are not only animals but also people and symbols. Theories suggest that the artwork depicts successful hunting or possibly a ritual to improve the yield of future hunts.

The Cave of **Altamira** in northern Spain also contains Paleolithic art. This cave complex includes both charcoal and multicolored paintings from between 35,000 and 11,000 BC. The well-preserved petroglyphs, pictographs, and paintings show bison, bulls, and horses, among other animals. This was the first European cave system with prehistoric paintings discovered within.

The **Chauvet-Pont-d'Arc** Cave in France contains artwork from the Upper Paleolithic time. The art is thought to date back to 30,000 BC. This cave was inhabited by humans during two separate periods. The cave's floor includes impressions of cave bear prints and of where the bears slept. The artwork includes animals not seen in other paintings from the time, like hyenas, leopards, bears, and rhinoceroses.

AFRICAN ART

African art includes painting, sculpture, pottery, masks, textiles, body decoration, jewelry, and rock art. Some African art is aesthetic, some is political or ideological, and some is used for rituals. Characteristics of African art include stylized realism, an emphasis on sculpture, geometric forms, and a focus on the human figure. African artists will tend to visually abstract, or stylize, figures rather than represent them in a naturalistic way. Sculpture is a preferred art form rather than working in two dimensions. The human figure has often been a main subject for African art, depicted in masks, paintings, and sculptures. Human figures tend to show youthful characteristics because of an emphasis on health and physical strength as well as youth. African artists use geometric forms and symmetry, with repeated geometric shapes throughout an artwork. This example of a mask is symmetrical and includes several geometric shapes.

Context and Purpose

Some African art was created for religious purposes. In addition to regional religions, Christianity and other religions have been practiced there. Some art objects were created for display on an altar or shrine. Other artworks could be used to present sacrificial offerings, to commemorate leaders, or to contact spiritual ancestors. African art objects could also be used to connect with spirits through religious rites or by a religious specialist. These spirits could be summoned for healing or for communicating with ancestors.

Masks were used in performances and rituals with the participation of musicians, dancers, and the audience. When the masked dancer put on the mask, they took on the role of a powerful spiritual being. Many African societies have names for their masks, and these names are connected to the dance, the meaning of the mask, and the spirits associated with the mask.

Examples of African Art

The **Great Zimbabwe birds**, a set of soapstone sculptures created between the 11th and 15th centuries AD, were discovered at the archaeological site of Great Zimbabwe, the capital of the Kingdom of Zimbabwe. The purpose of the birds is unknown, but they are thought to have had religious significance and to have possibly represented a link between the rulers and gods. The Zimbabwe Bird is now a national symbol for the country. It is shown on the country's coat of arms and flag.

The **Benin Bronzes** were created by the Edo people in the Kingdom of Benin, which is modern-day Nigeria. They date back to the 13th century, and they decorated the king's royal palace. The bronzes are plaques and sculptures that show scenes of historical events and important figures. They glorified the king and documented the history of the kingdom. The craftsmanship and intricate designs show high skill in metalworking.

The **Nkisi Nkondi** figures are wooden figures made by the Kongo people in the Democratic Republic of Congo. They have sharp objects, such as nails and blades, driven into them. These figures were used for spiritual and magical intervention and to cure illnesses, settle disputes, and protect villages. They were believed to contain spirits that were capable of punishing people or bringing about good outcomes.

Egyptian Art

Painting, sculpture, and jewelry created in ancient Egypt from 3000 BC to 30 AD has largely been found in monuments and tombs. The artwork is mostly formal, and it follows specific guidelines for depicting figures. The stone statues are rigid and formal, whereas wood figures are more expressive. Ancient Egyptians' two-dimensional art is a combination of people, animals, and symbols. The organization of this artwork depends on the context: For more formal, organized scenes, they are sorted with the more important figures at the top. For a chaotic scene, such as a battle, this organization is not used.

The art we are most familiar with was found in the tombs of wealthy leaders; however, items of lesser quality are found in the burial sites of people of lower status. Statues were used as a conduit for people to interact with their gods. A ka statue is a statue intended as the resting place for a person's life force. Certain conventions were used for the creation of these, such as the sky god Horus always being represented with a falcon head. This consistency gave the figures a timeless quality.

Characteristics and Purpose

Much of the artwork created in ancient Egypt was not meant to be seen; rather, it was mostly created for tombs, and it emphasized life after death. Tombs in ancient Egypt were packed with furniture and food, as well as art and jewelry. The more important and wealthy the person, the more precious artifacts were found in their tomb. These items were meant for the person in their afterlife.

Egyptians used a hierarchy of scale to depict people, leaders, and gods: The larger the figure, the more important they were. Kings and deities might be shown on the same scale. Another common element of Egyptian artwork was hieroglyphs, or images that were symbols for sounds and words. These were the writing system of ancient Egypt, and they often accompanied the artwork.

Two-dimensional scenes were organized in registers, or parallel lines that separated scenes and served as ground lines. People were depicted with a simultaneous profile view and front view.

MATERIALS

Ancient Egyptians used soft stones such as limestone, sandstone, and calcite for sculpture. Copper chisels and stone tools could be used on these softer stones, and ancient Egyptians used copper alloys on harder stones such as quartzite, basalt and granite. Most statues were painted, as evidenced by traces of paint left on them. For wood carving and sculpting, a variety of native woods was used, including acacia, fig, fir, and cedar.

For metalwork, Egyptians used copper, bronze, gold, and silver. Many metal statues were melted down, and the materials were reused. They were able to cut stones for jewelry with precision. They used many stones in jewelry including lapis lazuli, feldspar, jasper, amethyst, and quartz.

The pigments used for painting came from local minerals. They used carbon for black, gypsum for white, iron oxide for reds and yellows, azurite and malachite for blues and greens, and orpiment for bright yellow. Paints were applied directly, or they were layered to create other effects.

EXAMPLES OF ANCIENT EGYPTIAN ART

Ancient Egypt created many well-known examples of artwork. One is the bust of Nefertiti, which was created in the 14th century BC. This bust is made of limestone, coated in stucco, and painted decoratively. Nefertiti was the wife of a pharaoh and may have been a pharaoh herself after his death. The bust exemplifies a classical style of Egyptian art. While the purpose of the bust is unknown, it is thought to have been used for creating official portraits of her.

Tutankhamun's Golden Death Mask is an iconic symbol of ancient Egypt. This funerary mask was created around 1323 BC and was made in the likeness of the god Osiris, who is the Egyptian god of the afterlife. The mask was made of copper and covered with a thin layer of gold. It was decorated with semiprecious stones like turquoise, lapis, and obsidian. Tutankhamun's burial chamber in the Valley of Kings contained his sarcophagus, which was opened in 1925 to reveal this mask.

ASIAN ART

Eastern art does not follow the same aesthetics of the elements and principles as Western art. Asian art does not have a hierarchy of fine arts versus crafts; rather, the skill of craftsmanship is valued, and all types of arts and crafts will be exhibited simultaneously. The crafts of creating porcelain or textiles, for example, have a long and respected history in Asia. Calligraphy, or the art of writing, is also a valued art form, and it has included many different scripts from different times and cultures.

Eastern art focuses more on landscapes and spiritual ideas, rather than representational subjects or realism. It will often be shown on more of a flat plane, instead of showing traditional perspective that is used in Western art. Some common forms of traditional Asian art include silk painting, woodblock printing, and batik, as well as painting with ink on rice paper.

CONTEXT AND PURPOSE

Buddhism has had a great influence on Asian art. Mandalas, which are geometric artworks representing the universe, and Buddha statues are examples of this influence. Asian art has sought to depict man's understanding of natural forces and the pattern of nature. The creation of artwork, including calligraphy, could refresh the spirit of the artist. Portraits would attempt to highlight the subject's moral character rather than just faithfully depict the subject. Art showed inspirational themes, and it often stayed away from subjects such as war, violence, death, and nudes. All objects in nature were seen as "alive," and rather than depicting nature realistically, Asian artists would try to capture the inner essence of these things. The artwork is full of symbolism, such as a dragon representing an emperor, or a pine tree symbolizing endurance. In the 1800s, Asian artists began to experiment with Western artistic traditions but turned back to Eastern traditions and began to combine Eastern and Western ideas.

EXAMPLES OF ANCIENT FAR EASTERN ART

Ancient China has a rich history of artwork dating back to Neolithic pottery and jade art. This early art included decorated, unpainted pottery made without the use of pottery wheels. In early Imperial China in 211 BC, more than 8,000 life-sized terracotta warriors and over 500 horses were created to be buried with the First Qin Emperor in his mausoleum. The figures of this **terracotta army** are lifelike and show several different poses. The original colors faded over time, but some are still visible. Each of the figures was created with a uniquely formed head.

The **Jomon art** of **ancient Japan** was created by the Jomon people, who were some of the first settlers of the country. The art and vessels were decorated with cord markings. Some of the early figurines were thought to be fertility figures based on their size and proportions. **Dogu** figurines were created in the late Jomon period, and they were small humanoid and animal earthen figures that were mostly between 4 and 12 inches high. The majority of the figurines were women, and they were thought to be used as a form of sympathetic magic, similar to voodoo dolls.

EXAMPLES OF EASTERN ASIAN ART

The Great Wave off Kanagawa, by Katsushika Hokusai, was created in 1831. This color woodblock print was part of a series called "Thirty-six Views of Mount Fuji." It is an example of *ukiyo-e* or floating world woodblock prints. This Japanese style flourished from the 1600s to the 1800s and showed scenes from life, theater, and landscapes. The artwork has a limited color palette, and the wave takes up much of the composition, capturing the raw power of nature and the Buddhist theme of impermanence.

Mughal miniatures were small paintings created during the Mughal Empire in South Asia between the 16th and 18th centuries. They include Central Asian, Persian, and Indian techniques. These miniatures had vivid colors and meticulous craftsmanship. They were often only a few square inches and were used for illustrating manuscripts and books. Some lines were so fine that they needed to be painted with a brush made of one hair.

MIDDLE EASTERN ART

Middle Eastern or Islamic art includes artwork created by countries in the Middle Eastern region by Muslim and non-Muslim artists. This includes architecture, mosaics, calligraphy, manuscript illumination, metalworking, textiles, and more. Religion is the most important aspect of Islamic art, and the artwork will often include patterns that could be repeated into infinity. This concept is important to Muslims, contrasting the experience of infinity with man's finite existence on earth and disregarding this temporary presence. Another important concept is the dissolution of matter, which can be achieved by applying patterns and decoration to surfaces. Floral patterns were often used for patterns and decorations, and they could be highly intricate and ornate. Calligraphy was integrated into artwork and decorations as an important element, and the inscription is often a quote from the Qur'an.

This image is an example of a repeated infinite pattern as well as dissolution of matter by covering it with a pattern.

The Ardabil Carpet, created between 1539 and 1540 in the town of Ardabil in Iran, is the oldest dated carpet in the world. It is made of wool with silk highlights and has a high knot density. The precise weaving technique shows the artisans' skills. This Persian carpet, made during the Safavid Dynasty, was intended for a major religious shrine and demonstrated the wealth and power of the Dynasty.

SOUTH PACIFIC ART

South Pacific artwork from areas including Polynesia, Melanesia, and Micronesia often uses natural materials that are readily available. Carving wood is a main technique of this artwork, as well as textile work and weaving. Some of the common forms of art include statues and figures carved from stone or wood. These often represent ancestors, gods, or spirits. Elaborately decorated masks are another commonly found form, as well as tall wooden totem poles. Canoe prow ornaments decorate the prow, or front, of canoes.

Some of the regional variations include the tattoos, wood carvings, and tapa cloth designs of Polynesia, as well as their Moai statues and tiki figures. Melanesian art uses complex patterns for carvings and features both masks and totem poles. Micronesian art focuses on weaving and art related to navigation like stick charts, canoe prow ornaments, and paddle decorations.

PURPOSE AND CONTEXT

South Pacific artwork showcases the traditions of cultures from Polynesia, Micronesia, and Melanesia. Religious Polynesian art from regions like Hawaii, New Zealand, and Easter Island includes tiki figures used in ceremonies to honor ancestors and deities. The artists often served as priests since making art required adding spiritual powers to the work. Ancestor figures were made of wood and housed the spirits of those who had died. Polynesian tattoos and carvings show lineage and rank within the society. Their navigation-related art reflects their seafaring culture.

Melanesian art from countries like Papua New Guinea, Vanuatu, and Fiji includes figures and masks used for spiritual ceremonies to channel ancestors and other forces. Each object was created for a specific purpose or ritual and was not designed to last. Body painting and elaborate costumes were used in New Guinea, and totem burial poles honored significant family members after they passed.

Micronesia, which includes Palau and the Marshall Islands, has created art relating to navigation, including stick charts and weather charms. Few of their sculptures or paintings were intended to last. The stick charts show where the region's islands were and were used for navigation. Weather charms protected travelers against evil spirits. Canoe prow decorations showed the importance of canoes in their society.

Examples of South Pacific Art

The **Moai statues** of Easter Island are a well-known example of Polynesian art. The monolithic carvings were created between 1400 and 1600 AD. There are more than 900 of them, and they have oversized heads and no legs. The majority were carved from compressed volcanic ash called *tuff*. They are thought to be religious and political symbols, as well as vessels for sacred spirits.

The wooden figures found in Micronesia, called **Nukuoro sculptures** after their origin in Nukuoro, are deity sculptures that represent ancestors and gods. They were created in the late 18th and early 19th century. They were used in homes and temples to ward off bad spirits and ill fortune. These sculptures were made from breadfruit wood and were made smooth using pumice. Their faces are devoid of features, and they are mostly unornamented, but some have carved tattoos.

Bisj poles (also called Bis or Mbis) were created in Vanuatu and New Guinea. They have been created from about 1900 AD to the present. They are made from mangrove trees and are carved for memorial feasts honoring those who passed away recently. Each pole is carved from one piece of wood, and all the roots are removed except for one. The tree is then inverted so that the root projects out from the top. The carvings feature figures of those who have died, and the poles are thought to help the dead pass on to the afterlife.

Aboriginal Art

Early Aboriginal art from Australia included rock paintings (shown) and carvings now found throughout the country, and many are protected in national parks. The rock art is thought to be for decoration or ceremonial purposes. Indigenous art is still created today in Australia and has become popular again since the 1970s.

The European colonization of Australia had a large impact on its artwork. Since the 1700s, Europeans began depicting Australian scenes, landscapes, and natural history illustrations. They attempted to capture the difference in lighting and scenery from the European landscape to the Australian landscape. The Victorian gold rush of the 1850s prompted wealthy landowners and merchants to commission landscape paintings. A distinctly Australian style of painting arose in the late 1800s, focusing on idealized landscapes and plein air painting. The main themes included working and conquering the land, the Australian outback, and the rural pioneer.

Latin American or Precolonial/Mesoamerican Art

Latin American art, from Central and South America, begins with the indigenous people. The first art objects were utilitarian, but eventually they began to produce artwork that represented the values and religions of the different regions. When South America was colonized by Europe, the art forms began to merge and blend. Latin American art is a blend of three cultures: Native American, African, and European. Prior to colonization, many Native Americans lived in Latin America, but then European settlers arrived and brought African slaves. During colonial times, art was usually religious, and it resembled traditional European artwork.

In the 1800s, artists began to develop their own regional styles that departed from European styles and traditions. One important artistic movement is muralism, which began in the 1920s. Hundreds of murals were painted in public places, with social and political messages, ideas of identity, and a theme of unity.

Characteristics

Mesoamerican artwork used a lot of natural materials. Stone was used for sculptures, feathers were used to decorate ceremonial attire, and stones like jade and obsidian were used for carving masks, figures, and tools. Some of the artwork was very colorful, such as the Aztec Portrait of Moctezuma II. Metals such as gold, copper, and silver were used for jewelry and ceremonial items, but not as extensively as in some other ancient cultures. They also created ceramic pottery that was decorated with elaborate designs.

The artwork included themes of mythology and religion with images of gods, scenes from mythology, and religious rituals. It also included plants, animals, and celestial bodies, as well as portraits of people in power. Skeletal figures and underworld scenes highlighted a focus on the afterlife.

Mesoamerican artwork used a mix of realistic depictions of human figures as well as idealized representations. They included stylized geometric patterns and abstract motifs on pottery, textiles, and architecture. They also used artwork to show sequences of events or stories in codices, which were a form of book, and murals.

Purpose and Context

Mesoamerican artwork was created for a variety of **purposes**. One such purpose was ceremonial and religious. Sculptures, masks, and ceremonial items were created for religious practices. Some objects were used for sacrifices and rituals to appease deities. Some art showed significant astronomical events.

The art showing rulers was used for political propaganda. It showed the divine right of rule and legitimized those in power. It was also used to show the history of the ruling dynasties. Art was used to document legends, myths, and historical events, as well as observations of astronomical events. Art also helped to keep genealogical records of significant families.

These materials and themes were influenced by the diverse environments of the regions, including rainforests and plateaus. Artistic motifs spread through trade and alliances, allowing the cultural heritage to be shared while regional variations were maintained. Mesoamerica's complex system of beliefs and gods remained a central theme throughout the artwork.

Examples of Precolonial/Mesoamerican Art

The **Maya Stelae** are tall stone slabs created by the Mayans during the Classic period, which was from 250 to 900 AD. They were carved from limestone, sandstone, or volcanic tuff. These structures are rectangular and measure anywhere from several feet to over 30 feet high. They include elaborate carvings of gods, rulers, and scenes of events. They have hieroglyphic text that explains the events with dates and names.

The **Olmec Colossal Heads** were created from 1400 BC to 400 BC by the Olmec civilization. This area is now the Gulf Coast of Mexico. The heads are carved from basalt boulders and are anywhere from 4.8 to 11 feet high. Many have helmets, and each head is unique. They are considered to be portraits of important figures or rulers. They show the civilization's skill at carving and transporting large stones.

The **Aztec Calendar Stone** was found under the main plaza in Mexico City. It is thought to date back to the early 16th century. The stone is about 12 feet in diameter and has detailed carvings showing elements of Aztec mythology and cosmology. The sun god Tonatiuh is in the center, and the outer rings show the 20 days in the Aztec month as well as other astrological and mythological symbols.

Western Art through the Ages

Relationship Between Western Tradition and Non-Western Tradition Art

Western art is created in America and Europe, while **non-Western** art is the artwork created in other regions of the world. Western art has historically valued individualism and realism, while non-Western art has valued communal identity and symbolism. Despite their differences, both Western and non-Western art have been used for religious ceremonies, to record historical events, and to portray important people. Both types of art have been enriched by their exposure to each other. However, questions about Western art appropriating non-Western artwork and issues of cultural power have also arisen.

Thanks to trade, like through the Silk Road and colonial expansion, Westerners were exposed to non-Western forms of art like Chinese silk painting. Certain Western art movements were influenced by non-Western art, like the influence of Japanese woodblock prints on Impressionists and Post-Impressionists.

Modern artists in the early 20th century found inspiration in the stylization and abstract forms from Oceanic and African art.

Large museums like the Louvre include diverse collections that juxtapose non-Western and Western work. The internet has facilitated the exchange of ideas across the world, and virtual exhibitions now allow audiences to easily engage with both Western and non-Western art.

European Art

European artwork began with prehistoric rock painting and carving, and it has developed over the centuries through many different artistic movements. Beginning in the Middle Ages, art would be commissioned by a patron, usually by the church or state. This artwork mainly showed historic, biblical, and religious scenes and religious and political leaders. Secular artwork included landscapes and still lifes. Academies trained artists in methods, materials, and anatomy. They attempted to elevate art from a craft to fine art and began to exhibit artwork. Art was created in workshops by master artists and their apprentices. As the importance of the church and royalty declined, the subject matter changed. The industrial revolution brought changes in technology that included premade, portable paints. Artists became independent and could use their own creativity. Because the academies resisted these changes, innovative artists became avant-garde while academic art stuck to traditions.

North American Art

Traditional Native American art flourished in North America prior to colonization. **Early colonial** art was based on European traditions, and artists mainly painted portraits and landscapes. In the 18th century, artists such as Benjamin West, John Singleton Copley, and Gilbert Stuart became some of the first significant American painters. Starting in 1820, the Hudson River School produced romantic landscape painting artists. The American Revolution brought a demand for patriotic artwork, and artists began to document rural America. Prominent 19th-century painters created portraits and painted a wide range of subjects including pioneers, soldiers, and sailors. American impressionism flourished in the 19th century, and in the 20th century, European art continued to impact America. This influence gave rise to the abstract art scene. Many art genres have risen in North America since the beginning of the 20th century, including pop art, minimalism, and photorealism.

Greek and Roman Art

The great classical art period began in Greece, and this art later greatly influenced Roman artwork. Romans borrowed many elements of their religion from Greece, and they also borrowed art and architectural styles. Ancient Greeks used art to express noble ideas and emotions. They wanted to highlight the great accomplishments of man and honor their gods through their artwork. Sculptures included nude athletes in realistic poses, as shown, as well as gods and goddesses. The artwork was mostly sponsored by the government and made for the public to see, and it was a great source of pride for the people. Art from ancient Greece includes stone and wood statues and pottery in red figure and black figure styles. They also painted on panels and pottery.

Ancient Romans used their artwork more for aesthetics and decoration, rather than for lofty ideals like the Greeks. In Rome, art lost its spiritual quality and was used more to adorn homes. They did copy the

Greek statues of gods and goddesses, but they also created skillful and realistic portrait sculptures. In addition to sculptures, they created paintings and mosaics for homes, showing scenes of daily life.

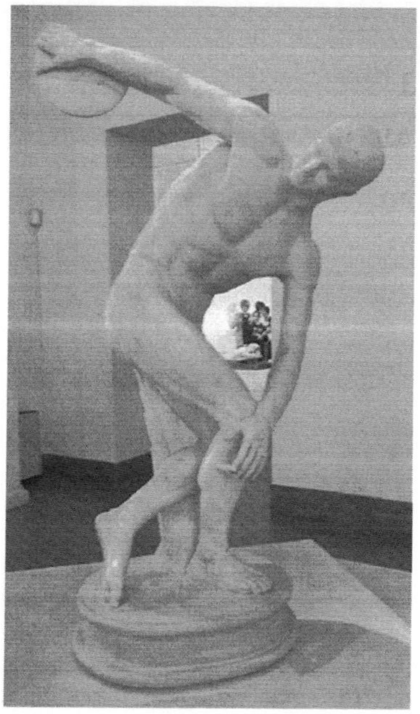

MATERIALS

The Greeks and the Romans used marble and bronze for sculptures. Roman artists used encaustic (pigment mixed with hot wax) and tempera for painting scenes on panels, and they created fresco paintings on architectural surfaces. For mosaics, Romans used small cut pieces of glass, tile, pottery stone, and shells. The pieces were called tesserae, and they were stuck to the surface with mortar.

The ancient Greeks also created wood sculptures in their early period, although few of these have survived. The preferred sculpture materials were marble and limestone, as well as cast bronze. They created figurines from terra cotta and bronze. The Greeks also painted on panels with encaustic and wax, and they painted their sculptures as well as parts of their temples. Most of the paintings that have survived are on pottery. Their pottery had a high iron oxide content, giving it a red color. This example is of the Greek red figure pottery.

Characteristics and Purpose of Ancient Greek/Roman Art

While the art of **ancient Greece** and **ancient Rome** include some similarities, their purposes and characteristics differ. The art of ancient Greece was intended to celebrate the philosophical ideals of beauty, the divine, and heroism. Greek art and sculpture emphasized proportion, beauty, and balance. It featured mainly gods, athletes, and mythological figures. The Greeks paid attention to details of the human form, including posture and musculature. The artwork was lifelike and made gods more relatable.

The art of ancient Rome mainly commemorated individuals, especially those in power. The sculptures and busts included people's imperfections in their realistic portrayals. The artwork was more utilitarian and individualistic, showing age as well as unique features. The artwork communicated the achievements and power of Roman leaders. The artists adapted their style from the art of ancient Greece, associating themselves with the prestige of Greek artwork and culture while changing it to make it their own.

Examples of Ancient Greek and Ancient Roman Art

The **Discobolus**, or Disc Thrower, is a well-known example of **ancient Greek** sculpture. This bronze sculpture by Myron was created during the Classical period, around 450 BC. It shows a nude male athlete throwing a discus, standing in a twisted pose. The face shows the Greek ideal of athletes with calm, controlled expressions.

Venus de Milo was created by an unknown sculptor between 130 and 100 BC. This marble sculpture portrays Aphrodite, the goddess of love, in a contrapposto stance with the weight shifted onto one leg. The arms of the statue are missing, and it is unknown what pose they had or what they might have held. She is partially draped in a cloth with her upper body exposed. It was designed to show the divine beauty of the goddess in a human form.

The **Colosseum** of ancient Rome is an iconic piece of architecture located in the center of Rome. Also known as the Flavian Amphitheatre, it was built between 70 and 80 AD and was made from mainly concrete and sand with a limestone facade. The elliptical building was used for public events and had tiered seating that reflected the hierarchy of society.

The statue of **Augustus of Prima Porta** was made of marble and created around 20 BC. This statue portrayed the first Roman emperor, Augustus, in a detailed military breastplate and cloak. His face shows idealized eternal youth, much like Greek tradition, and his right arm extends as if addressing his troops. This powerful piece of political propaganda presented Augustus as an ideal ruler.

Early Christian Art

Early Christian artwork was created from the late second century to the sixth century. It shows the formation of religious identity and theological ideas of early Christians. Since Roman authorities often persecuted the early Christians, much of the art was created secretly. Once Christianity was legalized, Christian art became more visible. The spread and public presence of its artwork accelerated when Christianity was adopted as a state religion of the Roman Empire under Theodosius I in 380 BC.

The purpose of this artwork was to educate faithful followers, most of whom were illiterate, about biblical narratives through visual storytelling. They used allegories and symbols to convey ideas and maintain secrecy during the times they were persecuted. Art was used to adorn worship spaces and to honor martyrs and saints. It helped Christians to develop a distinct identity and fostered a sense of unity.

Medieval and Byzantine Art

The period of medieval art spans more than 1,000 years, from the fall of the Roman empire to the Renaissance period. Subjects explored during this time include mythology, Christian themes, and biblical stories. The medieval period can be separated into Byzantine, Romanesque, and Gothic. Byzantine art was from the Eastern Empire called Byzantium, and it was highly stylized. Byzantine art favored symbolism over realism, and the subject matter included imperial and religious subjects. This example of Byzantine painting shows religious subject matter.

Romanesque art included massive churches built with stone arches, similar to Roman architecture. Romanesque painters created frescoes and used encaustic on panels. Gothic art began in Paris and spread throughout Europe. Its greatest contribution was the cathedral and elaborate architecture with complicated decoration. Painting during the Gothic period included animated figures and expressions, painted small in relation to their backgrounds.

Examples of Medieval and Byzantine Art

There are several notable examples of **medieval art**. The **Bayeux Tapestry,** from the 11th century, is an embroidered tapestry almost 70 meters long showing the events leading to the Norman conquest of England and the Battle of Hastings in 1066. It was commissioned by Bishop Odo of Bayeux, William the Conqueror's half-brother, to serve as a record of the conquest. It legitimized William's claim to the throne of England.

The **Ghent Altarpiece**, from the 15th century, is a polyptych altarpiece made by Hubert and Jan van Eyck for the Saint Bavo Cathedral located in Ghent, Belgium. It was the centerpiece for liturgical ceremonies and meant to inspire devotion by depicting Christian themes in a detailed and symbolic way.

The **Hagia Sophia**, constructed in the sixth century under Emperor Justinian I, was built in Constantinople as a Christian cathedral. It served as the central church of the **Byzantine** Empire as well as a symbol of religious devotion and imperial power. Notable aspects include a massive dome and intricate mosaics.

The **Icon of Christ Pantocrator**, an icon created in the sixth century, is one of the earliest icons of Christ. It is now found in Mount Sinai, Egypt. Icons were used in worship, serving as a focal point for prayer.

Byzantine Characteristics and Purpose

Byzantine art is influenced heavily by Christian themes. This style is a subset within the broader medieval art movement, and it is the artwork specifically of the Byzantine Empire from the 4th to the 15th century. It often shows scenes from the Bible, scenes of the lives of saints, and other Christianity-related events. Icons were the main focus of Byzantine art. An icon is usually a painting of Jesus Christ or another holy figure. They were painted on wooden panels and used for both private and public worship.

Byzantine art is stylized and abstract. It focuses on conveying ideas rather than showing realistic representations. Figures in Byzantine art are shown on a hieratic scale, with more important figures depicted as larger than others to show their significance.

Byzantine art was created mainly for the Eastern Orthodox Church and was used in rituals and religious services as well as private devotional practices. The artworks were focal points for prayer. They were also used as teaching tools to educate people about biblical stories. The saints and holy figures depicted in artwork served as models of virtuous behavior for others to follow.

Medieval Art Characteristics and Purpose

The medieval period of art covered over 1,000 years and several styles from the 2nd century to the 16th century when the Renaissance began. Medieval art mainly depicts Christian subjects, including images of Christ, the saints, and biblical scenes. Much of the art was created to decorate churches, including stained glass, frescoes, altarpieces, and illuminated manuscripts. The art contains allegories and symbols that convey moral and spiritual meaning. It uses symbols or icons for subjects, such as a lamb for Christ, to convey complex ideas. Medieval art lacks linear perspective and often appears flat. Objects and figures are stylized, and they often have vibrant colors and bold outlines. Figures are shown using a hieratic scale, with important figures being larger than those that are less important. Figures placed centrally are more significant than those placed on the sides.

Medieval art was used to educate people on Christianity and convey ethical and moral lessons. The artwork showed the consequences of sin and the benefits of piety. The art was an important part of religious services and was used for personal devotion as well. Artwork in churches and cathedrals inspired awe and helped bring the soul closer to the divine. Some of the tapestries and manuscripts served as a visual record of historical events.

Renaissance Art

The **Renaissance** was a revival of classical learning during the 14th, 15th, and 16th centuries in Europe. Renaissance artists sought to capture the value of the individual and the beauty of the natural world. This revival of drawing, painting, sculpture, and architecture was partly driven by humanism, which is a philosophy that attached importance and worth to the individual. Artists looked to the past for inspiration, while innovating and producing some of the best-known art in history. Artists used naturalism, attempting to portray figures realistically rather than exaggerating or stylizing them. Renaissance artists studied anatomy and perspective, as well as light and shadow, to use them accurately in their artwork. They took ideas from the mythology of classical civilizations and used them as a starting point to create their own monumental works.

During the Renaissance, the ambition of classical civilizations was rediscovered, boundaries were pushed, and artists innovated to capture the beauty of humanity. The Greek idea of humanism was used to celebrate the accomplishments of man. Renaissance artists saw the classical period as the height of humanity and attempted to recreate and build upon this movement.

Increased prosperity during this time led to an increase in commissioned artwork from wealthy patrons (especially the Medici family). At the same time, the church was conflicted on spiritual and secular issues, which helped the spread of humanism. The church was also a big patron of the arts, and it spent a great deal on art and architecture at the time. In addition to the wealth of Italy, Italy also contained a lot of Roman architecture and artifacts, which contributed to the beginning of the Renaissance in this area.

Characteristics and Purpose

The ideas of humanism brought greater attention to detail and greater realism, as well as a focus on virtue. Artists began to use linear perspective foreshortening, bringing a natural realism to faces and figures. Sculptures, drawings, and paintings showed increased knowledge of anatomy. Most painters began to use oil paint rather than tempera at this time, which contributed to this realism.

Christianity was still the main subject of artwork at this time, reflected in the paintings and sculptures of many prominent artists including Michelangelo, Leonardo da Vinci, and Raphael. Stories from mythology were depicted, too, to promote the idea of humanism. During the Renaissance, artists were creating artwork for patrons and their status was raised to a level above craftsman. Because of the Renaissance movement, Western art developed from the ideals of classical artwork.

Altarpieces were commissioned often, and these would be the focal point of the space they occupied. Frescoes were often created in churches and in private buildings. This painting method was time consuming, with a prominent example being Michelangelo's Sistine Chapel ceiling (shown). Patrons also commissioned portraits of themselves and artworks for their homes.

Materials

Frescoes, that is, murals painted onto plaster walls, were painted during the Renaissance period. The pigments were mixed with water and applied to wet plaster, and once the plaster dried, the pigments were visible on the wall. This was a time-consuming process, but it was used for large works of art including the Sistine Chapel ceiling.

Artists also painted with oil paints, which became available in the 15th century. The slow drying time allowed artists to blend and paint with greater realism and detail than before. More colors were available, and the transparency allowed artists to use glazing techniques, layering transparent colors for greater depth and richness. Artists during this time also still painted on wood panels or rigid supports with tempera.

For sculpting, the most common material was marble. Michelangelo's famous sculptures, including *David*, *Moses*, and other notable works, were carved from marble.

Leonardo da Vinci, Michelangelo, and Raphael

Leonardo da Vinci, Michelangelo, and Raphael are a few of the best-known artists of the Renaissance period. Leonardo was a "Renaissance man," with knowledge of math, astronomy, architecture, art, inventing, literature, anatomy, and more. His well-known works include the *Mona Lisa* and *The Last Supper*. He pioneered a technique called sfumato, which uses subtle gradations to create a smoky look.

Michelangelo showed a mastery of anatomy in his artworks. His best-known works are his *David* statue and his painting of the Sistine Chapel ceiling. Unlike many artists, he achieved fame as an artist during his lifetime. He was accomplished in art, sculpture, and architecture, and he inspired the artist Raphael.

Raphael is known for his skillful composition, as well as his serene depictions of the greatness of human nature. One of his best-known works is the School of Athens, a monumental work from 1509–1511 depicting many ancient Greek philosophers (shown). This artwork also shows a mastery of perspective, as well as natural poses and lighting.

The Mannerism Style

The **mannerism** style of art and architecture emerged as a reaction to the high Renaissance. From the end of the Renaissance in the 1520s to the beginning of baroque art in 1590, mannerism focused more on style and technique than the meaning of the subject. Mannerism arose partly from new scientific discovery that man was not the center of the universe, but, rather, the earth revolves around the sun. At the same time, the Reformation movement highlighted a need for church reforms, bringing turmoil and religious uncertainty.

Mannerist artists reflected this uncertainty, attempting to solve artistic problems by changing proportions and portraying people in new and strange ways. These included elongated limbs, small heads, and dramatic, unnatural, contrived poses. Departing from the linear perspective and depth used in Renaissance art, mannerists flattened the composition and arranged the figures on a flat plane, as shown. Mannerism artists experimented with form, portraying emotions, and bright and unusual colors.

El Greco and Tintoretto

El Greco, a nickname meaning "the Greek," painted in the mannerist style, using elongated and strange proportions and portraying strong, dramatic emotions. The poses are strained and unnatural, heightening the emotion conveyed by the subjects. Rather than using accurate lighting, the lighting in his works seem to come from within the figures or from an unseen source. In his later works, he elongated figures even more, especially on altarpiece works. This work from 1600 shows his odd use of lighting and forced, strained poses that illustrate the mannerist style.

Tintoretto, another mannerist painter, created monumental religious works and emphasized the mystical nature of religion. He also used elongated forms and forced poses, but his works show a mastery of lighting along with a better idea of spatial depth. He sought for viewers to experience the divine through his religious depictions. Through lighting and composition, he created a supernatural atmosphere, portraying scenes not from this world.

BAROQUE ART

Baroque art dominated Europe in the 17th and 18th centuries. The style was propagated by the Catholic Church, often in the form of monumental works of public art. This style was meant to counter the rationality and simplicity of the Renaissance style and inspire a sense of awe. Many baroque artworks illustrated Catholic ideas, within biblical or mythological depictions. Architecture, painting, and sculpture all reflected these ideals successfully. Baroque sculpture also used a dramatic sense of movement, contrasting with the comparatively still and calm Renaissance sculptures.

Baroque paintings would often include allegories, which are stories with hidden meaning and messages. The educated viewer was expected to recognize and understand symbols and hidden meanings in the artwork.

The *Trevi Fountain in Rome* (1732, shown) is an example of the overly ornate baroque style in sculpture. Some of the major artists of this time include Rembrandt, Caravaggio, and Peter Paul Rubens.

CHARACTERISTICS AND PURPOSE

The **baroque** art style is characterized by exaggerated motion and attention to detail. The scenes are created to enhance a sense of drama and grandeur. The chiaroscuro technique is often used in baroque art. This is the use of strongly contrasting tones of light and dark, usually in a dramatic, high-contrast scene. Another technique used is tenebrism, which consists of keeping an area black, while a portion of the subject is brightly illuminated, as shown in this painting from 1636.

To set their artwork apart from the Renaissance artworks, artists departed from tranquil scenes and expressions of that time and instead showed intense emotion and movement in their work. Instead of the even lighting of Renaissance artwork, they used more dramatic lighting and they used asymmetry to enhance the sense of instability and movement. Clothing would be moving by wind or the motion of the person instead of draped and resting motionlessly.

NEOCLASSICISM

Neoclassicism occurred during the late 18th and early 19th centuries. This movement in art and architecture was an attempt to revive the classical Greek style and depart from the highly ornate baroque style. It also came about partly from the discovery of Roman ruins at Pompeii and Herculaneum. Neoclassical artwork was serious, stoic, and heroic. Artists portrayed moral narratives of ethical superiority, returning to classical subjects and motifs from Greek and Roman art. This art is characterized by somber colors, shallow space, balance, clarity, and restraint. Artists sought to show smooth paint surfaces with no brushstrokes visible in their artwork.

This movement coincided with the Age of Enlightenment, or Age of Reason, which was an intellectual and philosophical movement focused on reason as the main source of authority. These ideas were also reflected in the art at the time, as artists moved from ornate and frivolous art to more serious, classical subjects. Neoclassical artists had few surviving Greek paintings to model their work after, but they had many more examples of sculpture to follow for their work.

Jacques-Louis David and Jean-Auguste-Dominique Ingres.

One significant artist of the neoclassical style is Jacques-Louis David. His painting *Oath of the Horatii* is a prime example of the neoclassical movement. This painting (shown) tells a story from classical times, from a Roman legend in which the Horatii brothers take an oath to defend Rome. In this carefully organized composition, three arches with columns span the background, whereas all the figures and action are pushed into the foreground as if creating a sculptural relief.

Jean-Auguste-Dominique Ingres was a student of David, and he also created works in the neoclassical style. Unlike David, he began to favor more sensuous subjects and became known for portraits. His work *Oedipus and the Sphinx* (1808) was completed while Ingres worked in Rome. This scene is from the Greek myth of Oedipus, when Oedipus was guessing the riddle of the Sphinx. Ingres won the prestigious Prix de Rome for this painting. Keeping with classical standards, Oedipus is depicted as a beautiful and ideal young man.

Romanticism

The **romanticism** movement began in 1770 and encompassed art, literature, music, and culture. The term romantic refers not to love, but to intense emotion. This movement emphasized emotion and individualism, and it was a reaction against the rationalism of neoclassicism. Romantic artists often illustrated literary themes. They emphasized and depicted emotions such as terror, awe, and apprehension, and they attempted to capture the beauty and sublime feel of nature. This painting by

Thomas Cole from 1836, *The Course of Empire: Destruction*, embodies the focus on nature and destruction in a romantic artwork.

This style first manifested in landscape painting, and artists challenged the previously low status of landscape art by painting monumental works. History painters also created large works, portraying disaster, divine wrath, and natural catastrophe. Artists portrayed vast spaces with people dwarfed in comparison, mystical landscapes, and nature's triumph over man. No traditional religious art came from this period, but artists continued to portray small villages and the wilderness, despite the increase of urban spaces.

Eugène Delacroix, Theodore Gericault, Thomas Cole

Several significant artists worked in the romanticist style. Eugène Delacroix was at the forefront of the French school of romantic artwork. In *Liberty Leading the People*, he depicted the female figure of Liberty leading the French Revolution of 1830. It is a history painting, showing a violent, dramatic, catastrophic scene.

Theodore Gericault was another French romantic artist. His work *The Raft of the Medusa* is a significant romantic painting. This work is larger than life size, and it shows the aftermath of the wreck of a French naval frigate, with people escaping on a makeshift raft. It shows men dying and struggling to survive against nature, with strong emotions and an unfolding drama.

Thomas Cole was an American painter who portrayed the American wilderness in the romantic style. One of his well-known works is called *The Oxbow*, which shows a bend in the Connecticut River, in a valley after a thunderstorm. There is a juxtaposition of broken trees, violent cliffs, and dark rain clouds beside blue skies and a tranquil bend in the river.

Realism

The **realism** movement began in France in the 1850s, as a rejection of the ideas of romanticism. Rather than exaggerated scenes and heightened emotions, realism sought to portray ordinary scenes with accuracy and truth. The artists attempted to show people from all walks of life and social classes accurately and not smooth over or avoid unpleasant subjects. Realist artists did not portray people heroically or sentimentally; instead, they wanted to treat all subjects with equal seriousness. The advent of the camera helped to increase the desire to show subjects realistically.

The realism movement is thought to be the first modern art movement, because the artists rejected traditions and expanded the definition of what is considered art. They examined the political, cultural, and economic structure of society, and they used earthy tones to show what was happening in all parts of society. Realist artists painted real-life events, workers, street life, cafés, peasants, and nightclubs, rather than grand landscapes or posed scenes with extreme emotions.

Gustave Courbet, Jean-Francois Millet, and Honoré Daumier

The main realist artists in France were Gustave Courbet, Jean-Francois Millet, and Honoré Daumier. Courbet would paint ordinary scenes on vast canvases that were normally used for history paintings. Two of his well-known works include *The Stonebreakers* (shown) and *A Burial at Ornans. The Stonebreakers* was painted in 1849, and it shows ordinary workers in his native region of France. He uses natural color and lighting to portray his subjects.

In the United States, Thomas Eakins and Winslow Homer were significant realism painters. Winslow Homer began as a commercial illustrator, but then he was inspired by Courbet, Millet, and Daumier and began to paint ordinary subjects in America. Eakins painted his friends and local people in outdoor sports, including his work *Max Schmitt in a Single Scull, from 1871.* His most well-known work is *The Gross Clinic*, which showed a scene from a surgical operation, and this was received unfavorably by critics due to its subject matter.

IMPRESSIONISM

The **impressionism** movement began in the late 1800s as artists in Paris began to practice plein air painting together. The artists included Claude Monet and Pierre-Auguste Renoir. Impressionists departed from a faithful depiction of a scene, and instead they attempted to capture their impression of it, or the momentary effect of lighting on the scene. Artists used small brushstrokes and pure color. They tried to capture the optical effects of light, and the differences that weather and sun position create in a scene.

The recent invention and availability of paint in a tube helped spur on this movement. Artists were able to paint outside more easily and capture scenes as they saw them. The emphasis in the painting was as much on the artist's perception of the scene as it was on the scene itself. The painting by Claude Monet, *Haystack. End of Summer. Morning.* from 1891, shows how Monet used color and brushstrokes to capture the lighting of a summer morning on the haystack.

CLAUDE MONET, EDGAR DEGAS, MARY CASSATT, AND AUGUSTE RENOIR

Claude Monet is the most well-known impressionist painter, and some of his subjects include cathedrals, haystacks, landscapes, water lilies, and his garden in Giverny, France. The paintings of his garden included a Japanese footbridge that spanned over water lilies. His paintings became increasingly abstract in later years due to his failing eyesight.

Edgar Degas was an impressionist painter best known for his paintings of ballerinas and dancers. He captured his impression of dance lessons and performances, showing the movement of the moment with visible brushstrokes. This example from 1873–1876, *The Dance Class*, shows a dance class being instructed by the man in the center. He did not capture outside light like other impressionists, but he still captured fleeting moments in time.

Mary Cassatt was the best-known female impressionist painter, and she often painted domestic scenes with a child and mother as the subjects. Cassatt was invited to exhibit with the impressionists by Degas, and she began to be influenced by their work.

Auguste Renoir captured stunning landscapes and beautiful portraits in the impressionist style. The visible brushstrokes, soft edges, and pure colors follow the patterns of impressionist painters, and he shows a masterful understanding of how light affects his subjects.

POSTIMPRESSIONISM

Postimpressionism was a French art movement from 1886 to 1905 that followed impressionism and preceded fauvism. Postimpressionism sought to explore the emotional response of the artist and depart from the naturalism of impressionism. These artists still used bold and pure colors as well as real-life subject matter, but they also leaned toward more geometric shapes, distorted forms, exaggerated or arbitrary colors, and sometimes heavy outlines.

Neoimpressionist Georges Seurat departed from the spontaneous nature of impressionism for a more planned approach that included the optical blending of spots of color. This is now known as pointillism, but it falls under the postimpressionist movement. Paul Signac carried on Seurat's ideas; he helped Seurat develop the pointillism style.

This work by Henri de Toulouse-Lautrec from 1889, titled *Monsieur Fourcade*, shows several major ideas of postimpressionism. Although the artworks and artists of this period are fairly varied, this work does show the bold, arbitrary colors and outlines used in postimpressionist artwork.

VINCENT VAN GOGH, PAUL GAUGUIN, AND PAUL CÉZANNE

Vincent van Gogh, a prominent Dutch postimpressionist artist, exhibited many of the ideas of this movement. He used bold colors, sometimes arbitrarily or in odd ways, as well as bold lines to express his emotion through his paintings. In this 1890 painting, *Portrait of Dr. Gachet*, van Gogh expresses emotion through the pose, facial expression, and colors. Bold colors and brushstrokes, along with heavy outlines, are visible in this artwork.

Paul Gauguin used bold and unusual colors, sometimes in flat planes and flattened spaces. This French artist's work includes many paintings of landscapes and people of French Polynesia, where he lived for 10 years.

Paul Cézanne was another French postimpressionist painter, and he is known as the father of postimpressionism. His exploration of geometric shapes and bold colors prompted Picasso and others to eventually experiment with multiple views of forms. He sought to reduce nature to geometric shapes and find new ways of modeling space and volume.

FAUVISM AND EXPRESSIONISM

The **fauvism** movement, from about 1905 to 1908, followed the postimpressionism movement and included some similar ideas. Fauvism emphasized strong and unusual colors, using color to express mood without being representational of actual colors. Fauvism also emphasized the flatness of the canvas, and it valued individual expression over naturalistic representation. The leaders of the fauvism movement were Henri Matisse and André Derain.

Expressionism began in Germany at the beginning of the 20th century, and it spanned from roughly 1905 to 1920. Artists of this movement used strong colors and distorted forms to express their feelings in their artwork. Artwork came from within the artist, rather than being copied from what they observed. They used swirling and exaggerated brushstrokes and sought to evoke emotional responses to their works. Edvard Munch's *The Scream* (1893) is an example of the Expressionist style, with its unusual, nonrepresentational colors, distorted form, and desire to express a strong feeling of despair or agony.

Fauvist and Expressionist Artists

Henri Matisse was a fauvist artist who pioneered the movement. He applied large, flat areas of color to his paintings and worked with bright colors directly from the tubes to convey emotions. He is also considered a leader in defining the 20th-century modern art movement. One of his best-known works of this period is called *Woman with a Hat* (1905). He used unusual colors, including green on the woman's face.

Expressionism began with works of artists such as Vincent van Gogh and Edvard Munch, and then in 1905, German artists formed a group called Die Brücke that began the main wave of expressionism. This group included artists Erich Heckel, Fritz Bleyl, and Karl Schmidt-Rottluff, and they were later joined by Otto Müller, Emil Nolde, and Max Pechstein. Wassily Kandinsky was a notable Russian expressionist painter, and he went on to work in abstract art.

Cubism and Futurism

Cubism is an early-20th-century art movement in which several viewpoints are shown simultaneously, and simple geometric shapes or interlocking planes are used to construct a scene. Cubism began in 1907 and ended around 1915. Pablo Picasso and Georges Braque pioneered this movement, influenced partly by the three-dimensional representations in works by Paul Cézanne. Cubist artists would analyze a form, break it apart, and reassemble it visually in a more abstracted format.

Futurism, an early-20th-century movement that began in Italy in 1909, emphasized movement, technology, speed, and violence. The artwork included objects such as cars, airplanes, and industrial elements. Like cubists, these artists expressed dynamic elements in artwork. They also praised originality, admired technology over nature, and sought to convey movement through space. Futurist artists praised war and valued nationalism, and they would depict urban scenes such as riots and construction in the city.

Pablo Picasso, Marcel Duchamp, Giacomo Balla

Pablo Picasso is one of the most recognizable names of cubism. His cubist works include flat planes of color, distorted forms, geometric shapes, and reassembled faces with both eyes on one side of a profile.

Marcel Duchamp's work spanned both the cubist and futurist movements. His work, *Nude Descending a Staircase, No. 2*, from 1912, shows a dynamic scene of repeated abstracted and geometric forms of a nude descending from left to right in the painting. The repetition and form convey movement and rhythm.

Giacomo Balla's *Dynamism of a Dog on a Leash* from 1912 embodies some of the tenets of the futurist movement. The painting shows the feet of a woman, plus a leash and a walking dog. Through the repetition of the feet, leash, and tail, Balla shows the dynamic movement of the woman and the dog. The dynamic elements show almost a blur of movement, conveying speed and direction.

Constructivism and De Stijl

The constructivism movement began as a Russian abstract style of art and architecture that started in the 1910s. This movement consisted of constructing dynamic three-dimensional forms from objects such as plastic, wood, glass, or iron. This movement began with Vladimir Tatlin, who was influenced by Picasso's cubist constructions and wanted to "construct" art with dynamic components. Tatlin began to make abstracted still lifes out of scrap materials.

De Stijl is Dutch for "the style," and this Dutch art movement that started in 1917 is also known as neoplasticism. This art movement promoted the reduction of artwork into geometric shapes, lines, and primary colors. Artists attempted to turn this style into a universal form of expression, departing from individual expression. Piet Mondrian is the most recognizable de Stijl artist. Neoplasticism refers to the style and ideas developed by this artist, promoting a new, abstract form of artwork for modern times.

Vladimir Tatlin, Piet Mondrian

The **constructivism** movement began with artist Vladimir Tatlin in 1913. Tatlin was a Soviet architect and painter, and he constructed three-dimensional "counter-reliefs" of wood and metal. His intention was to question the traditions of art. His main constructivist work was the *Monument to the Third International* (*Tatlin's Tower*), which joined the dynamic components of technology with the aesthetics of machines. This construction included searchlights and projection screens, and it was criticized for being a combination of functional items and art. This tower sparked an exchange of ideas between Russia and Germany on the ideas of revolutionizing art.

The main artist from the de Stijl movement is Dutch painter Piet Mondrian. He sought to create pure abstractions with horizontal and vertical lines, as well as primary colors. He wanted to reduce his artwork to the most basic elements, using them to represent the essence of the energy and forces of nature. The pure abstraction and minimal palette was meant to express an ideal and universal harmony in the art world. His idea of neoplasticism, which guided his work, relied on color, line, and form to express universal ideas. This is an example of Mondrian's work, showing his use of black lines, geometric shapes, and primary colors.

Dada and Surrealism

The **Dada** art movement began around 1915 in Zurich, New York, Germany, and Paris. The movement came about as a reaction of disgust and revolt to the horrors of World War I, and the movement was also antibourgeois. This wasn't so much of a cohesive style as it was a group of artists looking to collaborate and create art with spontaneity. This group actually mocked the established art scene, and they started debates about the definition of art. They sought to depart from so-called traditional values of art and create a new kind of artwork. Dada is considered antiart, challenging the definition and conventions of art. Dada techniques include readymades, which involves presenting a premade object as art, and the photomontage, using scissors and glue to assemble images from images printed in the press. Dada artists issued publications and created photomontages to stand up against political ideas. Dada art critiqued society, politics, and previously established rules for art, and their penchant for the strange, satirical, and irrational was later picked up and used by surrealist artists.

Surrealism began in the 1920s in France, and the movement included paintings of strange, dreamlike, and unnerving scenes with realistic accuracy. Surrealism sought to express unconscious thoughts and resolve contradictions between reality and dreams. This movement eventually affected literature, music, and film in many countries as well. This art movement drew heavily on Freudian theories of sexuality, fantasy, dreams, and irrationality.

Marcel Duchamp, Salvador Dali, and René Magritte

As part of the Dada movement, Marcel Duchamp began creating artwork called "readymades," made from items that were already created and he just declared them to be art. One well-known example is his 1917 *Fountain*, which is an already-made urinal that he signed as "R. Mutt." Another Duchamp artwork from 1919, *L.H.O.O.Q.*, shows the departure from and irreverence toward traditional artwork. He took a postcard depicting the Mona Lisa and drew a moustache and face on the portrait, then labeled it *L.H.O.O.Q.* With this artwork, he challenged artistic conventions of the past, and the value of traditional artwork.

Salvador Dali, a well-known surrealist artist, created his best-known work, *The Persistence of Memory, in 1931. The painting depicts melted pocket watches* on a dreamlike landscape.

René Magritte, a Belgian surrealist artist, created thought-provoking artwork by juxtaposing ordinary objects in unusual ways. In *The Treachery of Images* (1928–1929) he depicts a pipe with the words, in

French, "This is not a pipe." The viewer is faced with the challenge of reconciling these words with the fact that this is a representation of a pipe, not an actual pipe.

Abstract Expressionism

Abstract expressionism refers to an art style from the 1940s and 1950s. The artists grouped under this style sought total freedom of expression through their artwork. They shared an outlook, rather than a specific style, and this is thought to be the first truly American art movement. Abstract expressionism is also called the New York School, because the movement was centered in New York. Its influence extended into the 1970s. Abstract expressionist artists were influenced by the surrealist idea of expressing the subconsciousness in artwork. Abstract expressionism includes color field painting and action painting, and mixes of these two, among other techniques.

Color field painting uses solid areas, or fields of color, on a large scale that extend to the edges of the canvas. The extension to the edges suggests the colors continuing to infinity, and the large scale helps to envelop the viewer in the colors. Action painting includes dribbling, splashing, and dripping paint onto a canvas using gestures and movements, while emphasizing the unconscious.

Artists of Abstract Expressionism

Jackson Pollock is known for his action paintings, or splatter paintings. The term "action painting" was coined to describe Pollock's methods of applying paint to a canvas. Pollock considered this technique to be a way to harness the capabilities of his unconscious, which expressed itself onto the canvas. He saw the drips and splatters not as random paint, but as a balance of chaos and control.

Mark Rothko, Barnett Newman, and Clyfford Still were all color field painters of the abstract expressionist movement. They were looking to get away from form and representation in artwork, and they did away with the figure/ground convention by turning the figure and ground into one. The color seemed to extend beyond the edges of the painting and was the focus of the artwork.

Helen Frankenthaler used a mix of techniques and invented the "soak-stain" technique, which involved creating large color washes by pouring thinned paint onto a canvas. She used Pollock's technique of pouring paint but also used elements of color field painting by incorporating large areas of pure color.

Pop Art

Pop art was a British and American movement in the 1960s that used items from popular culture and incorporated them into artwork. This was partly inspired by the readymades of Dadaism. The artists of this movement went against the disengagement of abstract expressionism and celebrated popular culture and consumer items. They used bright, flat colors from advertising and imagery from comic books as well. As a response to and departure from abstract expressionism, pop art used hard edges instead of painterly techniques and impersonal, everyday reality instead of personal symbolism.

Some of the significant artists of the pop art movement used commercial imagery such as Campbell's Soup cans, imagery directly from comic books, and even a direct representation of the American flag. They were inspired by everyday objects and mass consumerism, and they combined objects, text, and images to create new meaning in their artwork.

Roy Lichtenstein, and Jasper Johns

Roy Lichtenstein was a pop artist who is known for his comic book imagery. He altered images from comic books, added different text, and painted them on a large scale. He used Benday dots, the dots produced by mechanical means in printing, to create these images. One of his well-known works is *Drowning Girl* (1963), which depicts a comic image of a drowning girl and her boyfriend in a boat, along with text.

Jasper Johns was a pop artist known for his American imagery, especially the American flag. His *Three Flags* (1958) is a painting of three American flags layered upon each other. *Flag*, from 1954–1955, is a faithful reproduction of an American flag using encaustic.

Andy Warhol

Andy Warhol was a commercial artist who became a significant pop artist as he explored the connections between popular culture and art, and he gained international attention for his artwork and for himself. He created video art, installations, performance art, and paintings, and in 1961 he began producing pop art paintings, including the iconic *Campbell's Soup Cans.* He also painted portraits of many celebrities in bright and vivid colors.

Andy Warhol He used many different media types, including painting, screen printing, and even computers, to create iconic pop art. The allure and mystery of his personal life, combined with his public persona, helped to keep him in the spotlight and create interest in him and his work. He reproduced images from mass media that nobody had thought to use before for artwork, and he successfully became synonymous with pop art. His work appealed to a large audience, and he created some the most widely recognized artworks ever made. Warhol also changed the concept of being an artist by using his factory concept to produce artwork. He predicted the quick rise and fall of celebrities with his "15 minutes of fame" concept, which became the new norm in popular culture.

Warhol's Factory

The Factory refers to Andy Warhol's studio in New York City. This location became a hangout for artists and celebrities, and it was known for its raucous parties. Warhol decorated this location with aluminum foil, mirrors, and silver paint, and it was also called the Silver Factory. The Factory later occupied two other locations. Warhol's time at this Factory location was referred to as the Silver Era.

In addition to the artistic experimentation and musical performances at The Factory, an assembly-line production of artwork also occurred. Warhol questioned the idea of artist and art production by mass-producing artwork with his silkscreen method and having a group of helpers create his work for him. These helpers became known as "Warhol Superstars," and they included musicians, free thinkers, drag queens, socialites, and celebrities, among others. He paralleled and reflected the concept of mass consumerism and mass-produced commercial objects by creating his own artwork in this way.

Postmodernism

Postmodernism is a mid- to late-20th-century art movement that departed from modernism. Since the beginning of the 20th century, modernism had led art practice and theory and had promoted the ideas of progress, reason, and idealism. Postmodern artists would not recognize the authority of previous art movements, and this movement was skeptical and antiauthoritarian. This "anything goes" style cast aside all rules of style and included elements of confrontation, tongue-in-cheek humor, and ludicrousness. Postmodernist artists built on the ideas of previous movements such as pop art and feminist art, but they questioned the ideas and subjectivity, authorship, and originality in previous art movements. This movement also questioned the commodification of art production.

Postmodernism is a cross-disciplinary term with philosophical origins, and it was highly influenced by French philosopher Jacques Lacan. Lacan added a contemporary intellectual significance to the ideas of Sigmund Freud, and he suggested that the unconscious is just as complex and sophisticated as the conscious mind.

Sigmar Polke, and Gerhard Richter

Sigmar Polke, a German artist whose artwork pioneered a postmodern approach, departed from coherence in his art as well as the idea that art comes from the artist's personality. In his 12 canvases collectively called *The Fifties* (1963–1969), he portrays a combination of cynicism and nostalgia while commenting on German culture. The grouping of paintings goes against the concept of stylistic coherence because he used different styles throughout the works.

Gerhard Richter's photo paintings of the 1960s combined photography with painting. In doing this, he combined high and low art into one technique. Richter would project a photograph onto a canvas, then paint it in neutral shades of gray, leaving out the black and white tones. He then used a dry brush to soften the edges, degrading the image to give a blurry effect. He assigned neutral titles to his works. This method of mechanical reproduction took any artist style out of the equation, as well as any emotion expressed through the artwork.

FEMINIST ART

Feminist art came into prominence in the late 1960s as female artists sought to revise the history of a male-dominated art world and bring attention to the contributions of female artists. They sought to abolish stereotypes as well as challenge and influence cultural attitudes. Previously, female artists did not get the same publicity or status that their male counterparts did, and the art world was dominated by male artists. The feminist art movement expanded the definition and scope of art, the artists we recognize, and who is included in the conversation of art making. Feminist artists gave credit to artists before them, and they introduced new media in their artwork. These artists began to embrace and use materials in their works that were tied to their gender, such as textiles and embroidery. They also used newer styles such as video, body, and performance art that did not have such a long history as a male-dominated style. These newer types of media allowed these artists to deliver more direct and personal messages to their viewers. Whereas some feminist artists explored the objectification of women in media, or ideas of domesticity, others focused on the absence of recognition of female artists throughout history.

Due to the accomplishments of this movement, women artists no longer necessarily feel the need to identify themselves as such, or to specifically create artwork that addresses the perspective of women. Women artists began to express their individual concerns and feelings, rather than trying to address and contribute to the feminist viewpoint.

BARBARA KRUGER, CINDY SHERMAN, AND FAITH RINGGOLD.

Barbara Kruger uses mass communication and advertising techniques, pairing black-and-white photos with Helvetica or Futura text, to explore identity and gender issues. The text and slogans she uses challenge the viewer, and her phrases often include pronouns such as I, you, we, or they. She often appropriates images from magazines and adds text to frame the images in a new context to make the viewer think. This image shows her artwork *Belief + Doubt* from 2012 and its iconic and recognizable style of text.

Cindy Sherman is a feminist artist who is known for her self-portraits. She used makeup, wigs, and props to transform herself to represent various female stereotypes in her photographs. Her artworks question ideas of authenticity and identity.

Faith Ringgold is an African-American feminist artist who worked in themes of racial and gender identity and equality. She told stories through quilts, and she recognized a need for equality in the art world. Ringgold would often insist that 50% of the artists included in prominent art shows should be women.

Armory Show

The Armory Show was the first major exhibition of modern art in America. This show is also called the International Exhibition of Modern Art, and it was held in New York City's 69th Regiment Armory building in 1913. The art exhibited here was influential to American art because of the inclusion of modern art by European and American painters and sculptors. Prior to this, Americans were used to seeing realistic art, but this show exposed them to cubist, impressionist, and fauvist artworks. Marcel Duchamp's *Nude Descending a Staircase* was included in this show. This collection of more than 1,300 artworks shocked many, and it was ridiculed and declared insane and immoral by some. The inclusion of these works in this successful art show served as a catalyst for many artists to rethink their styles and experiment with new ways of creating art.

The Degenerate Art Exhibition

The Degenerate Art Exhibition was in held in Munich by Adolf Ziegler and the Nazi party in 1937. The Nazis had removed more than 20,000 artworks from state museums that had been deemed too modern or progressive. Works by foreign artists were also confiscated, including Pablo Picasso, Piet Mondrian, and Wassily Kandinsky, but these works were not exhibited. 740 of these confiscated works were shown in the Degenerate Art Exhibition to defame the artists and show the public the decay of culture. These works were thought to lack artistic skill or insult the German culture. The works were shown in the exhibition without frames and were accompanied by derogatory words or slogans. The art was divided into categories including "An Insult to German Womanhood," and "Nature as Seen by Sick Minds." More than two million visitors attended this show, and some works were destroyed after the show ended. Many other works were sold on the international market and found new homes in museums abroad.

The Guerrilla Girls

The Guerrilla Girls group formed in 1985 to speak out against sexism and racism in the art world. The group is still active today. These women wear gorilla masks to hide their identities while they speak out against powerful institutions. They also hide their identities by using pseudonyms, taking the names of deceased female artists. They have used posters, billboards, and books, as well as public appearances, to disseminate their messages. This group has gained attention for their protest art, and their first well-known poster asked, "Do women have to be naked to get into the Met. Museum?" The image on the poster was a copy of Ingres' *La Grande Odalisque*, with a gorilla head over the woman's face. This poster was in reference to the number of nude women exhibited in the museum and the lack of female artists represented. The Guerrilla Girls have repeatedly brought attention to issues of inequity through their clean designs and jarring images.

Minimalism Art

Introduced in the 1960s, the **minimalism movement** is characterized by an extreme form of abstract art. Like many other movements, minimalist artists sought to challenge the boundaries and conventions of art. By removing themselves and their feelings from their artwork, these artists distanced themselves from the work of the abstract expressionists who came before them. They were interested in creating a new kind of artwork that was unlike any other previous fine art, minimized to its simplest and barest form, not designed to represent anything. Minimalist artists used geometric shapes and challenged the previous conventions of creating and viewing artwork. They wanted their artwork to exist simply as its own form and material, not as a representational form. Minimalist artwork shows traits of simplicity, harmony, and purity.

These artists wanted their art to show no evidence of the artist who created it and stand on its own instead of having personal elements. Paintings lacked brushstrokes and had flat fields of color, and sculptures had clean, straight lines and geometric shapes. The minimalism label referred to artists using a minimal number of colors, shapes, or forms in their artwork and the artwork was stripped of decoration and refined to its simplest form.

Although minimalist art can be two-dimensional, it is often three-dimensional, using simple, sometimes repeated, geometric shapes. Early abstract ideas, as well as the constructivist ideas of reducing artwork to its simplest and most essential form, inspired minimalist artists. This example from 1991 by Solomon "Sol" LeWitt is called *Open Cubes*, and it shows white repeated geometric forms. These forms exist only as themselves and are not meant to be representational. The viewer should only accept the artwork as its purest form of geometry and simplicity.

Street Art

Street art began with graffiti, but these artists have eventually shown their work in public areas and in galleries and museums in the 1970s and 1980s. Street art initially consisted of politically charged protest slogans and graphics illegally painted in public areas. Graffiti usually refers to vandalism, and street art was initially tied to hip-hop culture and lower income areas. In the 1970s, Jean-Michel Basquiat began spray painting his form of artwork in Manhattan. Later in the 1980s, Keith Haring was creating his distinctive artwork on the subway lines in New York City, and his well-known style of outlines and vivid colors, as shown, has persisted as popular artwork even now.

Banksy is another well-known street artist, although his identity is unknown. Banksy spray paints stencils designs onto walls and buildings throughout major cities, and those works have been turned into prints, t-shirts, and more. Street artist Shepard Fairey created the iconic Andre the Giant stencil which can be seen in many locations, and he went on to make the well-known Barack Obama graphic in red, white, and blue.

THE HARLEM RENAISSANCE ART MOVEMENT

Between 1920 and 1930, a new wave of artistic creativity poured out from a group of African American artists in Harlem, a neighborhood in the borough of Manhattan in New York City. This movement became known as the Harlem Renaissance, and its influence continued through and past the 1930s. This area of New York became a center of African-American immigrants, and the movement sparked a racial pride that challenged racism and stereotypes. The artwork of this time had aims to uplift African-Americans' spirits and the race as a whole. Some of the common themes represented in the artwork were racism, the effects of slavery, folk traditions, and how to convey the experience of black life or black neighborhoods.

Jacob Lawrence was the first well-known African-American artist, and his Migration series showed the migration of blacks from the rural South to the urban North.

Aaron Douglas was an artist who painted murals on buildings and created illustrations for the covers of black publications. In this work, *Aspiration* from 1936, Douglas shows the progression from slavery to the freedom of the industrialized North.

Ashcan School

The Ashcan School describes a group of American realist painters who decided to portray urban life of New York in an unidealized fashion. This was not an organized movement; rather, it was a collective desire to portray modern life in a new way. This group believed that poor and working-class people were a worthy artistic subject matter, and they sought to portray these people in an authentic way. They used a dark palette, a sketchy quality, and visible brushwork to show scenes of everyday modern life in New York City, with subjects including street kids, alcoholics, subways, crowded tenements, and theaters. These artists challenged refined and idealized artwork, moving away from American impressionism and the more polished academic realism. After the Armory Show in 1913, as well as the advent of cubism and fauvism, the work of the Ashcan School no longer seemed as radical as it initially did.

The Hudson River School

The Hudson River School was an American art movement in the mid-19th century that included landscape painters intent on painting in a romantic style. The paintings of this movement depict the Hudson River Valley and areas surrounding it. The themes reflected in these artworks are exploration, discovery, and settlement. These landscapes are detailed and somewhat idealized, often showing a juxtaposition and harmony of settlers or agriculture with nature. They were also showing their belief in nature as a revelation of God.

This movement was the first native art movement in America. Thomas Cole is credited as the founder, and the movement spanned two generations of painters. The second generation was not as tied to a geographical location as the first, but rather followed the style. Albert Bierstadt was a notable artist of this second generation. This painting by Bierstadt, *A River Landscape, Westphalia* (1855), shows the accord of man with the beauty and grandness of nature.

Folk Art and Outsider Art

Folk art is the art of peasants or a native culture. Folk art is generally characterized by simple or naive subject matter, and it is utilitarian or decorative in purpose. Folk art is not influenced by art movements or styles, and it will not include the work of professional artists. This type of art shares and expresses the values of a community as well as their cultural identity. Pottery, jewelry, paintings, sculpture, needlework, and costumes can all be folk art.

Outsider art is artwork created by untrained artists who learned their craft and methods on their own. These artists are not part of an artistic establishment and can include the mentally ill or even rural artists outside of urban areas. Outsider art is sometimes called "naive art." An increased interest in outsider art is in line with the general rejection of traditional values and methods of art by modernist artists.

OP ART

The **op art movement** of the 1960s used geometric forms to create visual effects and optical illusions. Op art is abstract and nonrepresentational, and many works were created in just black and white. Viewers often were given the feeling of movement, vibration, hidden images, or swelling within the artwork. Op artists consider how our vision works and how the planes of the figure and the ground can work with or against each other. Op artists also work with colors and how they can function together to produce different effects on the viewer's eye. As an early op artist, Bridget Riley worked in black and white and later began working in color op art. Josef Albers is another well-known op artist who worked in color, and he would nest geometric shapes of contrasting colors within each other, making visual effects of the shapes receding and advancing against each other.

ART DECO MOVEMENT

The **art deco movement**, taking its name from the Exposition Internationale des Arts Décoratifs et Industriels Modernes held in Paris in 1925, began in Paris with architecture and decorative arts in the 1920s. It later became a major style in the 1930s throughout America and Western Europe. The art deco style is characterized by streamlined forms, symmetry, geometric shapes, smooth lines, and bright vibrant colors. This movement was influenced by the geometric forms of cubism, the industrial components of futurism and constructivism, and the bright colors of fauvism. The style was used during the roaring twenties as well as the Great Depression of the 1930s. Art deco was used to improve the style of mass-produced objects, and it was also used for posters and some fine arts. This poster from 1925 is an example of the art deco style, with hard lines, streamlined forms, and geometric shapes with vibrant colors. The style was meant to be pleasing to the eye.

Art Nouveau

Art nouveau sought to distance itself from historical styles, as well as challenge the hierarchy of fine arts over decorative arts. Art nouveau was a decorative style that focused on linear contours and outlines, and it used muted, limited colors such as blues, greens, yellows, and browns. Art nouveau artists wanted to revive good craftsmanship, lift the status of crafts, and skillfully create modern designs that did not rely on past design. This international style was popular between 1890 and 1910, and it was applied to art, architecture, as well as everyday objects such as furniture, lamps, and jewelry.

One prominent art nouveau artist was Alphonse Mucha, a Moravian artist who created many illustrations, posters, paintings, and other designs. This example shows his signature style, which was considered outdated by the time of his death. His designs often showed beautiful women surrounded by a symmetrical, flowing, floral and ornate design and muted colors.

The Impressionist Movement

The impressionist movement marked a departure from the traditional notions of art. At the time, the narrow ideals of art were controlled by institutions such as the Salon and the French academy. These institutions also held control over the careers of artists. The impressionists cast the old rules aside and painted how they wanted to, capturing the changing qualities of light in new ways and scenes as they looked at a particular moment. They captured scenes as they saw them, on the spot, rather than taking sketches back to the studio to complete a painting. Impressionism also began when photography was catching on, and it served as an imitation of and reaction against it. Impressionism imitated the capturing of fleeting moments, while reacting against a faithful photographic reproduction of a scene. This art movement transformed landscape painting, and impressionism influenced artists to later express their artistic freedom and experiment with methods and media.

The Postimpressionist Movement

Postimpressionist artists rejected the ideas of depicting the world around them, as the impressionists did, and instead sought to explore their emotions and memories to depict highly personal meanings through their artwork. Instead of showing scenes from life, as the impressionists did, postimpressionist artists wanted to go further and show their feelings through abstracted forms and new uses of color. They used symbolism and attempted to evoke emotion in their viewers. Postimpressionist artists did not seek to create a cohesive style; rather, the movement was more about the departure from a faithful depiction of the world or events, and it was about beginning to relay information from the artist's subconscious mind. Postimpressionists used saturated colors and unnatural hues to express emotion in their artwork, taking a new, imaginative approach to representing their subjects. The painterly quality and distinct brushstrokes added to the notion that this was not a faithful representation, but rather an interpretation.

The Social Realism Movement

Social realism began in the early 1900s with the aim of portraying everyday life, especially that of the working class. It became an important art movement in the 1930s in the United States during the Great Depression. At this time, urban areas were growing, and slums also grew. Social realism artists were motivated by reacting against the idealism of the romantic period. These artists revealed the realities of contemporary life, and they sympathized with the poor and working class. They recorded the realities of what they saw, without glorifying scenes or heightening emotions. While documenting the realities of the poor and working class, social realists were also critical of the government and structures that created these conditions. They wanted to use this new style as a weapon to fight against the government and capitalism, as well as the exploitation of workers, while transforming society.

Chapter Quiz

Ready to see how well you retained what you just read? Scan the QR code to go directly to the chapter quiz interface for this study guide. If you're using a computer, simply visit the online resources page at **mometrix.com/resources719/ftcehumank-12** and click the Chapter Quizzes link.

Interrelatedness of Arts and Ideas

Purpose of Art

A common perception of art in the modern era is that artwork serves only to entertain. Historically, this has not been so. Art has historically served to recreate reality as a historical medium. Especially before the advent and popularization of the camera, artforms like drawing, painting, and sculpture were sometimes used as a means of recording what people looked like. Some forms of art embody only a decorative purpose, such as jewelry. Others, such as clothing, furniture, and architecture, have their roots in utility, but over time have morphed into elaborate or decorative forms as an expression of beauty.

Fine Art vs Applied Art

Fine art is art with no purpose other than being aesthetically pleasing or for expressive purposes. This can include drawing, painting, sculpture, and other media. **Applied art** is art that serves a purpose. Applied arts are useful objects with artistic design applied to their creation. This includes graphic design, interior design, fashion design, decorative arts, and architecture. Graphic design and illustration are also categorized as commercial arts, which fall under applied art. Decorative arts is the creation of jewelry, metalwork, ceramics, embroidery, carpets, furniture, and more. Sometimes applied arts are used in fine art works, so the line between fine arts and applied arts can be blurred, depending on the creator and their intent. In the 1960s, artists such as Andy Warhol began to blur the division between the two, which had been clear in previous years. Warhol used commercial art techniques to mass-produce works that were considered fine art.

Various Roles of Art

Storytelling vs Documentation

When art is used for **storytelling**, the artist creates a narrative that tells a story, expresses a theme, or communicates a message. The artwork guides the viewer through the narrative with composition, characters, and symbols. Art for storytelling often engages the viewers' emotions while connecting with them on a cultural or personal level. This type of art has historical and cultural significance because it passes down stories, legends, and myths while preserving cultural identity. Egyptian hieroglyphs are an example of art with the role of storytelling. This art gives stories of pharaohs, gods, and the afterlife. Renaissance artwork like da Vinci's *The Last Supper* expresses a religious narrative through its composition.

When art is used for **documentation**, it attempts to accurately show an event, a moment in time, or the likeness of a person or place. Art for documentation can serve as a historical record. It helps to ensure that details, people, and events are preserved so that future generations can see and understand them. This type of art is realistic and focuses on the accurate representation of perspective, proportion, and likeness. It avoids the use of symbolism, and the artist avoids adding his or her interpretation by maintaining accuracy and objectivity. Portraits of significant historical figures are examples of art for documentation. Da Vinci's illustrations of human anatomy are another example.

Decoration vs Utility

Art with a **decorative** purpose is intended to enhance a space aesthetically. It is created with the goal of pleasing the viewer's eye or adding color or texture to a space. This type of art shows the personal, social, or cultural tastes of an individual or society. It can influence a person's mood by creating feelings like calmness, agitation, or inspiration. This type of art can be found in a variety of forms, including drawings, paintings, tapestries, mosaics, and sculptures. It increases the visual appeal of a place but does not serve a practical function otherwise.

Art that is **utilitarian** is created to serve a functional purpose while also being artistic. This art combines function with beauty and can enhance the user's everyday life. Many cultures have traditions of making finely crafted utilitarian objects that are also symbols of their cultural heritage. These include furniture, textiles, and pottery. Even though this type of art is pleasing to the eye, it is made primarily to serve a practical purpose. These types of art are often durable enough for regular use so that they will last over time.

Purposes and Origins of Art

Art is used to record **history**. It gives a viewer insight into the political, cultural, and social conditions from different periods of time. Historical events and figures inspire artists to create art that depicts or comments on them. Art is used to help historians understand past civilizations.

Art can be inspired by **literature**. Literature and art converge with book cover graphics and illustrations. Both art and literature use symbolism and narratives to convey meanings and emotions to the reader or viewer.

Advancing **technology** helps to reshape art practices. Technologies like photography, digital media, and virtual reality have expanded what is possible when creating art. New forms and mediums have been created from the advancements of technology. Art can be displayed in online galleries and social media, and some artists create art digitally. Art is also used to comment on or critique technology and its impact on society.

Scientific advances have influenced art. Art created during the Renaissance shows an increased understanding of human anatomy. Art is used to depict complicated concepts visually, such as medical diagrams and scientific illustrations.

Artists have been led to explore dreams and the unconscious mind because of theories from **psychologists** like Jung and Freud. The psychology practice of art therapy helps people improve their mental health by expressing themselves through artwork. Psychological principles help people understand how artwork is perceived.

Some **philosophical** ideas have influenced artists and art movements. For example, some artists focused on absurdity in modern art due to the philosophical movement of existentialism. Art can help people express and explore philosophical concepts. It can challenge the viewer to contemplate deep ideas.

Sociology has led to artworks that highlight or critique social issues. Social realism and protest art influence and reflect changes in society. Sociology can help the viewer understand the cultural values and collective identities depicted in artwork.

Both **anthropology** and art explore the practices, beliefs, and cultures of humans. Anthropology has helped people to understand indigenous and traditional artwork. Art is a cultural artifact that gives the viewer insights into the values and rituals of the societies that created it.

Value and Role of Art in Modern Society

Art serves many roles and values within **society.**

- The various cultural groups that make up the society in the United States use art to express parts of their identity. The art shows their history and traditions, and it is used to celebrate the heritage of communities. This art helps others appreciate cultural diversity.
- Art can help promote activism and social change. It provokes thoughts and emotions in the viewer while also inspiring public discussions and social movements.

- Art education helps students with their cognitive, emotional, and social development. It promotes critical thinking, creativity, and problem-solving while helping students learn empathy and self-expression.
- Public art increases the aesthetic appeal of public areas. It creates spaces that a community can be proud of. Installations, sculptures, and murals are accessible to all people. The art helps give neighborhoods unique identities and can revitalize urban areas.
- Art industries within the US help contribute to the economy. They generate jobs and drive tourism to areas. Museums, festivals, and galleries stimulate economic activity and attract visitors from other places.
- Iconic artworks created by American artists reflect the values, struggles, and triumphs of America. They remind people of the nation's values.

THEMES

Themes are universal ideas explored and represented in artwork. One popular recurring example is identity. Identity includes the characteristics and behaviors that put an individual in a certain group. Some of the factors for identity include race, religion, culture, and language.

Photographer Cindy Sherman explored identity by photographing herself in different roles and costumes, essentially erasing her own identity and taking on the identity of other people. In doing this, she focused on the stereotypes of these female roles, addressing feminism, youth, aging, and obsession with status, ultimately questioning identity.

Kara Walker, an artist working with silhouettes, explores ideas of identity through race and gender. She portrays racism and historic scenes of slavery, getting past the romanticized notions of the past and exploring its reality. Her silhouettes simplify forms and focus on the topic at hand. She seeks to get past misconceptions and portray the true nature and identities behind tough subjects.

REALISM

The **realism movement** began in France in the 1850s, and it attempted to document people and ordinary life faithfully, rather than avoiding unpleasant subjects or romanticizing them. Realist artists depicted laborers and ordinary people engaged in everyday life activities, realistically documenting and preserving life and culture at that time.

This example by Gustave Courbet is called *The Grain Sifters* (1855). It shows a mundane scene of workers sifting grain, using dark and natural colors to portray the scene realistically. Courbet led the realism movement in France. The realism movement challenged the narratives and depictions of history paintings, which was an academic style with posed action scenes. Realism artists documented manual labor and the plight of everyday people, using dark, serious tones to show serious-looking people. Realism artists were not interested in depicting history or anything that they did not personally see or experience; they were only documenting the present-day struggles of the common man.

Emotions and Ideas

Emotions and ideas can be expressed through artwork in many ways, including the imagery, subject matter, or colors used. Frida Kahlo is a Mexican artist who used the subject matter and imagery in her artwork to express her physical and emotional pain and frustration. Throughout her life, Kahlo experienced abuse as well as a near-fatal bus accident that caused many physical problems. She began to paint self-portraits and explore ideas related to her pain and injuries, including emotional pain from her divorce from artist Diego Rivera. In her paintings, she often depicted her physical problems as well as open wounds to portray her pain. She sometimes included imagery of roots, to symbolize growth and a feeling of being trapped. Kahlo would also depict issues of childbirth and miscarriage, to communicate her frustration over her own failed pregnancies. She would often mix reality with elements of fantasy and paint scenes relating to pain and death. She used self-portraits to communicate her emotions and ideas relating to her pain as well as to explore her identity.

Political Ideas

Artists can use their artwork to support or criticize **political ideas**. Political protest is an often-used theme in artwork. The imagery in artwork can show the devastation caused by political decisions and the harm they can cause to innocent people. Pablo Picasso's *Guernica* (1937) is one of the best-known antiwar paintings in history. Picasso created this to depict the violence, chaos, and suffering of war. Picasso focused on how war affected innocent civilians, and he depicted this in his work, showing the pain and suffering inflicted by the Spanish Civil War. The imagery and title reflect the bombing of the town Guernica by German and Italian war planes. *Guernica* was painted in black, white, and gray, and it depicts a wounded horse, a woman holding a dead child, and a woman with her arms raised in horror, among other imagery. The woman's hand suggests the shape of an airplane. The color scheme allows the viewer to concentrate on the imagery without being distracted by other colors. To many, this painting has become a symbol of the devastation and horrors of war.

Social Ideas

Artists will often reflect the social climate surrounding them through the subjects that they portray in their artwork. They can choose to portray marginalized populations, bringing social issues to the attention of a larger population. Romare Bearden is an African-American artist known for capturing the social and cultural climate of African-American neighborhoods in his collages. During the civil rights movement in the 1960s, he began to use cut paper and magazine clippings to portray the culture and community in African-American neighborhoods and to celebrate themes such as jazz music, the rural South, blues musicians, religion, and spirituality. He focused on unity and cooperation within the African-American community.

Another example of art reflecting society and culture is the social realism movement. Social realism artists sought to highlight the "forgotten" members of society, such as the poor, immigrants, and racial minorities. During the 1920s and 1930s, these artists portrayed the common worker as the backbone of society, and their artwork showed political corruption, materialism, joblessness, and poverty, among other social and political issues at the time. This example by Ben Shahn is a mural called *The Meaning of Social Security*, and it is an attempt to depict Franklin D. Roosevelt's speech on the upcoming social security legislation and the ambitions of the New Deal programs.

Women's Emerging Role

During the medieval era, women would work with men to create manuscript illuminations and embroideries. During the Renaissance, though, some women artists gained international reputations, thanks to shifts in culture such as humanism. Humanism emphasized the value of all people. During the baroque period, women began depicting women as strong figures, and they also began painting still-life artworks. In the 18th century, women began to be accepted as students by famous artists and two women founded the Royal Academy of Arts in London. In the 19th century, women began to gain access to formal art education and more women began to exhibit their artwork. Photography was an accessible medium for women, with no formal training or traditions to constrict their creativity. In the 20th century, particularly the 1960s onward, feminism played a role in increasing the focus on women artists as well as their presence in formal training and prominent exhibitions. In 1985, the anonymous female artist group the Guerrilla Girls spoke out strongly about gender inequalities, especially in the art world.

Reflecting the Current Economy

Artists can use their artwork to show how the economy is affecting certain populations and bring this awareness to a wider audience. One example of this is the visual depiction of the economic ruin caused by the Dust Bowl. In the 1930s, dust storms swept through the American West and wiped out many farms and ranches. The land was ravaged by drought and rolling clouds of dust. Farmers lost everything and had no way to make a living. The Dust Bowl, as it was called, was reflected in the artwork of the time. The artists who depicted this event attempted to show how it affected farmers and the economy. Below is Thomas Hart Benton's lithograph *Prodigal Son* from 1939, which shows the desolate and wasted land as well as the farmer mourning it. The farmer is meant not to represent one single man, but all farmers who were affected by this tragic event. Benton approached the topic symbolically, showing the ruined land and home, animal carcass, and the man who will have to move on from his land.

Another artist who depicted the Dust Bowl was Alexandre Hogue. Whereas Benton saw this event as something happening to passive victims, Hogue saw it as something created by man's effect on nature. Hogue showed the slashes and furrows made in the land and the ruined green plains.

Influences in Popular Culture

Pop art served as both an art movement and a cultural movement. Pop art used images and objects from popular culture and blurred the line between "high art" and mass-produced cultural objects. This movement elevated common items to fine art, rather than sticking to traditional art themes. Andy Warhol took mundane Campbell's soup cans and Brillo boxes, creating repeated images and objects based on them, and showing them as artwork. Many pop artists, including Andy Warhol and James Rosenquist, began as commercial artists.

Warhol began to mass-produce his artwork, much like the products he was depicting were also mass-produced. In doing this, he equated artwork to a commodity that can be bought and sold, just like these products. Warhol would use bright colors, high contrast, and multiple prints of the same image, as if you were seeing the product repeated on a store shelf. The repetition, bright colors, and contrast of pop art are still used today in advertisements, perpetuating the link between art and culture.

Technology and Art

Technology is used in conjunction with art in many different ways. Some artists use technology within their art, such as video artists. Others use computers, digital cameras, and scanners to create art, such as electronic artists or graphic designers. This art can be printed repeatedly, and multiple copies can be shown or sold. For those who do not use a form of technology to create their art, they might use it to compose a scene. An artist can use digital photography to capture images to work on, or he or she could use computer software to compose the artwork before drawing or painting it. An artist might draw or paint from life with no assistance from technology, but then he or she may use technology to document the work and put it online on a website for others to view. Technology can also be used to keep records of work or to submit artwork to art competitions across the world.

Chapter Quiz

Ready to see how well you retained what you just read? Scan the QR code to go directly to the chapter quiz interface for this study guide. If you're using a computer, simply visit the online resources page at **mometrix.com/resources719/ftcehumank-12** and click the Chapter Quizzes link.

Cultural Beliefs and Values and their Expression in the Humanities

Genres in Fiction

Common Genres in Prose Fiction

- The **mystery** genre includes stories with plots that follow a protagonist as they work to solve an unexplained situation, such as a murder, disappearance, or robbery. Protagonists of mysteries may be hired professionals or amateurs who solve the mystery despite their lack of experience and resources. Mysteries allow the reader to solve the case along with the protagonist, and often grant the reader an advantageous perspective, creating dramatic irony. The *Sherlock Holmes* novels by Sir Arthur Conan Doyle are examples of mystery novels.
- **Science fiction** is a genre that is based on the manipulation and exaggeration of real scientific discoveries and processes. These works are speculative and frequently depict a world where scientific discoveries and society have progressed beyond the point reached at the time of the work's creation. Works of science fiction often take place in a distant location or time, allowing for the dramatic advancements and conveniences they often depict. *Dune*, written by Frank Herbert, is an example of a science-fiction novel.
- The **fantasy** genre includes stories that feature imaginary creatures and supernatural abilities, but often take place in settings that resemble real places and cultures in history. Fantasy novels usually follow a gifted protagonist from humble beginnings as they embark on a quest, journey, or adventure and encounter mystical beings and personally challenging obstacles. Common themes in the fantasy genre include personal growth, good versus evil, and the value of the journey. J.R.R. Tolkien's *The Lord of the Rings* trilogy belongs to the fantasy genre.
- **Realistic fiction** describes fictional narratives that include events and characters that do not exist, but could appear in reality. Within the narrative, these characters and events may be depicted in real places. For example, Pip, the protagonist of Charles Dickens's *Great Expectations*, was not a real person, but the novel shows him living in London, England for much of his young adulthood. Realistic fiction contains no far-fetched or impossible elements and presents situations that can or do occur in real life. A contemporary example of realistic fiction is *Wonder* by R.J. Palacio.
- **Historical fiction** includes works that take place in the past and model their setting after real historical cultures, societies, and time periods. These works may include real historical figures and events, but they also may not. Works of historical fiction must be fully informed by the period and location they are set in, meaning both the major and minor details of the work must be historically compatible with the work's setting. Examples of historical fiction include Kathryn Stockett's *The Help* and Markus Zusak's *The Book Thief*.
- The phrase **literary nonfiction** describes nonfiction narratives that present true facts and events in a way that entertains readers and displays creativity. Literary nonfiction, also called creative nonfiction, may resemble fiction in its style and flow, but the truth of the events it describes sets it apart from fictional literature. Different types of books may be considered literary nonfiction, such as biographies, if they appear to employ creativity in their writing. An example of literary nonfiction is *The Immortal Life of Henrietta Lacks* by Rebecca Skloot.

Realism and Satire

Realism

Realism is a literary form with the goal of representing reality as faithfully as possible. Its genesis in Western literature was a reaction against the sentimentality and extreme emotionalism of the works written during the Romantic literary movement, which championed feelings and emotional expression. Realists focused in great detail on immediacy of time and place, on specific actions of their characters, and the justifiable consequences of those actions. Some techniques of **realism** include writing in vernacular (conversational language), using specific dialects, and placing an emphasis on character rather than plot. Realistic literature also often addresses ethical issues. Historically, realistic works have often concentrated on the middle classes of the authors' societies. Realists eschew treatments that are too dramatic or sensationalistic as exaggerations of the reality that they strive to portray as closely as they are able. Influenced by his own bleak past, Fyodor Dostoevsky wrote several novels, such as *Crime and Punishment* (1866) that shunned romantic ideals and sought to portray a stark reality. Henry James was a prominent writer of realism in novels such as *Daisy Miller* (1879). Samuel Clemens (Mark Twain) skillfully represented the language and culture of lower-class Mississippi in his novel *The Adventures of Huckleberry Finn* (1885).

Satire

Satire uses sarcasm, irony, and humor as social criticism to lampoon human folly. Unlike realism, which intends to depict reality as it exists without exaggeration, **satire** often involves creating situations or ideas that deliberately exaggerate reality to appear ridiculous to illuminate flawed behaviors. Ancient Roman satirists included Horace and Juvenal. Alexander Pope's poem "The Rape of the Lock" satirized the values of fashionable members of the 18th-century upper-middle class, which Pope found shallow and trivial. The theft of a lock of hair from a young woman is blown out of proportion: the poem's characters regard it as seriously as they would a rape. Irishman Jonathan Swift satirized British society, politics, and religion in works like "A Modest Proposal" and *Gulliver's Travels*. In "A Modest Proposal," Swift used essay form and mock-serious tone, satirically "proposing" cannibalism of babies and children as a solution to poverty and overpopulation. He satirized petty political disputes in *Gulliver's Travels.*

Types of Stories

Other Common Types of Prose

- A **narrative** is any composition that tells a story. Narratives have characters, settings, and a structure. Narratives may be fiction or nonfiction stories and may follow a linear or nonlinear structure. The purpose of a narrative is generally to entertain, but nonfiction narratives can be informative, as well. Narratives also appear in a variety of structures and formats.
- **Biographies** are books written about another person's life. Biographies can be valuable historical resources. Though they provide a narrow view of the relevant time period and culture, their specificity can also provide a unique context for that period or culture. Biographies, especially those whose subject was a well-known and influential figure, can provide a more complete picture of the figure's life or contributions. Biographies can also serve as a source of inspiration or communicate a moral because of their focus on one person over an extended period of time.
- **Myths** that explain how the world works, its creation, and human behavior exist in most ancient cultures and continue to influence modern cultures. Myths are stories that are part of a certain **mythology**, such as Norse mythology. Myths are so influential that they have even inspired numerous pieces of modern literature and media in popular culture. While popular culture most clearly references myths from the Ancient Greek and Roman cultures, literature has been influenced by mythologies from around the entire world. Since myths are so prevalent in ancient literature, it makes sense that universal themes and morals often appear in mythologies from different cultures. The similarities and parallels in different mythologies (e.g., Greek myths about Zeus are very similar to Roman myths about Jupiter) suggest connections between cultures.

- **Folktales** are stories that have withstood time and are usually popular in a particular region or culture. Folktales often depict the clever success of a common person, though the story may, alternatively, end poorly for the protagonist. A collection of folktales relevant to a particular region or culture is referred to as that culture's **folklore**. There are three common types of folktales: fables, fairy tales, and legends.
    - **Fables** are short, didactic stories that typically feature imaginary creatures or talking animals. The famous story "The Tortoise and the Hare" is a fable. Fables are still told and used today because of their universally understandable morals and characters, which also make them suitable for children's literature and media.
    - **Fairy tales** are stories that involve fictional creatures or realistic characters with fantastical traits and abilities. Fairy tales often end happily and depict the victory of good over evil. The plots and characters in fairy tales are often far-fetched and whimsical.
    - **Legends** are stories that typically focus on one character and highlight their victory over a particular enemy or obstacle. Legends often feature some facts or are inspired by true events, but are generally considered both unproven and unprovable. Heroes are often the protagonists of legends, and they generally save or protect others as they conquer enemies and obstacles.
- A **short story** is a fictional narrative that is shorter than a novel. However, there is not a definite page or word count that defines the short story category. Short stories tend to focus on one or few elements of a story in order to efficiently tell the story. Though they are often brief, short stories may still contain a moral or impact their readers.

Review Video: Myths, Fables, Legends, and Fairy Tales
Visit mometrix.com/academy and enter code: 347199

Historical Forms of Prose

Historical, Picaresque, Gothic, and Psychological Fiction

Historical fiction is set in particular historical periods, including prehistoric and mythological. Examples include Walter Scott's *Rob Roy* and *Ivanhoe*; Leo Tolstoy's *War and Peace;* Robert Graves' *I, Claudius;* Mary Renault's *The King Must Die* and *The Bull from the Sea* (an historical novel using Greek mythology); Virginia Woolf's *Orlando* and *Between the Acts;* and John Dos Passos's *U.S.A* trilogy. **Picaresque** novels recount episodic adventures of a rogue protagonist or *pícaro,* like Miguel de Cervantes' *Don Quixote* or Henry Fielding's *Tom Jones.* **Gothic** novels originated as a reaction against 18th-century Enlightenment rationalism, featuring horror, mystery, superstition, madness, supernatural elements, and revenge. Early examples include Horace Walpole's *Castle of Otranto,* Matthew Gregory Lewis' *Monk*, Mary Shelley's *Frankenstein*, and Bram Stoker's *Dracula.* In America, Edgar Allan Poe wrote many Gothic works. Contemporary novelist Anne Rice has penned many Gothic novels under the pseudonym A. N. Roquelaure. **Psychological** novels, originating in 17th-century France, explore characters' motivations. Examples include Abbé Prévost's *Manon Lescaut;* George Eliot's novels; Fyodor Dostoyevsky's *Crime and Punishment;* Tolstoy's *Anna Karenina;* Gustave Flaubert's *Madame Bovary;* and the novels of Henry James, James Joyce, and Vladimir Nabokov.

Novels of Manners

Novels of manners are fictional stories that observe, explore, and analyze the social behaviors of a specific time and place. While deep psychological themes are more universal across different historical periods and countries, the manners of a particular society are shorter-lived and more varied; the **novel of manners** captures these societal details. Novels of manners can also be regarded as symbolically representing, in artistic form, certain established and secure social orders. Characteristics of novels of manners include descriptions of a society with defined behavioral codes; language that uses standardized, impersonal formulas; and inhibition of emotional expression, as contrasted with the strong emotions expressed in romantic or sentimental novels. Jane Austen's detailed descriptions of English society and characters struggling with the definitions and restrictions placed on them by society are excellent models of the novel of manners. In the 20th century, Evelyn Waugh's *Handful of Dust* is a novel of social manners, and his *Sword of Honour* trilogy contains novels of military manners. Another 20th-century example is *The Unbearable Bassington* by Saki (the pen name of writer H. H. Munro), focusing on Edwardian society.

Western-World Sentimental Novels

Sentimental love novels originated in the movement of Romanticism. Eighteenth-century examples of novels that emphasize the emotional aspect of love include Samuel Richardson's *Pamela* (1740) and Jean-Jacques Rousseau's *Nouvelle Héloïse* (1761). Also in the 18th century, Laurence Sterne's novel *Tristram Shandy* (1760-1767) is an example of a novel with elements of sentimentality. The Victorian era's rejection of emotionalism caused the term "sentimental" to have undesirable connotations. However, even non-sentimental novelists such as William Makepeace Thackeray and Charles Dickens incorporated sentimental elements in their writing. A 19th-century author of genuinely sentimental novels was Mrs. Henry Wood (e.g., *East Lynne,* 1861). In the 20th century, Erich Segal's sentimental novel *Love Story* (1970) was a popular bestseller.

Epistolary Novels

Epistolary novels are told in the form of letters written by their characters rather than in typical narrative form. Samuel Richardson, the best-known author of epistolary novels like *Pamela* (1740) and *Clarissa* (1748), widely influenced early Romantic epistolary novels throughout Europe that freely expressed emotions. Richardson, a printer, published technical manuals on letter-writing for young gentlewomen; his epistolary novels were fictional extensions of those nonfictional instructional books. Nineteenth-century English author Wilkie Collins' *The Moonstone* (1868) was a mystery written in epistolary form. By the 20th century, the format of well-composed written letters came to be regarded as artificial and outmoded. A 20th-century evolution of letters was tape-recording transcripts, such as in Irish playwright Samuel Beckett's drama *Krapp's Last Tape.* Though evoking modern alienation, Beckett still created a sense of fictional characters' direct communication without author intervention as Richardson had.

Pastoral Novels

Pastoral novels lyrically idealize country life as idyllic and utopian, akin to the Garden of Eden. *Daphnis and Chloe*, written by Greek novelist Longus around the second or third century, influenced Elizabethan pastoral romances like Thomas Lodge's *Rosalynde* (1590), which inspired Shakespeare's *As You Like It*, and Philip Sidney's *Arcadia* (1590). Jacques-Henri Bernardin de St. Pierre's French work *Paul et Virginie* (1787) demonstrated the early Romantic view of the innocence and goodness of nature. Though the style lost popularity by the 20th century, pastoral elements can still be seen in novels like *The Rainbow* (1915) and *Lady Chatterley's Lover* (1928), both by D. H. Lawrence. Growing realism transformed pastoral writing into less ideal and more dystopian, distasteful and ironic depictions of country life in George Eliot's and Thomas Hardy's novels. Saul Bellow's novel *Herzog* (1964) may demonstrate how urban ills highlight an alternative pastoral ideal. The pastoral style is commonly thought to be overly idealized and outdated today, as seen in Stella Gibbons' pastoral satire, Cold Comfort Farm (1932).

Bildungsroman

Bildungsroman is German for "education novel." This term is also used in English to describe "apprenticeship" novels focusing on coming-of-age stories, including youth's struggles and searches for things such as identity, spiritual understanding, or the meaning in life. Johann Wolfgang von Goethe's *Wilhelm Meisters Lehrjahre* (1796) is credited as the origin of this genre. Two of Charles Dickens' novels, *David Copperfield* (1850) and *Great Expectations* (1861), also fit this form. H. G. Wells wrote *bildungsromans* about questing for apprenticeships to address the complications of modern life in *Joan and Peter* (1918) and from a Utopian perspective in *The Dream* (1924). School *bildungsromans* include

Thomas Hughes' *Tom Brown's School Days* (1857) and Alain-Fournier's *Le Grand Meaulnes* (1913). Many Hermann Hesse novels, including *Demian, Steppenwolf, Siddhartha, Magister Ludi,* and *Beneath the Wheel* are *bildungsromans* about a struggling, searching youth. Samuel Butler's *The Way of All Flesh* (1903) and James Joyce's *A Portrait of the Artist as a Young Man* (1916) are two modern examples. Variations include J. D. Salinger's *The Catcher in the Rye* (1951), set both within and beyond school, and William Golding's *Lord of the Flies* (1955), a novel not set in a school but one that is a coming-of-age story nonetheless.

Roman à Clef

Roman à clef, French for "novel with a key," refers to books that require a real-life frame of reference, or key, for full comprehension. In Geoffrey Chaucer's *Canterbury Tales,* the Nun's Priest's Tale contains details that confuse readers unaware of history about the Earl of Bolingbroke's involvement in an assassination plot. Other literary works fitting this form include John Dryden's political satirical poem "Absalom and Achitophel" (1681), Jonathan Swift's satire "A Tale of a Tub" (1704), and George Orwell's political allegory *Animal Farm* (1945), all of which cannot be understood completely without knowing their camouflaged historical contents. *Roman à clefs* disguise truths too dangerous for authors to state directly. Readers must know about the enemies of D. H. Lawrence and Aldous Huxley to appreciate their respective novels: *Aaron's Rod* (1922) and *Point Counter Point* (1928). Marcel Proust's *Remembrance of Things Past (À la recherché du temps perdu,* 1871-1922) is informed by his social context. James Joyce's *Finnegans Wake* is an enormous *roman à clef* containing multitudinous personal references.

> **Review Video: Major Forms of Prose**
> Visit mometrix.com/academy and enter code: 565543

Poetry

Poetry Terminology

Unlike prose, which traditionally (except in forms like stream of consciousness) consists of complete sentences connected into paragraphs, poetry is written in **verses**. These may form complete sentences, clauses, or phrases. Poetry may be written with or without rhyme. It can be metered, following a particular rhythmic pattern such as iambic, dactylic, spondaic, trochaic, or **anapestic**, or may be without regular meter. The terms **iamb** and **trochee**, among others, identify stressed and unstressed syllables in each verse. Meter is also described by the number of beats or stressed syllables per verse: **dimeter** (2), **trimeter** (3), **tetrameter** (4), **pentameter** (5), and so forth. Using the symbol ᴗ to denote unstressed and / to denote stressed syllables, **iambic** = ᴗ/; **trochaic** = /ᴗ; **spondaic** =//; **dactylic** =/ᴗᴗ; **anapestic** =ᴗᴗ/. **Rhyme schemes** identify which lines rhyme, such as ABAB, ABCA, AABA, and so on. Poetry with neither rhyme nor meter is called **free verse**. Poems may be in free verse, metered but unrhymed, rhymed but without meter, or using both rhyme and meter. In English, the most common meter is iambic pentameter. Unrhymed iambic pentameter is called **blank verse**.

> **Review Video: Different Types of Rhyme**
> Visit mometrix.com/academy and enter code: 999342
>
> **Review Video: Evocative Words and Rhythm**
> Visit mometrix.com/academy and enter code: 894610

Major Forms of Poetry

From man's earliest days, he expressed himself with poetry. A large percentage of the surviving literature from ancient times is in **epic poetry**, utilized by Homer and other Greco-Roman poets. Epic poems typically recount heroic deeds and adventures, using stylized language and combining dramatic and lyrical conventions. **Epistolary poems**, poems that are written and read as letters, also developed in ancient times. In the fourteenth and fifteenth centuries, the **ballad** became a popular convention. Ballads often follow a rhyme scheme and meter and focus on subjects such as love, death, and religion. Many ballads tell stories, and several modern ballads are put to music. From these early conventions, numerous other poetic forms developed, such as **elegies**, **odes**, and **pastoral poems**. Elegies are mourning poems written in three parts: lament, praise of the deceased, and solace for loss. Odes evolved from songs to the typical poem of the Romantic time period, expressing strong feelings and contemplative thoughts. Pastoral poems idealize nature and country living. Poetry can also be used to make short, pithy statements. **Epigrams** (memorable rhymes with one or two lines) and **limericks** (two lines of iambic dimeter followed by two lines of iambic dimeter and another of iambic trimeter) are known for humor and wit.

Haiku

Haiku was originally a Japanese poetry form. In the 13th century, haiku was the opening phrase of renga, a 100-stanza oral poem. By the 16th century, haiku diverged into a separate short poem. When Western writers discovered haiku, the form became popular in English, as well as other languages. A haiku has 17 syllables, traditionally distributed across three lines as 5/7/5, with a pause after the first or second line. Haiku are syllabic and unrhymed. Haiku philosophy and technique are that brevity's compression forces writers to express images concisely, depict a moment in time, and evoke illumination and enlightenment. An example is 17th-century haiku master Matsuo Basho's classic: "An old silent pond… / A frog jumps into the pond, / splash! Silence again." Modern American poet Ezra Pound revealed the influence of haiku in his two-line poem "In a Station of the Metro." In this poem, line 1 has 12 syllables (combining the syllable count of the first two lines of a haiku) and line 2 has 7, but it still preserves haiku's philosophy and imagistic technique: "The apparition of these faces in the crowd; / Petals on a wet, black bough."

Sonnets

The sonnet traditionally has 14 lines of iambic pentameter, tightly organized around a theme. The Petrarchan sonnet, named for 14th-century Italian poet Petrarch, has an eight-line stanza, the octave, and a six-line stanza, the sestet. There is a change or turn, known as the volta, between the eighth and ninth verses, setting up the sestet's answer or summary. The rhyme scheme is ABBA/ABBA/CDECDE or CDCDCD. The English or Shakespearean sonnet has three quatrains and one couplet, with the rhyme scheme ABAB/CDCD/EFEF/GG. This format better suits English, which has fewer rhymes than Italian. The final couplet often contrasts sharply with the preceding quatrains, as in Shakespeare's sonnets—for example, Sonnet 130, "My mistress' eyes are nothing like the sun…And yet, by heaven, I think my love as rare / As any she belied with false compare." Variations on the sonnet form include Edmund Spenser's Spenserian sonnet in the 16th century, John Milton's Miltonic sonnet in the 17th century, and sonnet sequences. Sonnet sequences are seen in works such as John Donne's *La Corona* and Elizabeth Barrett Browning's *Sonnets from the Portuguese*.

Review Video: Structural Elements of Poetry
Visit mometrix.com/academy and enter code: 265216

Structure and Meaning in Poetry

Carpe Diem Tradition in Poetry

Carpe diem is Latin for "seize the day." A long poetic tradition, it advocates making the most of time because it passes swiftly and life is short. It is found in multiple languages, including Latin, Torquato Tasso's Italian, Pierre de Ronsard's French, and Edmund Spenser's English, and is often used in seduction to argue for indulging in earthly pleasures. Roman poet Horace's Ode 1.11 tells a younger woman, Leuconoe, to enjoy the present, not worrying about inevitable aging. Two Renaissance Metaphysical Poets, Andrew Marvell and Robert Herrick, treated *carpe diem* more as a call to action. In "To His Coy Mistress," Marvell points out that time is fleeting, arguing for love, and concluding that because they cannot stop time, they may as well defy it, getting the most out of the short time they have. In "To the Virgins, to Make Much of Time," Herrick advises young women to take advantage of their good fortune in being young by getting married before they become too old to attract men and have babies.

"To His Coy Mistress" begins, "Had we but world enough, and time, / This coyness, lady, were no crime." Using imagery, Andrew Marvell describes leisure they could enjoy if time were unlimited. Arguing for seduction, he continues famously, "But at my back I always hear/Time's winged chariot hurrying near; / And yonder all before us lie / Deserts of vast eternity." He depicts time as turning beauty to death and decay. Contradictory images in "amorous birds of prey" and "tear our pleasures with rough strife / Through the iron gates of life" overshadow romance with impending death, linking present pleasure with mortality and spiritual values with moral considerations. Marvell's concluding couplet summarizes *carpe diem*: "Thus, though we cannot make our sun / Stand still, yet we will make him run." "To the Virgins, to Make Much of Time" begins with the famous "Gather ye rosebuds while ye may." Rather than seduction to live for the present, Robert Herrick's experienced persona advises young women's future planning: "Old time is still a-flying / And this same flower that smiles today, / Tomorrow will be dying."

Effect of Structure on Meaning in Poetry

The way a poem is structured can affect its meaning. Different structural choices can change the way a reader understands a poem, so poets are careful to ensure that the form they use reflects the message they want to convey. The main structural elements in poetry include **lines** and **stanzas**. The number of lines within a stanza and the number of stanzas vary between different poems, but some poetic forms require a poem to have a certain number of lines and stanzas. Some of these forms also require each line to conform to a certain meter, or number and pattern of syllables. Many forms are associated with a certain topic or tone because of their meter. Poetic forms include sonnets, concrete poems, haiku, and villanelles. Another popular form of poetry is free verse, which is poetry that does not conform to a particular meter or rhyme scheme.

The arrangement of lines and stanzas determines the speed at which a poem is read. Long lines are generally read more quickly since the reader is often eager to reach the end of the line and does not have to stop to find the next word. Short lines cause the reader to briefly pause and look to the next line, so their reading is slowed. These effects often contribute to the meaning a reader gleans from a poem, so poets aim to make the line length compatible with the tone of their message.

For example, Edgar Allan Poe's poem "The Raven" is written with mostly long lines. The poem's speaker experiences troubling events and becomes paranoid throughout the poem, and he narrates his racing thoughts. Poe's use of long lines leads the reader to read each line quickly, allowing their reading experience to resemble the thoughts of the narrator:

> Deep into that darkness peering, long I stood there wondering, fearing,
> Doubting, dreaming dreams no mortal ever dared to dream before;
>   But the silence was unbroken, and the stillness gave no token,
>   And the only word there spoken was the whispered word, "Lenore?"
> This I whispered, and an echo murmured back the word, "Lenore!"—
>   Merely this and nothing more.

The poem's meter also contributes to its tone, but consider the same stanza written using shorter lines:

> Deep into that darkness peering,
> long I stood there wondering, fearing,
> Doubting, dreaming dreams no mortal
> ever dared to dream before;
>   But the silence was unbroken,
> and the stillness gave no token,
>   And the only word there spoken
> was the whispered word, "Lenore?"
> This I whispered, and an echo
> murmured back the word, "Lenore!"—
>   Merely this and nothing more.

Breaking the lines apart creates longer pauses and a slower, more suspenseful experience for the reader. While the tone of the poem is dark and suspense is appropriate, the longer lines allow Poe to emphasize and show the narrator's emotions. The narrator's emotions are more important to the poem's meaning than the creation of suspense, making longer lines more suitable in this case.

Concrete Poetry

A less common form of poetry is concrete poetry, also called shape poetry. **Concrete poems** are arranged so the full poem takes a shape that is relevant to the poem's message. For example, a concrete poem about the beach may be arranged to look like a palm tree. This contributes to a poem's meaning by influencing which aspect of the poem or message that the reader focuses on. In the beach poem example, the image of the palm tree leads the reader to focus on the poem's setting and visual imagery. The reader may also look for or anticipate the mention of a palm tree in the poem. This technique allows the poet to direct the reader's attention and emphasize a certain element of their work.

Free Verse

Free verse is a very common form of poetry. Because **free verse** poetry does not always incorporate meter or rhyme, it relies more heavily on punctuation and structure to influence the reader's experience and create emphasis. Free verse poetry makes strategic use of the length and number of both lines and stanzas. While meter and rhyme direct the flow and tone of other types of poems, poets of free verse pieces use the characteristics of lines and stanzas to establish flow and tone, instead.

Free verse also uses punctuation in each line to create flow and tone. The punctuation in each line directs the reader to pause after certain words, allowing the poet to emphasize specific ideas or images to clearly communicate their message. Similar to the effects of line length, the presence of punctuation at the end of a line can create pauses that affect a reader's pace. **End-stopped** lines, or lines with a punctuation mark at the end, create a pause that can contribute to the poem's flow or create emphasis. **Enjambed** lines, or lines that do not end with a punctuation mark, carry a sentence to the next line and create an effect similar to long lines. The use of enjambment can speed up a poem's flow and reflect an idea within the poem or contribute to tone.

POETIC STRUCTURE TO ENHANCE MEANING

The opening stanza of Romantic English poet, artist and printmaker William Blake's famous poem "The Tyger" demonstrates how a poet can create tension by using line length and punctuation independently of one another: "Tyger! Tyger! burning bright / In the forests of the night, / What immortal hand or eye / Could frame thy fearful symmetry?" The first three lines of this stanza are **trochaic** (/᠎ᴗ), with "masculine" endings—that is, strongly stressed syllables at the ends of each of the lines. But Blake's punctuation contradicts this rhythmic regularity by not providing any divisions between the words "bright" and "In" or between "eye" and "Could." This irregular punctuation foreshadows how Blake disrupts the meter at the end of this first stanza by using a contrasting **dactyl** (/ᴗᴗ), with a "feminine" (unstressed) ending syllable in the last word, "symmetry." Thus, Blake uses structural contrasts to heighten the intrigue of his work.

In enjambment, one sentence or clause in a poem does not end at the end of its line or verse, but runs over into the next line or verse. Clause endings coinciding with line endings give readers a feeling of completion, but enjambment influences readers to hurry to the next line to finish and understand the sentence. In his blank-verse epic religious poem "Paradise Lost," John Milton wrote: "Anon out of the earth a fabric huge / Rose like an exhalation, with the sound / Of dulcet symphonies and voices sweet, / Built like a temple, where pilasters round / Were set, and Doric pillars overlaid / With golden architrave." Only the third line is end-stopped. Milton, describing the palace of Pandemonium bursting from Hell up through the ground, reinforced this idea through phrases and clauses bursting through the boundaries of the lines. A **caesura** is a pause in mid-verse. Milton's commas in the third and fourth lines signal caesuras. They interrupt flow, making the narration jerky to imply that Satan's glorious-seeming palace has a shaky and unsound foundation.

COUPLETS AND METER TO ENHANCE MEANING IN POETRY

When a poet uses a couplet—a stanza of two lines, rhymed or unrhymed—it can function as the answer to a question asked earlier in the poem, or the solution to a problem or riddle. Couplets can also enhance the establishment of a poem's mood, or clarify the development of a poem's theme. Another device to enhance thematic development is irony, which also communicates the poet's tone and draws the reader's attention to a point the poet is making. The use of meter gives a poem a rhythmic context, contributes to the poem's flow, makes it more appealing to the reader, can represent natural speech rhythms, and produces specific effects. For example, in "The Song of Hiawatha," Henry Wadsworth Longfellow uses trochaic (/ ᴗ) tetrameter (four beats per line) to evoke for readers the rhythms of Native American chanting: "*By* the *shores* of *Gitch*e *Gum*ee, / *By* the *shin*ing *Big*-Sea-*Wat*er / *Stood* the *wig*wam *of* No*ko*mis." (Italicized syllables are stressed; non-italicized syllables are unstressed.)

REFLECTION OF CONTENT THROUGH STRUCTURE

Wallace Stevens' short yet profound poem "The Snow Man" is reductionist: the snow man is a figure without human biases or emotions. Stevens begins, "One must have a mind of winter," the criterion for realizing nature and life does not inherently possess subjective qualities; we only invest it with these. Things are not as we see them; they simply are. The entire poem is one long sentence of clauses connected by conjunctions and commas, and modified by relative clauses and phrases. The successive phrases lead readers continually to reconsider as they read. Stevens' construction of the poem mirrors the meaning he conveys. With a mind of winter, the snow man, Stevens concludes, "nothing himself, beholds nothing that is not there, and the nothing that is."

CONTRAST OF CONTENT AND STRUCTURE

Robert Frost's poem "Stopping by Woods on a Snowy Evening" (1923) is deceptively short and simple, with only four stanzas, each of only four lines, and short and simple words. Reinforcing this is Frost's use of regular rhyme and meter. The rhythm is iambic tetrameter throughout; the rhyme scheme is AABA in the first three stanzas and AAAA in the fourth. In an additional internal subtlety, B ending "here" in the first stanza is rhymed with A endings "queer," "near," and "year" of the second; B ending "lake" in the second is rhymed in A endings "shake," "mistake," and "flake" of the third. The final stanza's AAAA endings reinforce the ultimate darker theme. Though the first three stanzas seem to describe quietly watching snow fill the woods, the last stanza evokes the seductive pull of mysterious death: "The woods are lovely, dark and deep," countered by the obligations of living life: "But I have promises to keep, / And miles to go before I sleep, / And miles to go before I sleep." The last line's repetition strengthens Frost's message that despite death's temptation, life's course must precede it.

Effects of Figurative Devices on Meaning in Poetry

Through exaggeration, **hyperbole** communicates the strength of a poet's or persona's feelings and enhances the mood of the poem. **Imagery** appeals to the reader's senses, creating vivid mental pictures, evoking reader emotions and responses, and helping to develop themes. **Irony** also aids thematic development by drawing the reader's attention to the poet's point and communicating the poem's tone. Thematic development is additionally supported by the comparisons of **metaphors** and **similes**, which emphasize similarities, enhance imagery, and affect readers' perceptions. The use of **mood** communicates the atmosphere of a poem, builds a sense of tension, and evokes the reader's emotions. **Onomatopoeia** appeals to the reader's auditory sense and enhances sound imagery even when the poem is visual (read silently) rather than auditory (read aloud). **Rhyme** connects and unites verses, gives the rhyming words emphasis, and makes poems more fluent. **Symbolism** communicates themes, develops imagery, evokes readers' emotions, and elicits a response from the reader.

Review Video: Sensory Language
Visit mometrix.com/academy and enter code: 177314

Repetition to Enhance Meaning

A **villanelle** is a nineteen-line poem composed of five tercets and one quatrain. The defining characteristic is the repetition: two lines appear repeatedly throughout the poem. In Theodore Roethke's "The Waking," the two repeated lines are "I wake to sleep, and take my waking slow," and "I learn by going where I have to go." At first these sound paradoxical, but the meaning is gradually revealed through the poem. The repetition also fits with the theme of cycle: the paradoxes of waking to sleep, learning by going, and thinking by feeling represent a constant cycle through life. They also symbolize abandoning conscious rationalism to embrace spiritual vision. We wake from the vision to "Great Nature," and "take the lively air." "This shaking keeps me steady"—another paradox—juxtaposes and balances fear of mortality with ecstasy in embracing experience. The transcendent vision of all life's interrelationship demonstrates, "What falls away is always. And is near." Readers experience the poem holistically, like music, through Roethke's integration of theme, motion, and sound.

Sylvia Plath's villanelle "Mad Girl's Love Song" narrows the scope from universal to personal but keeps the theme of cycle. The two repeated lines, "I shut my eyes and all the world drops dead" and "(I think I made you up inside my head.)" reflect the existential viewpoint that nothing exists in any absolute reality outside of our own perceptions. In the first stanza, the middle line, "I lift my lids and all is born again," in its recreating the world, bridges between the repeated refrain statements—one of obliterating reality, the other of having constructed her lover's existence. Unlike other villanelles wherein key lines are subtly altered in their repetitions, Plath repeats these exactly each time. This reflects the young woman's love, constant throughout the poem as it neither fades nor progresses.

Drama

Early Development

English **drama** originally developed from religious ritual. Early Christians established traditions of presenting pageants or mystery plays, traveling on wagons and carts through the streets to depict Biblical events. Medieval tradition assigned responsibility for performing specific plays to the different guilds. In Middle English, "mystery" referred to craft, or trade, and religious ritual and truth. Historically, mystery plays were to be reproduced exactly the same every time they were performed, like religious rituals. However, some performers introduced individual interpretations of roles and even improvised. Thus, drama was born. Narrative detail and nuanced acting were evident in mystery cycles by the Middle Ages. As individualized performance evolved, plays on other subjects also developed. Middle English mystery plays that still exist include the York Cycle, Coventry Cycle, Chester Mystery Plays, N-Town Plays, and Towneley/Wakefield Plays. In recent times, these plays began to draw interest again, and several modern actors, such as Dame Judi Dench, began their careers with mystery plays.

Review Video: Dramas
Visit mometrix.com/academy and enter code: 216060

Defining Characteristics

In the Middle Ages, plays were commonly composed in **verse**. By the time of the Renaissance, Shakespeare and other dramatists wrote plays that mixed **prose**, **rhymed verse**, and **blank verse**. The traditions of costumes and masks were seen in ancient Greek drama, medieval mystery plays, and Renaissance drama. Conventions like **asides**, in which actors make comments directly to the audience unheard by other characters, and **soliloquies** were also common during Shakespeare's Elizabethan dramatic period. **Monologues** date back to ancient Greek drama. Elizabethan dialogue tended to use colloquial prose for lower-class characters' speech and stylized verse for upper-class characters. Another Elizabethan convention was the play-within-a-play, as in *Hamlet*. As drama moved toward realism, dialogue became less poetic and more conversational, as in most modern English-language plays. Contemporary drama, both onstage and onscreen, includes a convention of **breaking the fourth wall**, as actors directly face and address audiences.

Comedy

Today, most people equate the idea of **comedy** with something funny, and of **tragedy** with something sad. However, the ancient Greeks defined these differently. Comedy needed not be humorous or amusing; it needed only a happy ending. The classical definition of comedy, as included in Aristotle's works, is any work that tells the story of a sympathetic main character's rise in fortune. According to Aristotle, protagonists need not be heroic or exemplary, nor evil or worthless, but ordinary people of unremarkable morality. Comic figures who were sympathetic were usually of humble origins, proving their "natural nobility" through their actions as they were tested. Characters born into nobility were often satirized as self-important or pompous.

Shakespearean Comedy

William Shakespeare lived in England from 1564-1616. He was a poet and playwright of the Renaissance period in Western culture. He is generally considered the foremost dramatist in world literature and the greatest author to write in the English language. He wrote many poems, particularly sonnets, of which 154 survive today, and approximately 38 plays. Though his sonnets are greater in number and are very famous, he is best known for his plays, including comedies, tragedies, tragicomedies and historical plays. His play titles include: *All's Well That Ends Well, As You Like It, The Comedy of Errors, Love's Labour's Lost, Measure for Measure, The Merchant of Venice, The Merry Wives of Windsor, A Midsummer Night's Dream, Much Ado About Nothing, The Taming of the Shrew, The Tempest, Twelfth Night, The Two Gentlemen of Verona, The Winter's Tale, King John, Richard II, Henry IV, Henry V, Richard III, Romeo and Juliet, Coriolanus, Titus Andronicus, Julius Caesar, Macbeth, Hamlet, Troilus and Cressida, King Lear, Othello, Antony and Cleopatra,* and *Cymbeline.* Some scholars have suggested that Christopher Marlowe wrote several of Shakespeare's works. While most scholars reject this theory, Shakespeare did pay homage to Marlowe, alluding to several of his characters, themes, or verbiage, as well as borrowing themes from several of his plays (e.g., Marlowe's *Jew of Malta* influenced Shakespeare's *Merchant of Venice*).

When Shakespeare was writing, during the Elizabethan period of the Renaissance, Aristotle's version of comedies was popular. While some of Shakespeare's comedies were humorous and others were not, all had happy endings. *A Comedy of Errors* is a farce. Based and expanding on a Classical Roman comedy, it is lighthearted and includes slapstick humor and mistaken identity. *Much Ado About Nothing* is a romantic comedy. It incorporates some more serious themes, including social mores, perceived infidelity, marriage's duality as both trap and ideal, honor and its loss, public shame, and deception, but also much witty dialogue and a happy ending.

DRAMATIC COMEDY

Three types of dramas classified as comedy include the farce, the romantic comedy, and the satirical comedy.

FARCE

The **farce** is a zany, goofy type of comedy that includes pratfalls and other forms of slapstick humor. The characters in a farce tend to be ridiculous or fantastical in nature. The plot also tends to contain highly improbable events, featuring complications and twists that continue throughout, and incredible coincidences that would likely never occur in reality. Mistaken identity, deceptions, and disguises are common devices used in farcical comedies. Shakespeare's play *The Comedy of Errors,* with its cases of accidental mistaken identity and slapstick, is an example of farce. Contemporary examples of farce include the Marx Brothers' movies, the Three Stooges movies and TV episodes, and the *Pink Panther* movie series.

ROMANTIC COMEDY

Romantic comedies are probably the most popular of the types of comedy, in both live theater performances and movies. They include not only humor and a happy ending, but also love. In the typical plot of a **romantic comedy**, two people well suited to one another are either brought together for the first time, or reconciled after being separated. They are usually both sympathetic characters and seem destined to be together, yet they are separated by some intervening complication, such as ex-lovers, interfering parents or friends, or differences in social class. The happy ending is achieved through the lovers overcoming all these obstacles. William Shakespeare's *Much Ado About Nothing*, Walt Disney's version of *Cinderella* (1950), and Broadway musical *Guys and Dolls* (1955) are example of romantic comedies. Many live-action movies are also examples of romantic comedies, such as *The Princess Bride* (1987), *Sleepless in Seattle* (1993), *You've Got Mail* (1998), and *Forget Paris* (1995).

SATIRICAL COMEDY AND BLACK COMEDY

Satires generally mock and lampoon human foolishness and vices. **Satirical comedies** fit the classical definition of comedy by depicting a main character's rise in fortune, but they also fit the definition of satire by making that main character either a fool, morally corrupt, or cynical in attitude. All or most of the other characters in the satirical comedy display similar foibles. These include gullible types, such as cuckolded spouses and dupes, and deceptive types, such as tricksters, con artists, criminals, hypocrites, and fortune seekers, who prey on the gullible. Some classical examples of satirical comedies include *The Birds* by ancient Greek comedic playwright Aristophanes, and *Volpone* by 17th-century poet and playwright Ben Jonson, who made the comedy of humors popular. When satirical comedy is extended to extremes, it becomes **black comedy**, wherein the comedic occurrences are grotesque or terrible.

TRAGEDY

The opposite of comedy is tragedy, portraying a hero's fall in fortune. While by classical definitions, tragedies could be sad, Aristotle went further, requiring that they depict suffering and pain to cause "terror and pity" in audiences. Additionally, he decreed that tragic heroes be basically good, admirable, or noble, and that their downfalls result from personal action, choice, or error, not by bad luck or accident.

Aristotle's Features of Tragedy

In his *Poetics,* Aristotle identified various elements that appear in Greek tragedies:

- ***Anagnorisis***: Meaning tragic insight or recognition, this is a moment of realization by a tragic hero or heroine that he or she has become enmeshed in a "web of fate."
- ***Catharsis***: Meaning an emotional release on the part of the audience.
- ***Hamartia***: This is often called a "tragic flaw," but is better described as a tragic error. *Hamartia* is an archery term meaning a shot missing the bull's eye, used here as a metaphor for a mistake—often a simple one—which results in catastrophe.
- ***Hubris***: While often called "pride," this is actually translated as "violent transgression," and signifies an arrogant overstepping of moral or cultural bounds—the sin of the tragic hero who over-presumes or over-aspires.
- ***Mimesis***: This refers to the idea that works of art reflect the real world, including individuals, nature, human behavior, and social order.
- ***Nemesis***: translated as "retribution," this represents the cosmic punishment or payback that the tragic hero ultimately receives for committing hubristic acts.
- ***Peripateia***: Literally "turning," this is a plot reversal consisting of a tragic hero's pivotal action, which changes his or her status from safe to endangered.
- ***Spectacle***: Visual elements of the story, in the context of dramatic plays.

Hegel's Theory of Tragedy

Georg Wilhelm Friedrich Hegel (1770-1831) proposed a different theory of tragedy than Aristotle (384-322 BC), which was also very influential. Whereas Aristotle's criteria involved character and plot, Hegel defined tragedy as a dynamic conflict of opposite forces or rights. For example, if an individual believes in the moral philosophy of the conscientious objector (i.e., that fighting in wars is morally wrong) but is confronted with being drafted into military service, this conflict would fit Hegel's definition of a tragic plot premise. Hegel theorized that a tragedy must involve some circumstance in which two values, or two rights, are fatally at odds with one another and conflict directly. Hegel did not view this as good triumphing over evil, or evil winning out over good, but rather as one good fighting against another good unto death. He saw this conflict of two goods as truly tragic. In ancient Greek playwright Sophocles' tragedy *Antigone,* the main character experiences this tragic conflict between her public duties and her family and religious responsibilities.

Revenge Tragedy

Along with Aristotelian definitions of comedy and tragedy, ancient Greece was the origin of the **revenge tragedy**. This genre became highly popular in Renaissance England, and is still popular today in contemporary movies. In a revenge tragedy, the protagonist has suffered a serious wrong, such as the murder of a family member. However, the wrongdoer has not been punished. In contemporary plots, this often occurs when some legal technicality has interfered with the miscreant's conviction and sentencing, or when authorities are unable to locate and apprehend the criminal. The protagonist then faces the conflict of suffering this injustice, or exacting his or her own justice by seeking revenge. Greek revenge tragedies include *Agamemnon* and *Medea.* Playwright Thomas Kyd's *The Spanish Tragedy* (1582-1592) is credited with beginning the Elizabethan genre of revenge tragedies. Shakespearean revenge tragedies include *Hamlet* (1599-1602) and *Titus Andronicus* (1588-1593). A Jacobean example is Thomas Middleton's *The Revenger's Tragedy* (1606, 1607).

Hamlet's "Tragic Flaw"

Despite virtually limitless interpretations, one way to view Hamlet's tragic error generally is as indecision. He suffers the classic revenge tragedy's conflict of whether to suffer with his knowledge of his mother's and uncle's assassination of his father, or to exact his own revenge and justice against Claudius, who has assumed the throne after his crime went unknown and unpunished. Hamlet's famous soliloquy, "To be or not to be" reflects this dilemma. Hamlet muses "Whether 'tis nobler in the mind to suffer the slings and arrows of outrageous fortune, / Or to take arms against a sea of troubles, / And by opposing end them?" Hamlet both longs for and fears death, as "the dread of something after death ... makes us rather bear those ills we have / Than fly to others that we know not ... Thus, conscience does make cowards of us all." For most of the play, Hamlet struggles with his responsibility to avenge his father, who was killed by Hamlet's uncle, Claudius. So, Hamlet's tragic error at first might be considered a lack of action. But he then makes several attempts at revenge, each of which end in worse tragedy, until his efforts are ended by the final tragedy—Hamlet's own death.

World Literature

American Literary Periods

Dark Romantics

In American literature, a group of late Romantic writers are recognized as **Dark Romantics**. These authors' works may be associated with both the Romantic and Gothic movements. These works emphasize nature and emotion, aligning them with Romanticism, and include dark themes and tones, aligning them with Gothic literature. However, these works do not all feature the historically inspired characteristics of Gothic literature, and their morals or outcomes more closely resemble those of Romantic literature. The Dark Romantics include writers such as Edgar Allan Poe, Nathaniel Hawthorne, Emily Dickinson, and Herman Melville.

Transcendentalism

Transcendentalism was a smaller movement that occurred alongside the American Romantic movement. The **transcendentalists** shared the Romantic emphasis on emotion and also focused heavily on how a person experiences life through their senses. They extended these sentiments to suggest that through embracing one's senses, an individual could transcend, or experience a state of being above physical humanity. They also extended the Romantic emphasis on subjectivity through their praise of self-sufficiency, as exemplified through Ralph Waldo Emerson's *Self-Reliance*. Emerson was a prominent transcendentalist. His writings included an essay titled *Nature*, which explains a progression from the use of the senses to the achievement of transcendence. Transcendentalist literature includes several essays that discuss the value of the senses and emotions or the process of transcendence. Transcendentalists also wrote poetry that includes the frequent use of imagery, metaphors, and references to nature. These elements reflect the ideas of transcendentalism and create a resemblance to the alleged experience of transcendence. Ralph Waldo Emerson, Henry David Thoreau, and Walt Whitman were all prominent writers in this movement.

Colonial America

The **colonial era** in America was influenced by immigration from England to what is now New England. These immigrants were mainly Puritans who centered their society in New England on their religious beliefs, allowing those beliefs to inform all aspects of their lives. This is apparent in the literature of the time, as much of it includes essays and sermons that discuss religion or the way the Puritans believed one should live and conduct themselves. Colonial literature also includes many poems, and these works also discuss or reference religious ideas and themes. There was not much fiction written in Colonial America, as most of the literature was written to inform or persuade.

Romantic Period

The **American Romantic** movement is also known as the American Renaissance. This movement yielded several notable American writers and works that began characterizing American literature and differentiating it from British literature. This literature, written after the American Revolutionary War and until the end of the Civil War, praised individualism and featured an expression of national pride and patriotism. The transcendentalists' extreme ideas about self-sufficiency and subjectivity reiterated this individualism, and their recommendations about society and its structure furthered the separation of American literature from British literature. While this period shaped the definition of American literature, it is criticized for featuring a narrow view of American politics and social issues at the time, as well as promoting a small group of similar writers.

Review Video: Authors in the Romantic Period
Visit mometrix.com/academy and enter code: 752719

HARLEM RENAISSANCE

The **Harlem Renaissance** took place in America during the 1920s and 1930s. The changing economy and opportunities led African Americans in the south to seek new lifestyles in other parts of America at the beginning of the 20th century. Many moved to Harlem, a small area in New York City. This group of African Americans yielded highly influential scholarly and artistic works, including poetry, fiction, music, and plays. The Harlem Renaissance marked an opportunity for these intellectuals and artists, who were largely ignored in the aftermath of the Civil War, to use their talents and express themselves through their works. While artists often featured personal expression in their works, the Harlem Renaissance was unique in its volume of culturally expressive works. This cultural expression and the movement's main ideas also contributed to the Civil Rights movement by promoting a spirit of unity among African Americans. The Harlem Renaissance eventually ended in the wake of the stock market crash in 1929. As the Great Depression began, financial support for the arts dwindled, making it difficult for many artists to succeed financially. Some members of the Harlem Renaissance who influenced American literature include Langston Hughes, Zora Neale Hurston, and Paul Robeson.

BRITISH LITERARY PERIODS

NEOCLASSICAL

The **British Neoclassical** period began in the middle of the 17th century and ended in the late 18th century. The latter part of the movement also took place alongside the Enlightenment, a period of scientific discovery and study that influenced many Western cultures. The Enlightenment's concern with intellectual pursuits and improvement increased discussions of introspection, or an individual's analysis of their own behavior, thoughts, and self. These ideas also affected society in England, as they contributed to a general attitude of complacency and a desire to ignore the past. The period saw a slightly increased acceptance of female writers, as their works were viewed as a method of self-reflection and improvement. The changes in British society allowed several new forms of literature to gain popularity and acceptance, usually for their introspective qualities. Essays, diaries, and letters all displayed the author's thoughts and experience, aligning them with the culture's values. Novels also gained popularity, as many were fictional diaries or epistolary novels. Journalism flourished during the Neoclassical period, leading to the creation of the newspaper. Literary criticism also gained popularity, though it was used to criticize an author and their style rather than examine or analyze the content of the work.

VICTORIAN

The **Victorian Era** in England was influenced by a variety of events and ideas, many of which were influenced by the Victorians' economy. The Industrial Revolution in England changed the circumstances of work for the Victorians. The changing industries and lack of labor laws led to several problems and a wide division between Victorian social classes. These factors inspired and saturated much of Victorian literature. Many novels' plots and characters were heavily influenced by social and economic issues, and many poems referenced and criticized specific events that occurred during this period.

While the structure of Victorian society was a major influence on literature, there were other popular topics that appeared in literature. Topics like evolution, psychology, and colonization frequently appeared in Victorian literature, reflecting the concerns and interests of the Victorian culture. The Victorian society was also characterized by a strict moral code that supported the view of women as homemakers and criticized the idea of female writers. Not only did this affect the portrayal of women in literature, but it also led some female novelists, such as the Bronte sisters, to write under a pseudonym and present their works as having been written by a man. Victorian literature also popularized forms of literature, including the novel and the dramatic monologue, a poetic form developed by Robert Browning. Victorian writers include Charles Dickens, Oscar Wilde, Elizabeth Barrett Browning, Emily Bronte, Matthew Arnold, and Thomas Hardy.

World Literary Characteristics and Periods

While many other nations shared literary movements with America and England, there are numerous literary movements that are unique to other countries and cultures. Some of these literary movements can be understood as variations of movements like Romanticism or modernism, since they occurred at similar times and feature similar elements, but the political and cultural events of each country shaped their version of each movement. Most regions also have some type of mythology, and while different mythologies have similar characters and events, each region's mythology is unique and significant to the region's literature. Another common feature of world literature is colonialism. Many nations are former colonies of European countries, and the effects of colonization are present in modern literature from countries worldwide, making it a key feature of many regions' body of literature.

African Literature

Literature from some cultures was not recorded until the 19th century, causing any movements and trends to be informed by ideas told aloud. This is true of African literature, where stories and ideas were spoken and passed down through the generations. Early African poetry was often metaphorical, structured or written to form a paradox, and included a riddle or puzzling statement. Proverbs and didactic tales were also told frequently, reflecting the dominant religions in a given region and time period. These poems and stories also reflect the variety of languages spoken in Africa and the shifts in each language's usage. Early African literature, once people began writing it down, included stories and proverbs that had been passed down, translations of religious texts, and descriptions of the way of life in different African cultures or groups. These cultures and the events specific to each of them produce a unique body of literature that places emphasis on certain topics and ideas. For example, much of the modern literature written in South Africa discusses politics and issues of race, since the country's history is characterized by events and movements that revolved around these topics.

Asian Literature

Asian literature features writings from several different countries and languages and has spanned many centuries. Many popular forms of writing have come from Asia, such as the haiku. A couple of significant literary movements include The Hungry Generation in South Asia and the Misty Poets in China. The Hungry Generation is a literary movement involving literature written in the Bengali language, spoken mainly in West Bengal and Bangladesh. The literature is characterized by unique and innovative writing, which impacted the use of figurative language in the region. The Hungry Generation also discussed cultural issues, particularly colonization in the region, and many participants were arrested for their work. The Misty Poets in China were characterized by their expressive use of abstractions. Their name, Misty Poets, comes from their writings, which were difficult to interpret due to their use of abstract language and ambiguity. This movement was partly inspired by the Misty Poets' distaste for literary realism, though its influence is detectable within their poetry. Many of the Misty Poets were punished for their poetry, since the poetry of this movement was also politically critical.

Latin American Literature

Latin American literature has several literary movements, many of which occurred near the same time as American and British literary movements and share ideas and trends with their English counterparts. Despite these similarities, each of these movements is distinguishable as its own movement with unique impacts of Latin American literature. By the 17th century, written language was in use in Mexico, and Latin American literary trends and figures had been recognized. During the 18th century, Latin American literature featured a variety of ideas and themes within each form of literature. By the 19th century, literary themes were more unified throughout popular Latin American literature. In the early 19th century, Latin American literature embraced the Romantic movement as it came to an end in England and the United States. Several Latin American countries were also fighting for independence during this time, amplifying the Romantic idea of national pride and identity.

In the wake of the Romantic movement, Latin American literature introduced the unique *Modernismo* movement, which yielded a large volume of poetry and is characterized by the use of whimsical imagery and discussions of spiritual ideas. Following *Modernismo* was the *Vanguardia* movement, which was created to introduce diversity within Latin American literature after modernism permeated the literature of the time. *Vanguardia* involved writers taking risks in their writing and breaking the mold from typical Latin American literature. In the 20th century, *Estridentismo* followed the *Vanguardia* movement, marrying the *Vanguardia* movement with the European Avant-Garde movement. Other 20th century movements functioned similarly by adapting literary movements from other regions to suit the themes and trends in Latin American literature, reflect Latin American cultures, and set their literature apart from other cultures.

Literary Periods and Movements

Old English

The English language developed over a long period of time through interactions between different groups in Europe, including the Romans, the Germans, and the Celtics. The Anglo-Saxons, a group that left what is now Germany and settled in England, further established the English language by using what is now called **Old English**. While Old English laid foundations for modern English, its usage fundamentally differs from the way English is used today. For example, Old English relied on inflections to create meaning, placing little importance on the order of the words in the sentence. Its use of verbs and tenses also differs from modern English grammar. The Anglo-Saxons also used kennings, or compound words that functioned as figurative language.

Old English, as a language influenced by several cultures, had dialects from its inception. Differences in usage also came from the division between secular and religious cultures. This division heavily influenced Old English literature, as most of the literature from the time is categorized according to the set of beliefs it reflects. Most of the influential literature of the time includes riddles, poems, or translations of religious texts. Surviving Old English poetry mainly discusses real heroes and battles or provides a narrative about a fictional hero. Many of these fictional poems are considered *lays*, or *lais*, which are narrative poems that are structured using couplets of lines containing eight syllables each. The translations were often of passages from the Christian Bible, adaptations of Biblical passages, or copies of Christian hymns. Old English persisted until the 12th century, where it was eventually replaced with Middle English. Influential literature from this period includes *Beowulf*, "The Wanderer," "The Wife's Lament," and "The Seafarer."

Middle English

Old English was replaced by **Middle English**, which was used from the 12th century to the 16th century. Old English was not governed by a consistent set of grammatical rules until the Norse people, their language, and its structure influenced the integration of grammar into English, leading to Middle English. Middle English relied less on inflections than Old English, instead creating variations by using affixes and synonyms. The development of grammar was further facilitated by the printing press, which made it easier for writers to comply with grammar rules since the printing of identical copies reduced variation between texts.

Old English's evolution into Middle English can be narrowed down to three stages: Early, Central, and Late Middle English. Early Middle English, though it showed a change in the language, maintained the writing style of Old English. Central Middle English is characterized by the development of dialects within written communication, which is partly due to scribes who translated texts or parts of texts using terms from their own dialect, rather than the source. Late Middle English includes numerous developments that created the foundation for Modern English. *The Canterbury Tales*, "Sir Gawain and the Green Knight," and "Le Morte d'Arthur" are all Middle English texts that are still read and studied today.

The Renaissance

The **Renaissance** swept through Europe and lasted for multiple centuries, bringing many developments in culture, the arts, education, and philosophy. The Renaissance in England did not begin until the late 15th century. Though ideas and cultures of the past, especially those of the ancient Greeks and Romans, inspired the Renaissance, the period saw innumerable developments in the English language and literature. The Renaissance was characterized by a focus on the humanities, allowing the arts, including literature, to flourish. At the time, drama was possibly the most popular form of literature, as the popularity of plays and theatrical performances greatly increased. Much of Renaissance literature is still studied today, maintaining its influence on Western literature. Poetry was also popular, and the period saw the development of new forms of poetry, such as the sonnet. Sonnets are often recognized according to one of four styles, each of which was popularized by a Renaissance writer. Lyrical poetry, which discusses emotions and is often written using first-person point of view, was also popular during the Renaissance.

In addition to new forms and literary trends, the Renaissance period also impacted English literature by facilitating discussion over the translation of the Bible. Education at the time often included instruction in Greek and Latin, allowing those with an education to read ancient texts in their original language. However, this instruction did not reach the majority of the public. The Protestant Reformation encouraged discussions about translating the Bible to make it accessible to more people. This suggestion was challenged by those who doubted the ability of the English language to fully reflect the original text. Eventually, the Bible was translated to English, and William Tyndale's partial translation became especially influential for later translations and the continuing development of the English language. Influential writers of the English Renaissance include William Shakespeare, John Donne, John Milton, Edmund Spenser, and Christopher Marlowe.

Gothic

The Gothic literary movement, beginning in the 18th century and persisting through the 19th century, took inspiration from the architecture and cultures of the Late Middle Ages in Europe. The Late Middle Ages saw the popularity of Gothic architecture, most prominently in places of worship. These structures inspired many of the settings in **Gothic literature**, as a large volume of Gothic literature takes place in an impressive location, such as a castle or ornate mansion. Gothic works also are often set in the past, long before the time the story was written. This aligns with prominent themes in Gothic literature, as several pieces are informed by an event that occurred before the story begins or a character who died before the plot's first event.

Another common characteristic of Gothic literature is its eerie, dark, suspenseful tone. Authors of Gothic literature often created this tone by setting their works in secluded and strange locations and incorporating intense, unsettling, or even supernatural events and scenarios into the plot. This tone is also created through the theme of death or mortality that often appears in Gothic literature. These characteristics support the aim of many Gothic writers to create fiction that evokes a certain emotion from the reader or shapes their reading experience. Well-known authors of Gothic literature include Horace Walpole, Ann Radcliffe, Edgar Allan Poe, and Nathaniel Hawthorne. While the Gothic literary movement took place in the 18th and 19th centuries, many works have been published in more recent centuries that have several characteristics of Gothic literature and may be included within the overall Gothic genre.

Naturalism

Naturalism was an active literary movement in the late 19th century, taking place alongside movements such as realism and modernism. **Naturalism**, like realism, rejected the emotional focus and sentimentality of Romanticism and provided a type of social commentary. However, the naturalist movement stretched the ideas of realism, promoting literature that authentically depicts the life of the common man and criticizing the influence of morality on such literature. Naturalist literature often includes characters who belong to a lower class and experience circumstances beyond their own control and takes place in urban settings. Prominent themes in naturalist literature include nature as an apathetic force, the influence of heredity, and life as something to be endured and survived. One of the most influential naturalist writers is French writer Emile Zola. Influential American Naturalists include Stephen Crane, Hamlin Garland, and Theodore Dreiser.

Modernism

The Modernist literary movement was largely influenced by industrialization, which heavily impacted both the Unites States and England, primarily in the 19th century. **Modernism** in literature was characterized by an attempt to turn away from the norms and traditions of literature and use new techniques and methods. Modernist literature was often written in first person and used literary devices and techniques to reveal problems within society. For the American modernists, these societal changes came from industrialization and the first World War, which effected the general view of human nature and reliability. In England, there were additional factors contributing to this shift. Modernism began during Queen Victoria's reign, which defined the period known as the Victorian Era. The Victorian society was characterized by a strict moral code that permeated England's society at the time. This moral code was incompatible with the Modernist's desire to turn away from tradition, but the changes that accompanied Victoria's death in 1901 enabled the Modernist movement to grow in England. American Modernist writers include Ezra Pound, William Carlos Williams, and Gertrude Stein. British Modernist writers include Matthew Arnold, William Butler Yeats, T. S. Eliot, and Joseph Conrad.

Postmodernism

Postmodernism grew out of Modernism's reliance on science and universal assertions, but emphasized the individual's subjective perception of reality, as it is often more authentic to an individual's experience than a universally applied statement. Postmodernism asserts that since each person creates their own version of reality, fully and accurately defining reality is futile and impossible. Due to this skepticism, postmodern writers use many concrete details, rather than abstract details, because they can be objectively observed and are not left up to the individual. The postmodernist literary movement began around the 1960s. The literary movement included a variety of new genres and techniques, reflecting the postmodernist idea that things like art cannot be truly defined or simplified. Notable American writers of the postmodernist movement include Kurt Vonnegut, John Barth, and Thomas Pynchon. British postmodernist writers include John Fowles and Julian Barnes.

Public Speaking

Speeches

Speeches are written to be delivered in spoken language in public, to various groups of people, at formal or informal events. Some generic types include welcome speeches, thank-you speeches, keynote addresses, position papers, commemorative and dedication speeches, and farewell speeches. Speeches are commonly written in present tense and usually begin with an introduction greeting the audience. At official functions, specific audience members are named ("Chairperson [name]," "Principal [name], teachers, and students," etc.) and when audiences include a distinguished guest, he or she is often named as well. Then the speaker introduces him or herself by name, position, and department or organization as applicable. After the greeting, the speaker then introduces the topic and states the purpose of the speech. The body of the speech follows, similarly to the body of an essay, stating its main points, an explanation of each point, and supporting evidence. Finally, in the conclusion, the speaker states his or her hope for accomplishing the speech's purpose and thanks the audience for attending and listening to the speech.

Clearly Written Prose and Speeches

To achieve **clarity**, a writer or speaker must first define his or her purpose carefully. The speech should be organized logically, so that sentences make sense and follow each other in an understandable order. Sentences must also be constructed well, with carefully chosen words and structure. Organizing a speech in advance using an outline provides the writer or speaker with a blueprint, directing and focusing the composition to meet its intended purpose. Organized speeches enable audiences to comprehend and retain the presented information more easily. Humans naturally seek to impose order on the world by seeking patterns. Hence, when ideas in a speech are well-organized and adhere to a consistent pattern, the speaker communicates better with listeners and is more convincing. Speechwriters can use chronological patterns to organize events, sequential patterns to organize processes by their steps, and spatial patterns to help audiences visualize geographical locations and movements or physical scenarios. Also, comparison-contrast patterns give audiences insight about similarities and differences between and among topics, especially when listeners are more familiar with one than the other.

Evaluating Speeches for Concise Information

To convince or persuade listeners or reinforce a message, speeches must be succinct. Audiences can become confused by excessive anecdotes and details. If a speaker takes three minutes or more to get to the point, audience members' attention will start to fade and will only worsen when details deviate from the main subject. When answering a question, the asker and speaker may even forget the original question if the speaker takes too long. Speakers should practice not only rehearsing written speeches, but also developing skill for spontaneous question-and-answer sessions after speeches. Speakers should differentiate necessary from simply interesting information because audiences can become overwhelmed by too much information. Speakers should know what points they wish to make. They should not be afraid to pause before responding to questions, which indicates thoughtfulness and control rather than lack of knowledge. Restating questions increases comprehension and appropriate responses, and allows time to form answers mentally.

Organizational Patterns for Speeches

A speechwriter who uses an **advantages-disadvantages** pattern of organization presents the audience with the pros and cons of a topic. This aids writers in discussing two sides of an issue objectively without an argumentative position, enabling listeners to weigh both aspects. When a speechwriter uses a **cause-and-effect** pattern, it can help to persuade audiences to agree with an action or solution by showing significant relationships between factors. Writers may separate an outline into two main "cause" and "effect" sections or into separate sections for each cause, including the effect for each.

Persuasive writing also benefits from **problem-solution** patterns: by establishing the existence of a problem, writers induce audiences to realize a need for change. By supplying a solution and supporting its superiority above other solutions, the writer convinces audiences of the value of that solution. When none of these patterns—or **chronological**, **sequential**, **spatial**, or **comparison-contrast** patterns—applies, speechwriters often use topical patterns. These organize information by various subtopics and types within the main topic or category.

EFFECTIVE SPEECH DELIVERY

Speakers should deliver speeches in a natural, conversational manner rather than being rigidly formal or theatrical. Effective delivery is also supported by confidence. Speakers should be direct, building audience rapport through personal connection and vivid imagery. Speakers should be mindful of the occasion, subject, and audience of their speeches and take care to use appropriate language. Good speakers learn vocal control, including volume, speed, pitch, use of pauses, tonal variety, correct pronunciation, and clear articulation. They can express enthusiasm and emphasize important points with their voices. Nonverbal behaviors, such as eye contact, facial expressions, gestures, good posture, and body movements clarify communication, stress important ideas, and influence perceptions that the speaker is trustworthy, competent, and credible. Nonverbal communications should seem as spontaneous and natural as vocal or verbal ones. Speakers should know their speeches well and practice frequently, taking care to avoid nervous or irrelevant movements such as tapping or pacing.

Chapter Quiz

Ready to see how well you retained what you just read? Scan the QR code to go directly to the chapter quiz interface for this study guide. If you're using a computer, simply visit the online resources page at **mometrix.com/resources719/ftcehumank-12** and click the Chapter Quizzes link.

Instructional Techniques, Assessment, and Resources Appropriate to the Humanities

Classroom Participation

Techniques to Ensure Active Listening and Productive Participation

When assigning students to participate in cooperative learning projects or discussions, teachers should consider their **cognitive, emotional, behavioral, and social developmental levels.** If a teacher assigns a topic for age levels younger than the class, students will be bored and unengaged. If the topic assigned is for older age levels, they will be confused, overwhelmed, or lost. Before initiating class or group discussions, teachers should model and explain appropriate behaviors for discussions—particularly for students unfamiliar or inexperienced with group discussions. For example, teachers can demonstrate active listening, including eye contact, affirming or confirming the speaker's message, and restating the speaker's message for confirmation or correction. Teachers should establish **clear ground rules**, such as not interrupting others when they are speaking, not monopolizing the conversation, not engaging in cross-talk, not insulting classmates verbally, and taking turns and waiting for the appropriate time to make a comment. For young children and students with behavioral issues, this would also include refraining from physical contact like hitting, kicking, and biting.

Active Student Listening

Active listening has multiple dimensions. It involves constructing meaning out of what is heard, being reflective and creative in considering and manipulating information, and making competent decisions rich in ideas. The natural properties of speech and thought enable active listening: the typical speed of speaking is roughly 125 words per minute, whereas the estimated speed of thinking is roughly 500 words per minute. Therefore, students have around 375 words per minute of spare time to think about the speech they hear. Students' minds can wander during this extra time, so teachers should instruct them to use the time instead to summarize lecture information mentally—a form of active listening. Listening and learning are both social and reciprocal. They also both allow and require students to process and consider what they hear and stimulate their curiosity about subsequent information.

Incorporating Active Student Listening into Lessons

At the beginning of each day (or class), teachers should clarify the "big picture" and identify the learning objectives incorporated into the day's activities. They should also give students a single word or phrase to summarize the prior day's subject and a single word or phrase to preview the current day's subject. Teachers should not only establish this recall, retrieval, prediction, and planning process as a daily habit, but should also encourage students to develop the same daily habit in their note-taking. Teachers should review main concepts or have students summarize the last lecture's main ideas to make connections with preceding lessons. By encouraging and guiding student listening, teachers supply spoken transitions analogously to those in written research. By cueing students to take notes with questions or summaries at the ends of sections, teachers also help students demonstrate their comprehension.

> **Review Video: Learning Objectives**
> Visit mometrix.com/academy and enter code: 528458

Using Media to Review

Teachers can allow students to take photos, videos, and audio recordings of lessons to review as needed. To encourage students to reword and recall instructional input, teachers can let students download class outlines from Google Docs. These outlines may include hard-to-spell terminology or vocabulary words, jargon of specific disciplines, and links reminding students to follow up by accessing resources and readings to inform the notes they take. Teachers should give outlines a two-column format: on the right, a wider column with teacher notes, to which students can add, and on the left, a narrower column for students to record notes and questions about previous lectures and reading. Teachers should advise students to take their own notes in similar formats. Students and teachers alike can learn through speaking, writing, listening, and reading when they contribute narratives to supplement visual graphics (photos, concept maps, charts, advance organizers, illustrations, diagrams, etc.) that support the concepts they analyze and explain.

Whole-Class Learning Circles

Forming **whole classes** into learning circles requires students to apply their skills for listening to lectures, synthesizing information, and summarizing the information. Teachers can prepare students by articulating central discussion points; identifying next steps in thought, question forming, analysis, and action; guiding student analysis and construction of meaning from what they have read, observed, and experienced; and asking students questions beginning with "What?" "Why?" and "Now what?"

Basic ground rules for learning circles include:

1. No student interrupts another.
2. Students may skip a turn until others have taken turns, but no student speaks out of turn.
3. Each student has a certain length of time for speaking.
4. Each student starts by restating what was said previously (e.g., summarizing shared points, differing points, missed points, or points not discussed fully).
5. After every student has had one turn, general discussion is open, possibly guided by teacher-provided questions.

Procedures and Ground Rules for Smaller Groups

Teachers can develop student discussion skills integrating listening, reading, and speaking skills by assigning small discussion groups to tackle assigned problems. Teachers may use established groups, assign new groups, or allow students to form groups of 4-5 students. Teachers can read a text passage, describe a scenario, or pose a question for discussion. They can then give students several minutes to review homework and notes, briefly read new related material, and review essay drafts. Teachers then give each student in each group a specified number of uninterrupted minutes to speak in turn.

After every student has taken a turn, the teacher opens general discussion, setting the following ground rules:

1. Students can only speak about others' ideas.
2. Teachers and classmates can ask students to clarify their ideas, give examples, connect them more closely to what they read, or elaborate.
3. Small groups can summarize overall points for other groups, including shared points, differences, and potential topics they missed.

Educator Techniques for Classroom Discussions

Students who feel comfortable with the teacher and the class are more likely to engage in open discussion. Teachers can encourage student openness and creativity by learning students' names and by posing questions rather than making comments. Lively discussions with all students participating are evidence that students are comfortable. A variety of student answers is evidence that the questioning technique works. When student discussions stray off the subject, learning goals will not be met. Teachers can redirect discussion by restating topics and questions previously announced, and by introducing new questions related to identified topics. When conversation refocuses on stated topics, teachers can identify specified learning goals/objectives students are meeting in their discussion. In most classes, a few students will dominate conversations. Teachers can pose less challenging questions, which can be answered even without preparation, to engage more reticent students, and then graduate to higher-level questions. They can evaluate all students' participation using checklists generated from attendance sheets.

Teaching Strategies to Encourage Discussion

During class discussions, students often contribute erroneous information. Teachers must be tactful in correcting them. If students withdraw from the conversation or cease further contributions, the teacher has not corrected them appropriately. If corrected students continue to contribute, the teacher has succeeded in providing positive reinforcement rather than punishment with the correction. Some ways to do this include acknowledging how the student came to a conclusion but explaining that it does not apply to the current context, or explaining how the student's response might be correct in another situation. Teachers can also provide incentives for students to contribute to class discussions. They may include participation in the syllabus as part of the grade, keep records to tally when each student contributes to a discussion, or assign different students to lead class discussions in turn. These are some ways teachers can evaluate individual student participation in classroom discussions, as well as their own effectiveness in encouraging such participation.

Reducing Intimidation

Students often feel intimidated if "put on the spot" to answer questions without warning. Teachers can put them at ease by allowing time to prepare. They can announce topics and questions for class discussion, giving students five minutes to jot down notes for responses and another five minutes for exchanging and reflecting on notes with classmates before beginning whole-class conversation. Teachers may distribute discussion topics at the end of one class for the next day's conversation or post questions online the night before class. One technique for evaluating discussions is asking students early in the term to write papers about the characteristics of good and bad class discussions, and then discuss what they have written. Teachers then compose a list of classroom discussion goals and give copies to all students. Another technique is an informal survey: ask students midway through the semester to evaluate the overall quality of class discussions. Share responses with the class, and inform them of plans incorporating their feedback to enhance discussions.

Promoting Discussion Outside of Class

Teachers can encourage in-class discussion by promoting group meetings and discussions outside the classroom. Interacting with students outside of class also promotes a sense of community. Teachers can demonstrate to students that they care about them as individuals and about their educational development by asking them about their holiday or summer plans, about how they are feeling during midterm and final exam periods, and about their other classes. Teachers can find online articles related to class material and email or text links to these for review. They can allow time at the beginning of each class for announcements and arrange classroom chairs in a semicircle to encourage conversation. These methods have all been found effective in promoting a sense of community, which in turn encourages class discussions. To address different student learning styles and abilities, teachers can vary the levels and types of questions they ask their students: asking them to give simple information, describe, compare, analyze, justify, compare, generalize, predict, or apply information.

Assessment in English Language Arts

Rubric for Assessing Student Writing

A **rubric** is a checklist used to evaluate what students have learned or accomplished. Teachers can take lesson objectives to form the basis of a rubric. The teacher should explain the rubric to the students before they begin a writing assignment. During their writing exercise, the students can refer to the rubric to guide what and how they write. After the students have completed their writing assignments, the teacher can then apply the rubric to assess their work, checking to see if they have met all of the learning objectives. Students will be less confused and frustrated when teachers have given them well-planned, clearly expressed guidelines. In addition to clearly stating their learning goals, objectives, and expectations for each assignment, teachers should model the kind of performance they expect. Teachers should connect lesson and assignment goals obviously and clearly with student achievement.

Summative and Formative Assessments

Summative assessments evaluate what a student has learned at the end of a lesson, unit, course, or term. A final examination is an example of a summative assessment. **Formative assessments** are ongoing evaluations to demonstrate what a student is in the process of learning and what he or she has learned thus far. Formative assessments are not just for evaluation: they are also important for use in the classroom as a teaching tool. As teachers conduct ongoing evaluations via formative assessments, they should use both formal and informal assessment instruments. Teachers should never use the results of only one formal or informal assessment to form permanent student groups. They should only place students into groups after administering, scoring, and interpreting a number of different assessments. Teachers should also create student groups that account for individual differences among the students in every group and should accordingly make these groups sufficiently flexible to accommodate individual student differences.

Review Video: Formative and Summative Assessments
Visit mometrix.com/academy and enter code: 804991

Observation

Observational assessment is appropriate for evaluating student progress and the effectiveness of instruction. A teacher can create a checklist of skills, requirements, or competencies that students should attain. The teacher can then observe individuals or student groups and check off the skills or competencies demonstrated. For example, if a teacher has been instructing a class in listening carefully, he or she can compose a checklist with items such as paying attention, refraining from interrupting others, summarizing what ideas the other students have expressed, and asking questions of other students. The teacher can then initiate and observe student discussion, checking off the checklist items he or she observes the students performing. Or, when teaching interview skills, a teacher can make a checklist including confidence, personal appearance, mannerisms, and directly answering interviewer questions. He or she can also observe students participating in mock or real interviews and identify which items the students satisfy.

By observing students as they work on assignments or practice exercises, teachers can obtain valuable information. With kindergarten and first-grade classes, many school districts inform parents of children's progress by filling out "report cards" or inventories. Through experience, long-term teachers typically develop their own methods of making ongoing skills assessments of their students. Books about reading instruction typically include informal reading assessments. Teachers should assess student progress in naturalistic ways on a continual basis. Teachers and parents continually observing students regarding their status and progress in the physical, cognitive, emotional, and social domains yields the most relevant assessment—particularly with young children. Portfolio and performance assessments provide a more complete picture of overall progress than standardized test scores alone.

Additionally, writing narrative reports about young children depicts the whole child better than just giving them number or letter grades.

Review Video: Assessment Reliability and Validity
Visit mometrix.com/academy and enter code: 424680

Observational Checklists

In informal assessment, using **observational checklists** to identify skills attained has an advantage over formal written tests because informal, naturalistic observation enables teachers to record behaviors that traditional written tests cannot include. For example, if teachers want to know whether students can follow all steps of a science experiment in the correct sequence, how many baskets they can make in free throws on the basketball court, or whether they can remember all of the significant parts to include in a speech they write and deliver to the class, they can record these by observing and marking such items on a checklist they have designed in advance—but they could not record any such behaviors through standard "pencil-and-paper" tests. The structure of checklists has the advantage of being consistent, but also the disadvantage of being inflexible. Teachers can remedy the latter by including a place at the end of the checklist to write open-ended comments on their observations of student performance.

Running Record

To identify what students are able and unable to do, one informal assessment measure teachers can use is a **running record**. For example, the teacher can listen to a student reading aloud from text such as an essay, a speech, a novel, or a class subject textbook. While listening, the teacher marks a copy of the text to show words the student mispronounces. The teacher draws a line through each word the student skips and draws an arrow under words the student repeats. Teachers may also mark student hesitations at certain words. If the teacher then calculates that the student correctly read 95 percent of the words, the student reads this text at the "Independent" level. If the student correctly reads 90-94 percent of the words, he or she reads this text at the "Instructional" level, indicating satisfactory performance with teacher assistance. Correctly reading 89 percent or fewer words indicates the "Frustration" level, where comprehension may be inadequate. This group of assessment levels is also known as the reading continuum.

Anecdotal Records

Anecdotal records can provide good information for formative assessments. For example, when students conduct science experiments or complete class projects, teachers can use anecdotal records to instruct them in writing reports to explain the procedures they followed. When students in group learning activities solve a problem together, teachers can use anecdotal records to document the process used. Such anecdotal documents not only provide the teacher with formative assessment information, but teachers can also use them to give feedback to the group of students. Two disadvantages of using anecdotal records are that they can take more time for teachers to complete than other informal assessments and that they can be hard to use for assigning grades. Two advantages are that anecdotal records can encompass all pertinent information, whereas other assessments may not, and that teachers may use them only for giving students feedback, which eliminates the need to base grades on them.

Portfolio Assessment

In portfolio assessment, teachers or students create a folder or box and deposit a student's best work products, accumulated over time. In language arts, teachers often collect student writing samples in portfolios for a whole year. Some language arts teachers additionally transmit year-long portfolios to the following year's teacher to aid in student assessment. Teachers can use portfolio assessments in any subject to enable students to assume greater responsibility for planning, organizing, and implementing what they learn. The combined products in the portfolio afford concise depictions of what students have achieved during specific time periods. Portfolios can include handwritten or printed essays, stories, and articles; videos; or computer files of multimedia presentations. Teachers should help students develop guidelines about which materials to place in portfolios, and how to self-assess their own work. The advantages of portfolios over tests include helping students develop self-assessment skills, giving clearer pictures of student progress, and learning from mistakes without the damage of a bad test grade.

Research-Based Assessment Techniques

Assessment of Student Learning

To assess student attitudes, educators can create various situations and observe and document their responses, requiring students to choose which behaviors to demonstrate. To assess **cognitive strategies**, teachers can give students learning tasks, require them to select useful strategies for learning new information independently, and expect them to explain and discuss what methods they use for different learning tasks. To assess student **comprehension**, teachers give them topics and ask them to restate and summarize information. Or, teachers may have students apply information in new contexts, such as giving statements with words that are different than those used in the original lesson and asking students to identify their meanings. To assess student **concept understanding**, teachers give students new examples and "non-examples," having students classify these into the right categories. To assess student **creativity**, teachers can give students new problems—including products, presentations, or performances—to study, resolve, or "turn upside down." They can also have students fit solutions and products into specified resources and functions and give them situations that require novel responses or approaches.

Assessment of Different Student Outcomes

To assess students' **critical thinking**, teachers can ask students to evaluate outcomes or information and have them perform research and analysis. To assess student **insight**, teachers should give students opportunities to engage in inquiry and discovery activities, and offer situations for them to manipulate. To assess student **metacognition**, teachers should give a variety of problems or situations to address, and assign students to identify different kinds of thinking strategies for analysis and evaluation of their own thought processes. To assess **multiple intelligences** (Gardner), teachers should give students learning experiences in each of the modalities they target, like verbal, musical, and physical. They should offer students choices of several different modalities. They should also require students to perform in the modalities selected. To assess **motor skills**, teachers must supply resources and situations in which students can perform the skills while the teachers evaluate, using checklists. To assess **problem-solving**, teachers ask students to choose appropriate strategies to solve different problem situations including simple, complex, structured, and unstructured.

Procedural Knowledge, Scientific Inquiry, Thinking Skills, and Verbal Knowledge

To assess student **knowledge of principles, rules, and procedures**, teachers supply situations that require students to correctly apply these to everyday problems. Students are asked to state principles, rules, and procedures, and choose which apply to various scenarios. To assess student **scientific inquiry skills**, teachers give problems or situations that require students to speculate, inquire, and formulate hypotheses. Teachers should also give hands-on activities to conduct research and draw conclusions. To assess student **thinking skills**, teachers can ask students to give summaries of different kinds of thinking strategies. Teachers can provide situations in which students must select the best thinking strategies to apply. Teachers assign students to observe examples of open-mindedness versus closed-mindedness, accurate versus inaccurate, and responsible versus irresponsible applications of thinking methods. Teachers can design scenarios requiring student persistence for analyzing and discovering answers, as well as application of thinking strategies in real-life circumstances. To assess **verbal knowledge**, teachers require information recall, restatement, and comprehension.

Teaching Strategies to Address Student and Family Diversity

Teachers must recognize that each student is unique. When a teacher respects individual student differences, he or she communicates this attitude to the class. Cultural differences influence human behavior, and thus play a part in classrooms. Acknowledgement of cultural differences helps to prevent student isolation. To educate students from diverse backgrounds, teachers need to understand a student's culture and individual characteristics—as well as any existing disabilities. Teacher and school involvement with students' families promotes student success during and after school. This requires educators to avoid ethnocentric approaches. Diverse families may need instruction in the school culture of collaboration and communication. Schools also must initially meet family needs physically, socially, and economically to enable involvement, requiring school knowledge of supportive community programs. Communications must be translated for families speaking different languages. Educators need willingness to interact outside of school hours and grounds. They can also recruit parent liaisons with similar cultural backgrounds. Teachers should open parent communications with positive feedback about children.

Inclusive educational programs require meaningful, effective collaboration of educators, students, and families. Teachers must not only meet student and family needs, but they must also communicate their own needs effectively and be willing to find solutions through team-based approaches. Collaboration allows outcomes that individuals cannot achieve alone. Despite the challenges of cooperation among staff members, the more teachers interact with each other, the more educational change can be achieved successfully. Understanding of cultural communication differences, respectful disagreement, respect for confidentiality, willingness to compromise, responsible communication of opinions and emotions (such as using "I" statements), tolerance for others' various perspectives, and careful listening to others are communication skills needed for effective communication and collaboration. Some educators advocate multicultural awareness days involving all school personnel, families, and community members when each school year starts. Culturally responsive standards-based instruction (CRSBI) incorporates caring, communication, and curriculum. Educators must also foster positive student-teacher relationships, and assure positive role models for every student.

Creating Safe Educational Environments

Teachers need to establish and sustain classroom environments for students in which they feel nurtured and know that the teacher is open to hearing their feelings, thoughts, and ideas. Teachers are responsible for developing respect for individual differences and openness to discussions in their classrooms. They may need to explain the difference between fairness and equality. For example, students who need eyeglasses cannot be deprived of them, but neither should all students be made to wear them. Teachers can use such examples to illustrate to students that fairness does not mean everybody gets the same treatment: while every student deserves help, that help will differ for different students. Teachers must create student-teacher relationships of mutual trust, and ensure that all students know the teachers care about them, both academically and personally. Teachers' beliefs, attitudes, and performance expectations, and how they communicate these, establish this knowledge. Teachers must know student and family languages, communication styles, and home literacy practices and build on these in their classrooms.

Review Video: Equality vs Equity
Visit mometrix.com/academy and enter code: 685648

Chapter Quiz

Ready to see how well you retained what you just read? Scan the QR code to go directly to the chapter quiz interface for this study guide. If you're using a computer, simply visit the online resources page at **mometrix.com/resources719/ftcehumank-12** and click the Chapter Quizzes link.

FTCE Practice Test

Want to take this practice test in an online interactive format?
Check out the online resources page, which includes interactive practice questions and much more: **mometrix.com/resources719/ftcehumank-12**

1. Which of these is not a type of musical scale?

a. Chromatic
b. Diatonic
c. Triadic
d. Minor
e. Pentatonic

2. Which of the following are characteristic of the Baroque period?

I. It began with the invention of opera and ended with the death of Johann Sebastian Bach.
II. It began with the death of Johann Sebastian Bach and ended in the 1820s.
III. Franz Haydn was a major composer of the period.
IV. Imitative polyphony is characteristic of the period.
V. Antonio Vivaldi is a major composer of the period.

a. I and V
b. II and III
c. I and IV
d. III and V
e. III and IV

3. Nineteenth century opera was dominated by which two composers?

a. Samuel Barber and Benjamin Britten
b. Richard Wagner and Giuseppe Verdi
c. Christoph Gluck and Wolfgang Amadeus Mozart
d. Giacomo Puccini and Maurice Ravel
e. Claudio Monteverdi and George Frideric Handel

4. Moderato, vivace, andante and presto are all examples of...

a. Rhythms
b. Meters
c. Tempos
d. Dynamics
e. Intervals

5. Musical notes are arranged in meter, or a series of beats. When an unexpected accent occurs (either between beats or on a weak beat), it is called...

a. Duple meter
b. Pulse
c. A key signature
d. Timbre
e. Syncopatio

6. Which is true of jazz?

a. It is widely considered to be America's only original contribution to music
b. It originated in American Hispanic culture.
c. It originated around the middle of the nineteenth century.
d. It is atonal.
e. John Cage was a famous jazz composer of the twentieth century.

7. What is true of a key signature?

I. It indicates the meter of a piece of music.
II. It is indicated at the beginning of a piece of music, just before the time signature.
III. It indicates how a tune gets from one pitch to the next.
IV. It is the scale that a piece of music is built on.
V. It refers to how loud or soft a tone is.

a. I and II
b. I
c. III and IV
d. II and IV
e. V

8. Which shows the correct order of the periods of Western music history?

a. Medieval, Renaissance, Baroque, Classical, Romantic, and 20th century
b. Gregorian, Baroque, Renaissance, Classical, Romantic, and 20th century
c. Gregorian, Medieval, Renaissance, Classical, Opera, and 20th century
d. Medieval, Renaissance, Baroque, Classical, Expressionist, and 20th century
e. Gregorian, Medieval, Baroque, Classical, Expressionist and Atonal

9. During which period did Giovanni Bellini, Josquin Desprez, and William Shakespeare work?

a. Classical
b. Renaissance
c. Baroque
d. Medieval
e. Romantic

10. Which languages are used in music and ballet?

a. Italian for music and ballet.
b. Italian for music, French for ballet.
c. German for music, Italian for ballet.
d. French for music and ballet.
e. French for music, Italian for ballet.

11. Where will you find the terms recitative, aria, and oratorio used?

a. Symphony
b. Concerto
c. Sonata
d. Musical theater
e. Opera

12. Which of the following does not belong with the others?

a. *Giselle*, Adam
b. *Aida*, Verdi
c. *Orfeo*, Monteverdi
d. *Parsifal*, Wagner
e. *The Marriage of Figaro*, Mozart

13. "Scat" is a singing style in which...

a. Accents are put in unexpected places.
b. A leader sings a line and others respond sympathetically.
c. Performers sit in silence for the entire piece.
d. The voice sings syllables rather than words and is used as another instrument.
e. Computer-generated music is used.

14. Which of these composers wrote exclusively for the piano?

a. Frederic Chopin
b. Richard Wagner
c. Robert Schumann
d. Wolfgang Amadeus Mozart
e. Felix Mendelssohn

15. Which option correctly lists human voices from lowest to highest?

a. Bass, tenor, baritone, alto, mezzo soprano, soprano
b. Bass, baritone, tenor, alto, mezzo soprano, soprano
c. Bass, tenor, baritone, mezzo soprano, alto, soprano
d. Bass, tenor, baritone, alto, soprano, mezzo soprano
e. Baritone, bass, tenor, alto, mezzo soprano, soprano

16. What do the terms major, minor, diminished and augmented refer to?

a. They are types of key signatures.
b. They are types of scales.
c. They are types of dynamics.
d. They are types of triads or chords.
e. They are examples of syncopation.

17. Which is not a dynamic marking?

a. Forte
b. Fortissimo
c. Mezzopiano
d. Piano
e. Andante

18. What are the four ways that sounds differ from one another?

a. Duration, frequency, intensity and timbre
b. Texture, frequency, intensity and interval
c. Tempo, duration, frequency and timbre
d. Pulse, duration, frequency and timbre
e. Duration, frequency, intensity and dynamics

19. Which is not usually true of a symphony?

a. It has four movements.
b. The first movement is usually in sonata form.
c. The second movement is usually fast.
d. The third movement is in ternary form.
e. It is a work for full orchestra.

20. This classical composer was influenced by the French Revolution, and his music is considered revolutionary because it expanded all the elements of classical style and enlarged the range of expression. He wrote nine symphonies. Who is it?

a. Wolfgang Amadeus Mozart
b. Franz Josef Haydn
c. Johann Sebastian Bach
d. Ludwig van Beethoven
e. Pyotr Ilyich Tchaikovsky

21. Improvisation characterizes which musical style?

a. Folk
b. Jazz
c. Impressionist
d. Opera
e. Rock and roll

22. What is a dithyramb?

I. A forerunner of Greek tragedies.
II. A scene of action in a tragedy.
III. A frenzied and impassioned hymn performed by a chorus of men.
IV. The conclusion of a play during which the chorus continues to chant as the characters depart.

a. I only
b. I and IV
c. I and III
d. IV only
e. II only

23. Who developed the technique of "the Method," in which actors use emotions from their past to bring depth to their acting?

a. Eugene O'Neill
b. Stella Adler
c. Konstantin Stanislavsky
d. Henrik Ibsen
e. Auguste Comte

24. Which is true of ballet?

I. One of its principles is to keep the feet turned in.
II. It was established during the reign of King Louis XIV.
III. It is based on six different positions of the feet.
IV. Marius Petipa is often referred to as its father.

a. II only
b. IV only
c. I and IV
d. II and IV
e. II, III and IV

25. The Nutcracker, Sleeping Beauty and Swan Lake are all ballets composed by...

a. Peter Tchaikovsky
b. Felix Mendelssohn
c. Martha Graham
d. Wolfgang Amadeus Mozart
e. Igor Stravinsky

26. Which of the following terms will you not hear in a ballet class?

a. Plie
b. Releve
c. Grands battements
d. Sonore
e. Fouette

27. The Peabody, the foxtrot, the jitterbug and the mashed potato all have what in common?

a. They are all types of folk dances.
b. They are all types of ballroom dances.
c. They are all characterized by flat-footed steps and syncopated rhythms.
d. They are all popular forms of dance in American musicals.
e. They are all popular American dances of the 1930s, 1940s or 1950s

28. Jazz dance played a prominent role in all of the following American musicals except...

a. Oklahoma!
b. West Side Story
c. 42nd Street
d. Chicago
e. A Chorus Line

29. What do Don Juan, The Jazz Singer and Steamboat Willie have in common?

a. They are some of the first color films.
b. They are some of the first films with sound.
c. They are some of the first films to win Academy Awards.
d. They are all produced by Thomas Edison's motion picture company.
e. They are all produced by Walt Disney.

30. Which film genre was produced only in the 1950s?

a. Comedy
b. Westerns
c. Science fiction
d. Gangster
e. Anti-communist

31. The Sound of Music, Annie Get Your Gun, Brigadoon and The Wizard of Oz all represent which film genre?

a. Comedy
b. Drama
c. Science fiction
d. Western
e. Musical

32. Which of the following actors would be out of place at an Academy Awards presentation during the 1970s or 1980s?

a. Jane Fonda
b. Sally Field
c. Jack Nicholson
d. Grace Kelly
e. Jon Voight

33. Who composed *Der Ring Des Nibelungen*, a cycle of four epic operas based on Norse legends often referred to as "The Ring"?

a. Richard Wagner
b. Giuseppe Verdi
c. Gioachino Rossini
d. Gaetano Donizetti
e. Ludwig van Beethoven

34. Rebel Without a Cause, East of Eden and Giant all star...

a. Marlon Brando
b. John Wayne
c. James Dean
d. Nicholas Ray
e. Rock Hudson

35. All of the following are true about the kinetoscope except...

a. Thomas Edison invented it.
b. It is considered the first motion picture machine.
c. It is designed as a cabinet that holds revolving spools of film.
d. The average length of its films was five minutes.
e. Movies can be viewed in it by looking through a peephole.

36. The Classical period of architecture and art begins with...

a. The ancient Greeks.
b. The ancient Romans.
c. The ancient Egyptians.
d. Neolithic people.
e. The Byzantine Empire.

37. Euripides, Aeschylus, and Sophocles were all...

a. Moral philosophers.
b. Historians.
c. Tragic playwrights.
d. Founders of Athenian democracy.
e. Sculptors.

Refer to the following for questions 38–39:

38. The sculpture pictured here is

a. Venus de Milo
b. The Dying Gaul
c. Artemis Rospigliosi
d. Barberini Faun
e. Winged Victory of Samothrace

39. The sculpture is located in the...

a. Uffizi Gallery
b. Louvre
c. Parthenon
d. Palace of Versailles
e. Tate Gallery

40. The sculpture is from which artistic period?

a. Hellenistic
b. Byzantine
c. Romanesque
d. Italian Renaissance
e. Rococo

41. Romulus and Remus were...

a. Sculptors of the Hellenistic period.
b. Architects of the Renaissance.
c. Founders of the Romanesque style of art.
d. The traditional founders of Rome.
e. Actors in Elizabethan England.

42. Pompeii is a first century southern Italian city famous because...

a. It is the site of one of Christianity's earliest churches.
b. The *Laocoon* was sculpted there.
c. The Arch of Titus is there.
d. It was completely flooded within ten years of its founding.
e. It was destroyed by a volcanic eruption.

43. Where will you find the Arch of Titus, Trajan's Column, the Pantheon and Trevi Fountain?

a. Athens
b. Rome
c. Sparta
d. Paris
e. Florence

44. The photo below shows which type of architecture?

a. Byzantine
b. Romanesque
c. Gothic
d. Tudor
e. Spanish Colonial

45. Which is not a type of architectural column?

a. Tuscan
b. Doric
c. Obelisk
d. Corinthian
e. Ionic

46. Verticality, a reach toward heaven, and a soaring and airy feel are characteristics of which architectural style?

a. Medieval
b. Roman
c. Rococo
d. Gothic
e. Renaissance

47. This painter's work is often regarded as the beginning of Renaissance art in Florence. Some of his paintings include *Ognissanti Madonna, The Life of St. Francis* paintings in Florence's Bardi Chapel in Santa Croce, and *The Life of St. John the Baptist* in the Peruzzi Chapel of the same church. Who is he?

a. Giotto
b. Cimabue
c. Duccio
d. Nicholas of Verdun
e. Ghiberti

48. Which is a group of seventeenth century artists?

a. Michelangelo, Botticelli, Masaccio, Fra Angelico
b. Hans Holbein, Albrecht Durer, Lucas Cranach, Matthias Grunewald
c. Caravaggio, Peter Paul Rubens, Jacob Jordaens, Anthony Van Dyck
d. Henri Matisse, Pablo Picasso, Georges Braque, Juan Gris
e. Édouard Manet, Claude Monet, Edgar Degas, Camille Pissarro

49. Which is a group of German Renaissance artists?

a. Michelangelo, Botticelli, Masaccio, Fra Angelico
b. Hans Holbein, Albrecht Durer, Lucas Cranach, Matthias Grunewald
c. Caravaggio, Peter Paul Rubens, Jacob Jordaens, Anthony Van Dyck
d. Henri Matisse, Pablo Picasso, Georges Braque, Juan Gris
e. Édouard Manet, Claude Monet, Edgar Degas, Camille Pissarro

50. Which is a group of Italian Renaissance artists?

a. Michelangelo, Botticelli, Masaccio, Fra Angelico
b. Hans Holbein, Albrecht Durer, Lucas Cranach, Matthias Grunewald
c. Caravaggio, Peter Paul Rubens, Jacob Jordaens, Anthony Van Dyck
d. Henri Matisse, Pablo Picasso, Georges Braque, Juan Gris
e. Édouard Manet, Claude Monet, Edgar Degas, Camille Pissarro

Refer to the following for questions 51–53:

51. This work portrays...

a. The homecoming of Odysseus
b. The Holy Spirit's coming to the apostles on Pentecost
c. Jesus's Last Supper with his disciples
d. Jesus turning water to wine at the wedding at Cana
e. King Louis XIV and his court

52. This work is by...

a. Michelangelo
b. Raphael
c. Andrea Mantegna
d. Fra Filippo Lippi
e. Leonardo da Vinci

53. Where is this work located?

a. Louvre, Paris
b. Pitti Palace, Florence
c. Chicago Art Institute
d. Santa Maria della Grazie, Milan
e. National Gallery, London

54. Pop art, which features icons of American popular culture, was popularized by...

a. Jackson Pollock
b. Andy Warhol
c. Salvador Dali
d. Giorgio de Chirico
e. Alexander Calder

55. Hagia Sophia, in Constantinople, is a soaring structure with a prominent dome, and was commissioned by Emperor Justinian in the sixth century. What style is the church built in?

a. Greek
b. Byzantine
c. Christian
d. Romanesque
e. Gothic

56. The Book of Durrow, the Lindisfarne Gospels and the Book of Kells are all...

a. Early gospels
b. Inspired by Greek tragedy
c. Commissions by Charlemagne
d. Illuminated manuscripts
e. From the time of the First Crusade

57. Who is famous for painting the Sistine Chapel frescoes in the Vatican?

a. Michelangelo
b. Da Vinci
c. Raphael
d. Uccello
e. Botticelli

58. Mannerism...

I. Was an artistic style of the 18th century.
II. Was an artistic style of the 16th century.
III. Features exaggerations.
IV. Features realistic figures.
V. Was a style used by Parmigianino, El Greco and Pontormo.

a. I, III and V
b. II and IV
c. I, III and V
d. II, IV and V
e. II, III and V

59. This 17th century artist was famous for his expressive brushwork and mysterious contrasts in lighting. *The Night Watch*, *The Anatomy Lesson of Dr. Tulp*, and *Belshazzar's Feast* are some of his most famous works.

a. Caravaggio
b. Rubens
c. Velazquez
d. Rembrandt
e. Van Dyck

60. The painting below is an example of...

a. Pointillism
b. Impressionism
c. Expressionism
d. Postimpressionism
e. Cubism

61. Which is not an example of pointillism?

a. A Sunday Afternoon on the Island of La Grande Jatte
b. The Circus
c. Bathers at Asnieres
d. The Scream
e. The Papal Palace, Avignon

62. Which correctly pairs an artist with a work he created?

a. Caravaggio: The Conversion of Saint Paul
b. Van Dyck: The Laughing Cavalier
c. Boucher: Christ Healing the Sick
d. El Greco: The Raising of the Cross
e. Rembrandt: Women Bathing

63. Michelangelo worked in all of the following art forms except...

a. Poetry
b. Painting
c. Sculpture
d. Musical composing
e. Architecture

64. The Residenz at Wurzburg, the Munich Residenz, Amalienburg Pavilion and Residenz Theater are all examples of which style of architecture?

a. Versailles
b. Rococo
c. Classical
d. Greek
e. High Renaissance

65. The late 18th century saw the rise of democracy and republics, revolutions in France and America, and the discovery of the preserved Italian city of Pompeii. These events contributed to the following architectural trend:

a. A revival of Greek and Roman design
b. A return to Rococo style
c. The Bauhaus school of design
d. The development of villa gardens
e. A revival of ancient Egyptian design

66. Daniel Burnham is famous for...

a. Planning the city of Chicago
b. Designing the Eiffel Tower
c. Planning the 1893 World's Fair
d. Designing the blueprint for the White House
e. A and C

67. A triangular space just below the roof of some buildings in the Greek architectural style is called a...

a. Entablature
b. Frieze
c. Pilaster
d. Pediment
e. Facade

68. The illustration shown below depicts a...

a. Triglyph
b. Tympanum
c. Capital
d. Portal
e. Cornice

69. Monticello, Drayton Hall, Woburn Abbey and Chiswick House are all examples of the classical revival style of architecture known as...

a. Greek
b. Baroque
c. Palladian
d. Rococo
e. Impressionist

70. This architect rebuilt much of London after the fire of 1666 and designed St. Paul's Cathedral. His style featured Baroque and classical elements.

a. Christopher Wren
b. Inigo Jones
c. William Kent
d. Thomas Jefferson
e. Charles Le Brun

71. Which is not true of the Bauhaus movement?

a. It was founded by Walter Gropius.
b. It featured simplified, usually geometric-oriented designs.
c. It became one of the most influential components of modern design.
d. It featured objects being broken up, analyzed, and reassembled in an abstract form.
e. Ludwig Mies van der Rohe and Frank Lloyd Wright were influenced by this style.

72. Elizabethans were fond of this literary device which involves plays on words, and Shakespeare made frequent use of it as well.

a. Synecdoche
b. Paradox
c. Oxymoron
d. Puns
e. Personification

73. What is a hamartia?

a. A type of drama
b. A type of comedy
c. An audience for a Greek drama
d. An outdoor setting in a Shakespeare play
e. A tragic flaw

Refer to the following for questions 74–76:

Refer to the following lines.

a. "How sharper than a serpent's tooth it is to have a thankless child!"
b. "To be or not to be: that is the question."
c. "I will wear my heart upon my sleeve for daws to peck at."
d. "Fair is foul, and foul is fair."
e. "All the perfumes of Arabia will not sweeten this little hand."

74. Which of these terms refers to the emotional relieving of tensions that Aristotle felt should occur when watching a drama?

a. Farce
b. Catharsis
c. Hubris
d. Catastrophe
e. Tragedy

75. Who is the author of the quotes?

a. Anton Chekov
b. Christopher Marlowe
c. Ben Jonson
d. William Shakespeare
e. Henrik Ibsen

76. Each of the quotes is from a...

a. Tragedy
b. Comedy
c. History
d. Poem
e. Fantasy

Refer to the following for questions 77–78:

Whose woods these are I think I know.
His house is in the village though;
He will not see me stopping here
To watch his woods fill up with snow.

My little horse must think it queer
To stop without a farmhouse near
Between the woods and frozen lake
The darkest evening of the year.

He gives his harness bells a shake
To ask if there is some mistake.
The only other sound's the sweep
Of easy wind and downy flake.

The woods are lovely, dark and deep.
But I have promises to keep,
And miles to go before I sleep,
And miles to go before I sleep.

77. Which quote is from King Lear?

a. The story of a Southern family in crisis
b. An aging salesman reminisces about his past
c. A group of Russian characters are dissatisfied with their lives
d. The study of a man's need to cling to the hope for a better life, even if he must delude himself
e. A retired teacher visits with former students for one last time

78. Which describes a play by Arthur Miller?

a. The story of a Southern family in crisis
b. An aging salesman reminisces about his past
c. A group of Russian characters are dissatisfied with their lives
d. The study of a man's need to cling to the hope for a better life, even if he must delude himself
e. A retired teacher visits with former students for one last time

79. Which describes a play by Eugene O'Neill?

a. The story of a Southern family in crisis
b. An aging salesman reminisces about his past
c. A group of Russian characters are dissatisfied with their lives
d. The study of a man's need to cling to the hope for a better life, even if he must delude himself
e. A retired teacher visits with former students for one last time

80. Which is a three-act play about an average town's citizens as depicted through their daily lives, first performed in 1938?

a. Eugene O'Neill's Mourning Becomes Electra
b. F. Scott Fitzgerald's The Captured Shadow
c. Ernest Hemingway's The Fifth Column
d. Thornton Wilder's Our Town
e. Langston Hughes's Mule Bone

81. All are 20th century playwrights except...

a. Tom Stoppard
b. Noel Coward
c. George Bernard Shaw
d. Oscar Wilde
e. Samuel Beckett

82. Which of the following Shakespeare works is not a comedy?

a. Two Gentlemen of Verona
b. The Merchant of Venice
c. Coriolanus
d. Twelfth Night
e. As You Like It

83. This play, by Samuel Beckett, has been subject to many different interpretations and is considered one of the most prominent works in the Theatre of the Absurd movement.

a. Waiting for Godot
b. Look Back in Anger
c. Long Day's Journey Into Night
d. Pygmalion
e. The Homecoming

84. Where did Western drama originate?

a. Ancient Rome
b. Classical Greece
c. Renaissance Europe
d. Medieval Europe
e. Jacobean England

85. What do the two masks associated with drama represent?

a. Romance and satire
b. Monologue and chorus
c. Tragedy and expression
d. Romance and irony
e. Comedy and tragedy

86. Which is not true of a sonnet?

a. It has 14 lines.
b. It comes from the Italian *sonnetto*, meaning "little song."
c. There are three types: Petrarchan, Shakespearean and Lyrical.
d. Sir Thomas Wyatt and Geoffrey Chaucer were two early writers of the sonnet.
e. It is a closed form of poetry.

87. The following lines are an example of...

O could I flow like thee, and make thy stream
My great example, as it is my theme!
Though deep, yet clear, though gentle, yet not dull,
Strong without rage, without o'erflowing full.

a. An epic
b. A ballad
c. An elegy
d. A villanelle
e. A heroic couplet

88. A tercet is...

a. A group of three related poems.
b. A rhyme scheme with three feet.
c. Part of the lyric family of poetry.
d. A three-line stanza or poem.
e. A four-line stanza or poem.

89. Which is not true of a limerick?

a. It uses dactyl meter.
b. It has 5 lines.
c. It uses the rhyme scheme AABBBA.
d. It is a type of poetry.
e. It is named after a borough in Ireland.

90. The rhyme scheme of most of the stanzas is

a. ABAA
b. ABAB
c. AAAA
d. ABCC
e. AABA

91. Who wrote the poem?

a. William Shakespeare
b. Walt Whitman
c. Robert Frost
d. John Donne
e. Emily Dickinson

92. What is the meter used in this poem?

a. Iambic pentameter
b. Iambic tetrameter
c. Accentual meter
d. Anapestic
e. Trochaic

93. The third stanza lines:

"He gives his harness bells a shake
To ask if there is some mistake"

is an example of...

a. Personification
b. Simile
c. Alliteration
d. Assonance
e. Hyperbole

94. What poetic device does each of the following use?

"Old age **should burn and rave at close of day;**
Rage, rage, against the dying of the light."
"I must confess that in my quest I felt depressed and restless."

a. Alliteration
b. Assonance
c. Enjambment
d. Caesura
e. Oxymoron

95. The following is an example of...

"Here thou, great Anna! whom three realms obey,
Dost sometimes counsel take – and sometimes tea."

a. Bathos
b. Onomatopoeia
c. Conceits
d. Hyperbole
e. Metonymy

96. Which creature repeats the word "Nevermore" in Edgar Allan Poe's famous poem?

a. Crow
b. Raven
c. Eagle
d. Heron
e. Bluebird

97. Which is a collection of poem-formed stories written in Middle English, detailing the travels of a group of pilgrims to the Shrine of Saint Thomas Beckett?

a. The Decameron
b. The Bible
c. The Aeneid
d. The Canterbury Tales
e. The Odyssey

98. Which is not true of a haiku?

a. It consists of three lines.
b. Each line has a specified number of syllables.
c. It is usually written in present tense.
d. It is a form of Japanese poetry.
e. Its lines rhyme.

99. Anapest, caesura, trochee, and sestina are terms used in

a. Biography
b. Poetry
c. Ballet
d. Opera
e. Architecture

100. Which is not a 20th century poet?

a. Maya Angelou
b. Shel Silverstein
c. Ansel Adams
d. T.S. Eliot
e. Allen Ginsberg

101. The Lady of Shalott; Ring Out, Wild Bells; and The Charge of the Light Brigade were all written by...

a. Alfred, Lord Tennyson
b. Walt Whitman
c. John Keats
d. Giordano Bruno
e. William Wordswort

102. This work is considered a masterpiece of world literature and has been called the greatest Italian language literary work. It consists of three parts.

a. Dante's Divine Comedy
b. Boethuis's Consolation of Philosophy
c. Cicero's On the Republic
d. Cavalcanti's A Woman Asks Me
e. Dante's The Banquet

103. Prose includes all of the following except:

a. Fiction
b. Non-fiction
c. Poetry
d. Drama
e. Satire

104. Which of the following contains intercalary chapters alternating with chapters detailing the main plot?

a. William Golding's *Lord of the Flies*
b. Lorraine Hansberry's A Raisin in the Sun
c. Ambrose Bierce's An Occurrence at Owl Creek Bridge
d. John Steinbeck's The Grapes of Wrath
e. Kurt Vonnegut's Cat's Cradle

105. Freytag's Pyramid is a way of...

a. Characterizing satire.
b. Classifying poetry.
c. Interpreting allegories.
d. Classifying types of novels.
e. Diagramming a story's plot.

106. Which is an example of an allegorical character?

a. Aslan in The Lion, The Witch and The Wardrobe
b. Jane in Jane Eyre
c. Jo in Little Women
d. Professor Aronnax in Twenty Thousand Leagues Under the Sea
e. Mr. Darcy in Pride and Prejudice

107. A foil in literature refers to...

a. A clichéd or predictable situation or character.
b. A character who contrasts to another character in order to highlight features in the main character's personality.
c. A character who struggles against something.
d. A character who changes in the course of the story.
e. A character who struggles towards something.

108. A detail or element of a story which is repeated and may become symbolic is called a...

a. Style
b. Theme
c. Anagram
d. Motif
e. Setting

109. Speculative, argumentative, narrative and expository are all types of...

a. Initiation stories
b. Essays
c. Short stories
d. Monologues
e. Satire

110. This writing perspective exposes and ridicules, denounces and derides folly, evil, stupidity and vice.

a. Tragedy
b. Epic
c. Irony
d. Satire
e. Motif

111. Which work is not known for its use of satire?

a. Jonathan Swift's Gulliver's Travels
b. Voltaire's Candide
c. Mark Twain's Huck Finn
d. George Eliot's The Mill on the Floss
e. Oscar Wilde's The Importance of Being Earnest

112. Nick Adams, Santiago and Francis Macomber were characters created by which author?

a. Virginia Woolf
b. Truman Capote
c. Harper Lee
d. J.D. Salinger
e. Ernest Hemingway

113. Which is not true of *The Decameron*?

a. It is written by Giovanni Boccaccio.
b. It is a collection of 100 novellas.
c. It was said to have inspired Chaucer.
d. It was written around 750 A.D.
e. It is a medieval allegorical work.

114. Which Shakespeare character takes revenge on his uncle for murdering his father?

a. Macbeth
b. King Lear
c. Hamlet
d. Mark Antony
e. Romeo

115. All of the following correctly pair an author with a character they created, except...

a. J.D. Salinger: Holden Caulfield
b. Ernest Hemingway: Frederic Henry
c. F. Scott Fitzgerald: Ebenezer Scrooge
d. Kurt Vonnegut: Billy Pilgrim
e. J.K. Rowling: Draco Malfoy

116. Which was a Southern US writer, famous for an emphasis on Southern settings and Roman Catholic influences?

a. Gertrude Stein
b. Alice Walker
c. Willa Cather
d. Sylvia Plath
e. Flannery O'Connor

117. Which is not a work by one of the Brontë sisters?

a. Jane Eyre
b. *Pride and Prejudice*
c. *Wuthering Heights*
d. *The Tenant of Wildfell Hall*
e. *Villette*

118. This contemporary American author is famous for horror and suspense novels such as *Carrie*.

a. Stephen King
b. Tom Clancy
c. Truman Capote
d. Anne Rice
e. V.C. Andrews

119. Each of the following wrote during the 18th century European Age of Enlightenment, except...

a. Immanuel Kant
b. Jean-Jacques Rousseau
c. Voltaire
d. Nathaniel Hawthorne
e. Gotthold Ephraim Lessing

120. Which term refers to a group of American writers who came to prominence in the 1950s and whose writings showed a rejection of mainstream American values?

a. The Beat Generation
b. Generation X
c. Flappers
d. Objectivists
e. Black Mountain poets

121. This novel is set during the Great Depression and explores issues of rape, Southern life, and class. It is one of the most widely-read books dealing with race in America.

a. Lolita
b. The House of Mirth
c. Mrs. Dalloway
d. To Kill a Mockingbird
e. In Our Time

122. A.A. Milne is known for his creation of which childhood character?

a. Pippi Longstocking
b. Huckleberry Finn
c. Winnie the Pooh
d. Anne of Green Gables
e. Mickey Mouse

123. Which childhood classic explores the circle of life theme and is the best-selling children's paperback of all time?

a. Little House on the Prairie
b. Charlotte's Web
c. The Bridge to Terabithia
d. Harry Potter and the Sorcerer's Stone
e. The Lion, the Witch and the Wardrobe

124. This novel is one of the most important works of Modernist literature, and chronicles an ordinary day in the life of the protagonist.

a. *Rabbit, Run* by John Updike
b. *The Metamorphosis* by Franz Kafka
c. *Invisible Man* by Ralph Ellison
d. *Ulysses* by James Joyce
e. *My Antonia* by Willa Cather

125. Which was not written by Albert Camus?

a. *The Plague*
b. *A Happy Death*
c. *The Fall*
d. *The Big Sleep*
e. *The Stranger*

126. This children's author detailed life experiences as a pioneer in the expanding American West.

a. Ezra Jack Keats
b. Laura Ingalls Wilder
c. Tomie dePaola
d. Margaret Wise Brown
e. Norman Bridwell

127. Clarissa Dalloway, Mrs. Ramsay, and Septimus Warren Smith were all characters created by...

a. Theodore Dreiser
b. Edith Wharton
c. William Faulkner
d. E.M. Forster
e. Virginia Woolf

128. The first American dictionary was written by...

a. John Adams
b. Thomas Jefferson
c. George Merriam
d. Noah Webster
e. Philip Gove

129. Which of these is not known for their scientific books?

a. Charles Darwin
b. Stephen Hawking
c. Richard Dawkins
d. Carl Sagan
e. George Plimpton

130. Charles Darwin wrote all of the following except...

a. On the Origin of Species by Means of Natural Selection
b. The Expression of Emotions in Plants and Animals
c. General Psychological Theory
d. Insectivorous Plants
e. The Descent of Man

131. This author lived in England during the 17th century. He was a member of the British Navy and later of Parliament, but is most famous for his detailed private diary.

a. Samuel Pepys
b. Robert Latham
c. Thomas Bloodworth
d. Winston Churchill
e. Edward Montagu

132. Which describes *Night*, by Elie Wiesel?

a. It is an opera based on the psychological ennui of the late 1920s.
b. It is a book based on Wiesel's experiences as a prisoner in Buchenwald and Auschwitz concentration camps.
c. It is an essay based on Wiesel's experiences as a slave.
d. It is a book based on Wiesel's stint as a researcher in Antarctica.
e. It is a poem based on segregation.

133. Which correctly pairs a nonfiction author with a work he/she created?

a. William F. Buckley - How the Mind Works
b. Gloria Steinem - Heartbreak: The Political Memoir of a Feminist Militant
c. Steven Pinker - National Review magazine
d. Andrea Dworkin - Ms. magazine co-founder
e. Samuel Johnson - Dictionary of the English Language

134. This philosopher was a student of Socrates. His most famous theory is the Theory of Forms, which postulates that the world as we perceive it is not as it seems, but is only a shadow of the real world.

a. Thales
b. Plato
c. Heraclitus
d. Parmenides
e. Leucippus

135. This philosophy states that knowledge of the external world can be derived from reason alone, without reliance on experience.

a. Neoplatonism
b. Empiricism
c. Idealism
d. Rationalism
e. Scholasticism

136. Which rationalist philosopher famously said, "I think, therefore I am" (*cogito ergo sum*)?

a. Blaise Pascal
b. Jean-Jacques Rousseau
c. Adam Smith
d. Rene Descartes
e. Immanuel Kant

137. Adam Smith is famous for writing...

a. The Social Contract
b. The Wealth of Nations
c. Essay Concerning Human Understanding
d. Appearance and Reality
e. The World as Will and Idea

138. Which philosopher is famous for the theory of the dialectic, in which a thesis and its antithesis are combined to form a synthesis?

a. Georg Wilhelm Friedrich Hegel
b. Johann Christoph Friedrich von Schiller
c. Johann Wolfgang von Goethe
d. Baruch Spinoza
e. James Mill

139. Which philosophy stresses the freedom and responsibility of man to shape his own life?

a. Empiricism
b. Pragmatism
c. Idealism
d. Rationalism
e. Existentialism

140. Which is not true of Aristotle?

a. He lived in the third century B.C.
b. He criticized Plato's Theory of Forms.
c. He was a Roman philosopher.
d. He was the first to systemize logic.
e. A majority of his works are now lost.

141. This book, by Thomas More, depicts a fictional island society and its customs.

a. Republic
b. Utopia
c. Gulliver's Travels
d. Pilgrim's Progress
e. Walden

Answer Key and Explanations

1. C: A triad is a type of chord comprised of three notes. The remaining choices are all types of scales: a chromatic scale consists of twelve half steps, a diatonic scale consists of seven different pitches, a pentatonic scale consists of five different pitches, and a minor scale lowers the third pitch of a major scale by a half step.

2. A: The Baroque period began around 1600 with the invention of opera and ended around 1750 with the death of Johann Sebastian Bach. Antonio Vivaldi also wrote extensively for the violin during the Baroque period, establishing the three-movement concerto. The Classical period began with the death of Johann Sebastian Bach and ended in the 1820s. Franz Haydn was a major composer during this period. Imitative polyphony, in which voices sing the same text and the same music, entering one after another, was a characteristic of Renaissance music.

3. B: Richard Wagner and Giuseppe Verdi dominated opera during the nineteenth century, with Verdi composing 28 operas (including Rigoletto, La Traviata, and Aida) and Wagner writing his famous Der Ring des Nibelungen series, among others. Samuel Barber and Benjamin Britten are famous opera composers of the twentieth century. Christoph Gluck and Wolfgang Amadeus Mozart were famous opera composers of the eighteenth century. Giacomo Puccini and Maurice Ravel wrote operas in the nineteenth century, but not as prolifically as Wagner and Verdi. Claudio Monteverdi and George Frideric Handel composed operas in the sixteenth and seventeenth centuries.

4. C: These are all tempos, or speeds, in music: moderato (moderate), vivace (fast), andante (walking speed) and presto (extremely fast). Rhythm refers to the pattern of music's duration of notes. Meter refers to a musical piece's pattern of rhythms. Dynamics are the degree of loudness or softness in a series of notes. Intervals are the distances between two musical pitches.

5. E: Syncopation occurs when a melodic accent falls on a weak beat or between beats. It occurs commonly in jazz and swing musical styles. Duple meter is a rhythmic pattern in which a strong beat is followed by three weak beats. Pulse refers to a musical beat. A key signature indicates the scale a musical piece is based on. Timbre refers to the texture of sound made by a musical instrument or voice.

6. A: Jazz is widely considered to be America's only original contribution to music. Jazz originated in American black culture around the beginning of the twentieth century. Jazz is not atonal, or without key or tonal center. John Cage composed modern or "chance" music during the twentieth century, not jazz.

7. D: A key signature indicates the scale a piece of music is built on, and is located at the beginning of a piece of music, just before the time signature. The time signature denotes the meter of a piece of music. How a tune gets from one pitch to the next is called melodic motion. The loudness or softness of a tone is called intensity.

8. A: The six historic periods of Western music in chronological order are Medieval, Renaissance, Baroque, Classical, Romantic, and 20th century. Gregorian refers to a type of a capella liturgical music common in the medieval period. Opera was a musical form invented during the Baroque period. Expressionist was a type of painting popular during the Romantic musical period. Atonal music lacks a center, or key, and was popular during the 20th century period.

9. B: William Shakespeare was the most influential writer of the Renaissance period. Italian painter Giovanni Bellini was one of the Renaissance's most famous artists. Josquin Desprez was a famous composer of the Renaissance. He was called "master of the notes" by Martin Luther.

10. B: Italian terms are used in music (andante, forte, vivace, allegretto, etc.). French terms are used in ballet (plie, pas de chat, pas de deux, etc.).

11. E: A recitative is musical speech that occurs during an opera, an aria is a more poetic musical speech during an opera with a fuller orchestral accompaniment, and an oratorio is a musical piece performed by an opera chorus. These elements are not part of the other musical forms listed.

12. A: Giselle is a two-act ballet with music by Adolphe Adam and choreography by Jean Coralli and Jules Perrot. It was first performed in 1841. The other four choices are all operas.

13. D: Scat is a musical style in which the voice is used as an instrument, singing syllables rather than words. It was made popular by Louis Armstrong. Syncopation is the term for accents put in unexpected places. "Call and response" is a type of jazz music in which a leader sings a line and others respond sympathetically. Chance music is a 20th century musical technique involving several elements, one of which may be performers sitting in silence for an entire piece. Computer-generated music is another 20th century musical technique.

14. A: Frederic Chopin wrote exclusively for the piano. Richard Wagner was famous for his operas. Robert Schumann wrote for the piano and orchestras. Wolfgang Amadeus Mozart composed for many instruments and wrote for orchestras and chamber music groups. Felix Mendelssohn wrote for numerous instruments including the piano, and also for orchestras.

15. B: The lowest male voice is a bass, then baritone, and the highest is tenor. The lowest female voice is alto, then mezzo soprano, and the highest is soprano.

16. D: Major, minor, diminished, and augmented are the four possible types of triads, depending on the arrangement of major and minor thirds. Key signatures refer to the scale a piece of music is based on and are indicated by letters (A, B-Flat, etc.). Scales can be classified as major, minor, diatonic, pentatonic, chromatic, or blues. Dynamics refer to the intensity, or loudness, of a tone. Syncopation refers to beats falling in unexpected or unaccented places in music.

17. E: Andante is a tempo marking meaning slow, graceful, or walking speed. Forte means loud, fortissimo means very loud, mezzopiano means medium soft, and piano means soft.

18. A: Duration, frequency, intensity and timbre are the four ways that one sound can differ from another. Duration refers to how long a sound or a silence lasts and the rate at which one tone succeeds another. Frequency determines a note's pitch, or how high or low it is. Intensity refers to how loud or soft a tone is. Timbre refers to the source of a musical sound, such as which instrument or voice is supplying it. Texture refers to how melodies are presented within a piece. An interval is the distance between two pitches. Tempo is a measure of duration; it is the speed of the pulse (or beat) in a musical piece. Dynamics is the music term for intensity.

19. C: The second movement of a symphony is often a slow movement. Symphonies do generally have four movements, the first of which is usually in sonata form. The third movement is in ternary form, or having three parts diagrammed ABA. Symphonies are works performed by an entire orchestra.

20. D: Beethoven is famous for his nine symphonies, which expanded the elements of classical style. They are longer and composed for larger performing groups than Haydn's or Mozart's, who were also classical era composers. Bach composed during the Baroque period, while Tchaikovsky composed during the Romantic period.

21. B: Jazz music is characterized by improvisation, where performers agree on a tune, key, tempo and form, and then make up what they play or sing as they go along in a spontaneous way. Folk music, impressionist music, opera and rock and roll are not characterized by the use of improvisation.

22. C: A dithyramb is a frenzied and impassioned hymn performed by a chorus of 50 men costumed in goat-skins during the earliest period of Greek plays. Aristotle described the dithyramb as the forerunner of tragedy. A scene of action in a play is referred to as an episode. The conclusion of a play, during which the chorus continues to chant as characters depart, is called an exodus.

23. C: Russian Konstantin Stanislavsky developed "the Method," so dubbed because of its broad impact on the training of Western actors. Eugene O'Neill was a 20th century American playwright. Stella Adler was a teacher of Method acting. Henrik Ibsen was a 19th century European playwright. Auguste Comte was a French philosopher who influenced the theater of realism.

24. D: Ballet was established during the reign of Louis XIV of France, who was a great champion of dance. Marius Petipa was a dancer, teacher and choreographer who is often referred to as the father of classical ballet. Ballet is based on five different positions of the feet, not six, and it is a principle of ballet to keep the feet turned out, not in.

25. A: Peter Tchaikovsky composed three ballets during the Romantic period: The Nutcracker, Sleeping Beauty, and Swan Lake. Felix Mendelssohn was another Romantic era composer. Martha Graham was a 20th century American dancer and choreographer. Wolfgang Amadeus Mozart was a leading classical era composer of symphonies, concertos and operas. Igor Stravinsky was a prominent Russian composer of ballets and other instrumental works of the 20th century.

26. D: Sonore is a term used in instrumental music, meaning resonant or rich in tone. Plie, releve, grands battements and fouette are all ballet exercises or movements.

27. E: The Peabody, foxtrot, jitterbug and mashed potato were popular in America from the 1930s to the 1950s. The Peabody and foxtrot were popular in the 1930s, the jitterbug in the 1940s, and the mashed potato in the 1950s. They are not types of folk or ballroom dances. Jazz is characterized by flat-footed steps and syncopated rhythms, and is a popular form of dance in American musicals.

28. A: Oklahoma! is an American musical of the 1940s which includes a barn dance and other choreography, but not jazz. West Side Story, 42nd Street, Chicago, and A Chorus Line all incorporate jazz dance.

29. B: Don Juan was released in 1926, and was the first film to have orchestral accompaniment and sound effects. The Jazz Singer, released in 1927, was a part sound/part silent film. Steamboat Willie, produced by Walt Disney, was Disney's first musical cartoon and contributed to the sound film genre. None of the films were in color, won Academy Awards, or were produced by Edison's motion picture company. Only Steamboat Willie was produced by Walt Disney.

30. E: Anti-communist films appeared only in the 1950s, although their themes can be seen in later films. Comedies, Westerns, science fiction films and gangster films were all popular in the 1950s, but have also been produced in other decades.

31. E: All of these films are musicals, a genre which was highly popular among filmmakers of the 1950s and 1960s.

32. D: Grace Kelly was an Academy Award winner in the 1950s, but retired from acting permanently in 1956. Jane Fonda, Sally Field, Jack Nicholson and Jon Voight were all Academy Award winners during the 1970s and 1980s.

33. A: Richard Wagner composed Der Ring Des Nibelungen over a 26-year period, from 1848 to 1874. The operas comprising "The Ring" are titled Das Rheingold, Die Walkure, Siegfried and Gotterdammerung. Giuseppe Verdi, Gioachino Rossini, Gaetano Donizett and Ludwig van Beethoven all composed operas as well, during the 1750-1899 time frame.

34. C: James Dean was a film actor and cultural icon of the 1950s, based on his appearance in just these three films. Marlon Brando played similar cynical, rebellious youth roles in some of his films. John Wayne was an actor famous for his appearance in Westerns. Nicholas Ray directed the James Dean film Rebel Without a Cause. Rock Hudson was an actor who starred with James Dean in Giant.

35. D: The kinetoscope was invented by Thomas Edison, and played movies when a coin was inserted. An electric light was projected onto the rear of the cabinet and viewers could see the movie by looking through a peephole. The average length of a kinetoscope film was one minute, not five.

36. A: The ancient Greeks began and best represent the Classical period of art and architecture, with the city-state of Athens being the most dominant influence. The ancient Romans later adopted much of the art and architecture of Greece. Egyptian art and architecture and Neolithic structures such as Stonehenge all pre-date the Classical era. The Byzantine Empire existed for 1000 years after the fall of the Roman Empire.

37. C: Euripides, Aeschylus, and Sophocles were the three great tragic playwrights of classical Athens. Aeschylus is the first of the three and is known as the father of Greek tragedy. Sophocles is the second of the three major Greek tragedians whose work has survived. Seven of his tragedies survive today, including Ajax and Antigone. Euripides is the third of the three tragic playwrights and is known primarily for reshaping the formal structure of Athenian tragedy by including strong female characters, among other things.

38. E: This sculpture is known as Winged Victory of Samothrace; it was created around 190 B.C. and is one of the most celebrated sculptures in the world. The other works listed are all sculptures of the same artistic era.

39. B: Winged Victory of Samothrace is located in the Louvre Museum in Paris. The Uffizi, located in Florence, Italy, is one of the world's oldest and most complete art museums. The Parthenon is located in Athens, Greece and is the most important surviving building of ancient Greece. The Palace of Versailles was built by King Louis XIV of France. The Tate Gallery is located in London and houses 16th century British art and international modern art.

40. A: Winged Victory was created around 190 B.C., during the Hellenistic period which spans 323 B.C. to 146 B.C. It is one of the most representative sculptures of its era. It is an example of Hellenistic "sculpture in the round" which allows it to be viewed from all angles. The Byzantine period spans the fourth century through 1453. The Romanesque period spans 1000 A.D. to the 13th century time period. Italian Renaissance art spans the late 14th century to the late 16th century. Rococo art was created from 1720 to 1780.

41. D: Romulus and Remus were the mythical founders of Rome in 753 B.C. They appeared in Roman mythology as the twin sons of Mars, the god of war, and the Vestal Virgin Rhea Silvia. Plutarch recorded Romulus as the first king of Rome.

42. E: Pompeii and its sister city, Herculaneum, were completely buried by the catastrophic eruption of Mount Vesuvius over the course of two days in 79 A.D. The Laocoon was sculpted in Greece. The Arch of Titus is in Rome.

43. B: All of these landmarks are found in Rome, Italy. The Arch of Titus was constructed near the Roman Forum by the emperor Domitian and describes the emperor's triumph over Jerusalem. Trajan's Column is a carved column depicting the story of Trajan's campaigns against the Dacians. The Pantheon is one of the ancient world's best preserved buildings. The Trevi Fountain features elaborate carvings and is a famous spot for throwing coins.

44. B: The photo shows a cathedral with round arches, vaulted ceilings and heavy walls, all of which are common features of Romanesque churches. This architectural style was preeminent in the 11th and 12th centuries.

45. C: An obelisk is a tapering monument used by the ancient Egyptians. Tuscan columns are Roman and are characterized by a plain design, with no fluting or decorative carving. Doric columns are plain and have no base. They are the most common type of Greek column. The Romans created a Doric column as well, but theirs had bases. Corinthian columns have elaborate capitals and often feature carvings. Ionic columns are Greek in origin and have a shallow base and shallow capital decorated with curled designs.

46. D: Buildings in the Gothic style, particularly cathedrals, were soaring and airy with strong vertical lines. Prominent features of the style include flying buttresses, pointed arches and vaults, and a plethora of sculptures and stained glass windows.

47. A: Giotto di Bondone, or simply Giotto, lived from 1267 to 1337 and was generally considered the first in a line of great artists contributing to the Italian Renaissance. Cimabue was a Florentine painter during the Renaissance. Duccio was a Tuscan painter during the Renaissance. Nicholas of Verdun was also a painter of classical style during the end of the 12th century. Ghiberti was an Italian sculptor who designed the bronze doors of the Florence Baptistry during the 15th century.

48. C: Caravaggio was the most significant proponent of the Italian Baroque style of painting during the 17th century. Peter Paul Rubens was a Flemish painter of the same century. Jacob Jordaens, also Flemish, was a painter whose work portrayed figures in constant motion and who used lighting and shadow to intensify the emotional impact of his work. Anthony Van Dyck was a British painter of the seventeenth century.

49. B: Hans Holbein was born in Germany and became a famous court painter for Henry VIII, among others. Albrecht Durer is widely regarded as Germany's finest Renaissance era painter; he was influenced by Venetian art and had a great scientific curiosity about the world which influenced his paintings. Lucas Cranach is famous for several of his paintings of Martin Luther. Matthias Grunewald is another German Renaissance painter; his most famous work is the Isenheim Altarpiece of 1515.

50. A: Michelangelo was a famous Italian Renaissance painter, poet, sculptor and architect. Botticelli was another famous Renaissance painter of the Italian School; his Birth of Venus and Primavera are familiar works. Masaccio, born Tommaso Casser, was the first great painter of the Quattrocento period of the Italian Renaissance. Fra Angelico, born Guido di Pietro, was another Italian Renaissance painter. He worked under the patronage of the powerful Cosimo de Medici, and is famed for his Biblically-themed paintings. Group D (Henri Matisse, Pablo Picasso, Georges Braque, Juan Gris) are all artists of the 20th century. Group E (Édouard Manet, Claude Monet, Edgar Degas, Camille Pissarro) are all famous painters of the Impressionist era of the nineteenth century.

51. C: This work is entitled The Last Supper and features Jesus dining with his disciples the night before he is betrayed and crucified. It is based on the story found in the Gospel of John, 13.21, where Jesus announces that one of the disciples will betray him. The painting depicts the varied reactions of the disciples to this news.

52. E: The Last Supper was painted by Leonardo da Vinci from 1495 to 1498 and is one of his most famous paintings. It was created for his patron Duke Ludovico Sforza and his duchess Beatrice d'Este. Michelangelo, Raphael, Andrea Mantegna and Fra Filippo Lippi were all painters during the same High Renaissance period as Leonardo da Vinci.

53. D: The Last Supper covers the back wall of the refectory, or dining hall, at Santa Maria della Grazie, a church and Dominican convent in Milan, Italy. The Last Supper theme is a common one in refectory artwork. It was painted on dry rather than wet plaster, so it is not a true fresco.

54. B: Andy Warhol popularized pop art, in which American popular culture icons are incorporated into artwork. Some Warhol creations included multiple silk-screened images of Campbell Soup cans and images of Marilyn Monroe. Jackson Pollock was an artist in the field of Abstract Expressionism. Salvador Dali and Giorgio de Chirico were Surrealist artists, and Alexander Calder created floating creations known as mobiles.

55. B: Hagia Sophia is the most important church in Constantinople, which is today Istanbul, Turkey. It was built in the Byzantine style, which featured grandiose mosaics, glittering gold, sparkling color, and created a supernatural, otherworldly effect.

56. D: The Book of Durrow (680), the Lindisfarne Gospels (690) and the Book of Kells (800) are all illuminated manuscripts – texts noted for their sophisticated, flamboyant and decorative letters. Illuminated texts were often produced in the monasteries of Ireland, Scotland and northern Britain, and their design was influenced by Celtic metalwork.

57. A: Michelangelo excelled as a High Renaissance artist in the fields of poetry, painting, sculpture and architecture. Counted among his masterpieces are the frescoes in the Vatican's Sistine Chapel. The frescoes include paintings of various Biblical stories and themes, including The Creation of the World, The Creation of Adam, The Creation of Eve, and The Last Judgment. Da Vinci and Raphael were also famous artists of the High Renaissance period. Uccello was an important early Renaissance painter. Botticelli was a painter as well, epitomizing the spirit of the early Renaissance with his Biblical themes and allegorical images.

58. E: Mannerism was a European art style of the 16th century. It featured exaggerations such as floating angels, the confusion of reality and illusion, and awkward spatial relationships. Parmigianino (The Madonna with the Long Neck), El Greco (The Burial of the Count of Orgaz) and Pontormo (Visitation) all painted in the mannerist style.

59. D: Rembrandt Harmenszoon van Rijn is the artist. He lived from 1601 to 1669 and painted during the period known as the Dutch Golden Age. He first achieved success as a portrait painter and continued to paint portraits into adulthood, also painting numerous Biblical scenes. His empathy for the human condition, and his melding of the natural and the spiritual, have led some to call him "one of the great prophets of civilization." Caravaggio, Rubens, Velazquez and Van Dyck are all roughly contemporary with Rembrandt, and all painted during the Baroque era.

60. B: Star of the Ballet, by Edgar Degas, is an example of Impressionism. Impressionist painters used bright colors and concentrated on the effect of light in their paintings. Traditional means of composing an Impressionist painting were rejected in favor of quickly observed and sketched life moments. The relationship of shapes, forms and colors is emphasized.

61. D: Pointillism is a style developed by Georges Seurat (who created Sunday Afternoon on the Island of La Grande Jatte, The Circus, and Bathers at Asnieres) and Paul Signac (artist of The Papal Palace, Avignon. Pointillism creates paintings through a series of tiny individual dots which create the effect of a larger picture.The Scream is a painting by Edvard Munch and is an example of expressionist style, not pointillism.

62. A: Caravaggio was the most significant proponent of the Italian Baroque style, and painted The Conversion of Saint Paul. The Laughing Cavalier was painted by Frans Hals. Christ Healing the Sick was painted by Rembrandt. The Raising of the Cross was painted by Rubens. Women Bathing was painted by Jean Honore Fragonard.

63. D: Michelangelo did not compose music, but he did work in the fields of poetry, painting, sculpture and architecture.

64. B: The Residenz at Wurzburg, the Munich Residenz, Amalienburg Pavilion and Residenz Theater, all designed by Francois Cuvillies in the 1730s, are the major palaces built in Rococo style. Rococo style was influenced by the characteristics of the Palace of Versailles and features a profusion of elegant and fantastic decorative elements, often including scrolls and leaves.

65. A: The late 18th century saw the rise of democracy and republics, revolutions in France and America, and the discovery of the preserved Italian city of Pompeii. These events led to a revival of Greek and Roman design. Examples include the Bank of England by John Soane, the Temple of Possagno by Antonio Canova, and the Virginia State Capitol designed by Thomas Jefferson to mimic a Roman temple.

66. E: Daniel Burnham (1846-1912) was a Chicago architect. His firm, D.H. Burnham and Co., designed department stores such as Marshall Field's, office buildings and public buildings. He supervised the construction and layout of the World's Columbian Exposition, more famously known as the Chicago World's Fair, in 1893. In 1909 he and his partner developed an urban plan for Chicago, the basis of which is still in use. It was the first plan for the controlled growth of an American city.

67. D: A pediment is a low-pitched triangular gable found on the front of many Greek or Greek Revival style buildings. An entablature is a horizontal structure of moldings and bands occurring above columns in buildings of classical architectural styles. A frieze is the wide central portion of an entablature. It can be plain or can be decorated with bas-reliefs. A pilaster is a slightly-projecting column built into a wall's face. A façade is an exterior side of a building, usually the front.

68. B: The illustration shows a tympanum, or a decorated semicircular area above an entrance. A triglyph refers to vertical panels on a Doric frieze. A capital is the crowning member of a column, pier, or pilaster. A portal is an entrance, particularly an entrance in a grand structure. A cornice refers to molding along the top of a wall.

69. C: Monticello, Drayton Hall, Woburn Abbey and Chiswick House are all examples of the classical revival style of architecture known as Palladian. Palladian architecture began in Europe, inspired by Venetian architect Andrea Palladio. It is based on symmetry, perspective and classical elements.

70. A: Christopher Wren (1632-1723) was one of England's best known architects. He rebuilt 55 churches in London after the 1666 fire, his masterpiece being St. Paul's Cathedral. Inigo Jones was a British architect of grand classical buildings a generation prior to Wren. William Kent was a British architect and landscape designer who lived a generation after Wren. Thomas Jefferson was one of America's founders as well as an architect. Charles Le Brun was the French architect who designed the Palace of Versailles.

71. D: The Bauhaus was a German school which operated from 1919-1933 and was famous for its approach to design. It was founded by Walter Gropius and taught designs that were simplified and usually geometric. The Bauhaus movement influenced architecture, industrial and commercial design, sculpture and graphic arts for the first half of the twentieth century. Architects Ludwig Mies van der Rohe, Le Corbusier and Frank Lloyd Wright were all influenced by the Bauhaus movement. Cubism is an art style which features objects being broken up, analyzed, and reassembled in an abstract form.

72. D: Puns are plays on words (example: "Stir-fry cooks come from all woks of life"). Shakespeare used puns frequently, particularly in his comedies. Synecdoche is a literary device in which part of an object is used to represent the whole thing, such as "lend me a hand" being a request for an entire person. Paradox is a situation appearing contradictory but true nonetheless. An oxymoron is the joining of two contradictory terms ("sweet sorrow," etc.). Personification is the giving of human traits to an inanimate object.

73. E: Hamartia refers to a character's tragic flaw or frailty which leads him to make errors in judgment, causing a reversal of fortunes for himself and/or others, most often ending in death. It is a term developed by Aristotle in Poetics. An example of hamartia would be Macbeth's ambition.

74. B: Aristotle felt audiences should experience an emotional reaction or release called catharsis. The word comes from Greek roots meaning purging, cleansing, or purification. He used the term to describe the sensation that would come over the audience after watching a tragedy.

75. D: The quotes are from King Lear (A), Hamlet (B), Othello (C), and Macbeth (D and E); all plays written by William Shakespeare. Marlowe and Jonson were playwright contemporaries of Shakespeare. Chekov and Ibsen were 18th century playwrights.

76. A: Each of the quotes is from a tragedy written by William Shakespeare. (A) is from King Lear, (B) is from Hamlet, (C) is from Othello, and (D) and (E) are from Macbeth.

77. A: King Lear says this line in response to his disappointment in daughters Regan and Goneril. The play contains numerous themes; among them the idea that suffering can transform a contemptible person into a good one, that things are not always as they appear, and that greed can corrupt humans and bring about their downfall.

78. B: Death of a Salesman, a play written in 1949 by Arthur Miller, tells the story of Willy Loman, an aging salesman reminiscing about his past. The play won a Pulitzer Prize and a Tony Award, and made Miller a household name.

79. D: The Iceman Cometh was written in 1939 by Eugene O'Neill and has been described as his finest and most complex work. It tells the story of visitors to Harry Hope's saloon and is marked by religious symbolism. It suggests that the American Dream may be an illusion.

80. D: Our Town is Thornton Wilder's best known play. He also wrote novels such as The Bridge of San Luis Rey and was a contemporary and friend of Gertrude Stein, Ernest Hemingway and F. Scott Fitzgerald. Our Town won a Pulitzer Prize and became one of the most performed American plays of the 20th century. In it, Wilder presents a celebratory picture of the small American town while not idealizing it.

81. D: Oscar Wilde was an Irish playwright, poet and short story author who lived from 1854-1899. Tom Stoppard (1937-present) is a British playwright. Noel Coward (1899-1973) was a British playwright, composer, director, singer and actor. George Bernard Shaw (1856-1950) was an Irish playwright. Samuel Beckett (1906-1989) was an Irish playwright and poet.

82. C: Coriolanus is a tragedy by Shakespeare. It tells the story of a Roman hero in fifth century B.C. named Caius Marcius who considers himself better than others, but is killed in the end. The other works listed are all Shakespeare comedies.

83. A: Waiting for Godot was originally written in French in 1948. It began Beckett's association with the Theatre of the Absurd movement, a designation given to plays with themes of absurdity, often taking the form of man's reaction to an apparently meaningless world. In the play, Vladimir and Estragon wait for another character, Godot, who never arrives.

84. B: Western drama originated in classical Greece, where the theater-approving culture of the city-state of Athens produced tragedies, comedies and satyr plays. These were popular at least as early as the fifth century B.C.

85. E: The two masks associated with drama represent the division between comedy and tragedy. They are symbols of the ancient Greek muses Thalia, the muse of comedy, and Melpomene, the muse of tragedy. They represent the masks worn in ancient Greek dramas.

86. C: Sonnets, the most easily recognized closed form of poetry, always have 14 lines. The term sonnet comes from the Italian sonnetto, or little song. There are two types of sonnets, the Petrarchan, or Italian, and the Shakespearean, or English. Wyatt and Chaucer were two early authors of sonnets.

87. E: Heroic couplet is a stanza comprised of two rhymed lines in iambic pentameter. Epic poems have great size and range, and deal with the great deeds of heroes. A ballad is a story in song form. An elegy is a lament for someone's death. A villanelle is a courtly love poem structure from medieval times.

88. D: A tercet is a three-line stanza or complete poem. Haiku is perhaps the most famous type of tercet poem.

89. A: Limericks are a poetry type that is 5 lines long, follow the rhyme scheme AABBA, are named after an Irish borough and are written in anapest meter, not dactyl meter.

90. E: The rhyme scheme for the first three stanzas is AABA. In stanza one, "know," "though" and "snow" rhyme and form A, while "here" is B. The final stanza uses AAAA as a rhyme scheme.

91. C: The poem is "Stopping by Woods on a Snowy Evening," written by Robert Frost in 1922. William Shakespeare, Walt Whitman, John Donne and Emily Dickinson are also poets.

92. B: The poem is written in iambic tetrameter, meaning it has four groups (or feet) of two syllables per line. Iambic refers to the two-syllable groups consisting of a first syllable which is unaccented and a second syllable which is accented. Iambic pentameter consists of five groups of two syllables per line. Accentual meter is used in Old English poetry and features four stresses per line without attention to unstressed syllables. Anapestic meter consists of a foot with two unaccented syllables followed by an accented syllable. Trochaic meter is the opposite of iambic meter: an accented syllable is followed by one that is unaccented.

93. A: The lines are an example of personification, in which a non-human, in this case the horse, is given human qualities, in this case asking a question. A simile compares two dissimilar things using the words "like" or "as." Alliteration is the practice of repeating initial consonants in nearby words. Assonance is the repetition of the same vowel sound within words. Hyperbole is intentional exaggeration.

94. B: Both examples use assonance, or the repetition of a similar vowel sound within words. In the first example, note the long A sound in age, rave and day. In the second example, note the short E sound in confess, quest, depressed and restless. Alliteration refers to the repetition of consonant sounds within words. Enjambment is the running on of one line of poetry into another. Caesura is a pause within a line of poetry. Oxymoron is a device in which incongruous or contradictory terms are put together (for instance, "sweet sorrow").

95. A: These lines, from the Alexander Pope poem "Rape of the Lock," are an example of bathos. It describes using anticlimax deliberately to make a point or draw attention to falseness. In this example, the humor and contrast come from Anna, Queen of England, holding her meetings in the same rooms in which she also takes part in the English tradition of daily teatime. Onomatopoeia, conceits, hyperbole and metonymy are other literary and/or poetic devices.

96. B: "Quoth the raven, Nevermore" is a famous line in Edgar Allan Poe's poem The Raven. The poem was published in 1845 and is noted for its musical language and its supernatural feel. It describes a talking raven's visit to a distraught lover and chronicles the lover's descent into madness. Publication of The Raven made Poe famous during his lifetime.

97. D: The Canterbury Tales, by Geoffrey Chaucer, was written in 14th century England and is a collection of poetically-written tales depicting the travels of pilgrims to the Shrine of Saint Thomas Beckett in England's Canterbury Cathedral. The tales are told as part of a storytelling contest among the pilgrims as they travel. The Tales are Chaucer's most famous work and are considered a foundation of Western culture.

98. E: Haiku lines do not rhyme. These Japanese poems use language to impart the essence of an experience in nature. Most Haiku consist of three unrhymed lines of seventeen or fewer syllables, with the middle line being the longest.

99. B: These are all terms used in poetry. An anapest consists of two unaccented syllables followed by an accented one ("and the sheen of their spears," etc.). A caesura is a strong pause within a line of verse ("was out of work – had sold his traps"). A trochee is an accented syllable followed by an unaccented one (football, etc.). A sestina is a poem consisting of 39 lines in iambic pentameter

100. C: Ansel Adams was a 20th century photographer, famous for his striking black and white images. Maya Angelou is a poet and autobiographer. She won a Pulitzer Prize for her poetry volume, Just Give Me a Cool Drink of Water 'Fore I Diiie. Shel Silverstein is a poet famous for his books of poetry for children, Where the Sidewalk Ends and A Light in the Attic among them. T.S. Eliot has been called the most important English language poet of the 20th century, famous for poems such as The Hollow Men and Ash Wednesday. Allen Ginsberg was an American poet best known for his poem Howl, celebrating the "Beat Generation" of the 1950s.

101. A: The Lady of Shalott; Ring Out, Wild Bells; and The Charge of the Light Brigade are all poems by Alfred, Lord Tennyson (1809-1892). He was the United Kingdom's Poet Laureate during much of Queen Victoria's reign, and is one of the most popular poets in the English language. He authored many phrases that have become popular in English, such as "'Tis better to have loved and lost / Than never to have loved at all," and "Nature, red in tooth and claw."

102. A: Dante's Divine Comedy details a journey in three parts: through hell (Inferno), purgatory (Purgatorio), and paradise (Paradiso). In the work, Dante is guided first by Roman poet Virgil and then by his love interest, Beatrice. His writing of this work in Italian helped establish the language as one capable of the highest forms of literary expression.

103. C: Prose is defined as what is written and spoken in everyday life: unmetered, unrhymed language. As such, it does not include poetry. It can and does include all other types of written language, however, including fiction, non-fiction, drama and satire.

104. D: The Grapes of Wrath by John Steinbeck uses intercalary chapters, which are placed between chapters detailing the book's main plot. These intercalary chapters include peripheral or parallel stories.

105. E: Gustav Freytag was a 19th century German novelist. He saw common patterns in story plots and developed a pyramid as a way to analyze them. The stages in his pyramid include introduction or exposition, complication, rising action, climax, falling action and denouement or conclusion.

106. A: In C.S. Lewis's The Lion, The Witch and The Wardrobe (part of the Narnia series), Aslan the lion is an allegorical character regarded as a Christ-figure in the story, especially in his sacrificial death and resurrection. Lewis himself regards Aslan as more than an allegory: as the person Christ would be if he became incarnate in a different world as a different creature.

107. B: In literature, a foil is a character who contrasts to another character in order to highlight features in the main character's personality. An example would be Tom Sawyer as a romantic foil to Huck Finn's realism. A stereotype is a clichéd or predictable situation or character. A character who struggles against something is an antagonist. A character who changes in the course of a story is referred to as dynamic. A character who struggles towards something is a protagonist.

108. D: A motif is a detail or element of a story which is repeated and may become symbolic. An example would be Emma Bovary's shoes in Madame Bovary, which signify her obsession with material things. Style refers to language, syntax, the balance between description and dialogue, and other elements of a novel. Theme is the overriding "why" of a story, and is determined by the interplay of plot and characters. An anagram is a word or phrase made from the letters of another word or phrase, as "heart" is an anagram of "earth." The setting of a story tells when and where a story occurred.

109. B: Essays fall into four rough categories: speculative, argumentative, narrative and expository. Speculative essays look at and explore ideas. Argumentative essays present a point and provide evidence for it. Narrative essays recount events and are often autobiographical. Expository essays explain and clarify ideas.

110. D: Satire is a literary form or genre in which human shortcomings and abuses are held up to ridicule, often with the intent to bring about improvement. Irony is a common feature used in satire. A motif is a recurring theme, often symbolic, in literature. Tragedies and epics are other literary genres.

111. D: The Mill on the Floss does not use satire as a major device. Gulliver's Travels and Candide both use satire in attacking various aspects of religion, government and prevailing beliefs in their societies. The Importance of Being Earnest constantly ridicules the superficiality Wilde perceived relating to the British gentry. Twain skewers religion and his opinion of its hypocrisy in Huck Finn.

112. E: Nick Adams (In Our Time), Santiago (The Old Man and the Sea) and Francis Macomber (The Short Happy Life of Francis Macomber) were all characters in novels written by Ernest Hemingway. Hemingway lived from 1899–1961 and was a writer and journalist, receiving a Nobel Prize for The Old Man and the Sea.

113. D: The Decameron was written by Italian Giovanni Boccaccio, most likely between 1350 and 1353. It is known for its bawdy tales of love in all its possibilities, from tragic to erotic. Chaucer was said to have drawn inspiration from The Decameron, and it is classified as an allegorical work of the medieval period.

114. C: Hamlet, written by William Shakespeare around 1600, is the story of how Prince Hamlet of Denmark takes revenge on his Uncle Claudius for murdering his father, marrying Hamlet's mother, and taking the throne for himself. Themes explored in the play include justice, revenge, treachery, and moral corruption.

115. C: Ebenezer Scrooge is a character in Charles Dickens's A Christmas Carol. Holden Caulfield is a character in J.D. Salinger's The Catcher in the Rye. Frederic Henry was created by Ernest Hemingway in his story A Farewell to Arms. Billy Pilgrim is a character in Kurt Vonnegut's Slaughterhouse Five. Draco Malfoy is a young student wizard in J.K. Rowling's Harry Potter series.

116. E: Flannery O'Connor (1925-1964) lived on the family farm, Andalusia, in Georgia. She authored two novels and 32 short stories, most in a style known as Southern Gothic. Her writings rely on settings, often Southern, and grotesque/exaggerated characters. Her Roman Catholic faith heavily influenced her writings as well, which often explore themes of morality. Wise Blood and A Good Man is Hard to Find are two of her works.

117. B: Pride and Prejudice was written by Jane Austen, a British contemporary of the Brontë sisters, around 1813. Charlotte Brontë wrote Jane Eyre in 1847 and Villette in 1853. Her sister Emily Brontë wrote Wuthering Heights in 1847, and sister Anne wrote The Tenant of Wildfell Hall in 1848. The three

Brontë sisters lived together in their family home of Haworth in England for their entire lives, which were cut short by diseases of the time.

118. A: Stephen King (born 1947) has sold more the 350 million copies of his works, such as Carrie, the story of a girl with psychic powers. Many of his works have been adapted for television and film, and he has also written under the pen name Richard Bachman. The Dark Tower series and The Running Man are two of his works.

119. D: Nathaniel Hawthorne wrote during the late 19th century. Immanuel Kant, Jean-Jacques Rousseau, Voltaire and Gotthold Ephraim Lessing all wrote during the 18th century Age of Enlightenment. The modern novel was developed in Europe during this period. Literature of the time explored themes ranging from social upheaval, satire, and geographical exploration, to differences between the natural and civilized states of man.

120. A: Famous Beat Generation authors (or "beatniks") include Allen Ginsberg, William S. Burroughs, and Jack Kerouac. The original beatniks met in New York City, though most eventually moved to San Francisco. Beat generation authors were non-conformist and accepted experimentation with drugs and Eastern spirituality.

121. D: To Kill a Mockingbird was written by Harper Lee in 1960 and won the Pulitzer Prize for Fiction in 1961. The novel has become an American literature classic, and its character Atticus Finch has become a fictional moral hero and model for many in the legal profession. The book deals with a trial where Finch represents a black man accused of raping a white woman.

122. C: Alan Alexander Milne (1882-1956) was a British author and playwright, now mostly known for his creation of the character Winnie the Pooh. He named the Christopher Robin character in the Winnie the Pooh books after his own son, and created the Pooh animal characters based on stuffed animals his son owned. Winnie the Pooh was named after Winnipeg, or Winnie, a black bear military mascot during World War I.

123. B: Charlotte's Web, written by American author E.B. White in 1952, tells the story of a spider named Charlotte who uses her ingenuity to save a pig's life. The book has won numerous awards and has been praised for its simple, yet poetic, writing style.

124. D: James Joyce published Ulysses in 1922, and the novel has been called a "summation of the entire movement" of Modernism. The title alludes to the hero of Homer's Odyssey, and the book makes use of experimental prose, careful structuring, and a stream-of-consciousness technique.

125. D: The Big Sleep was written by Raymond Chandler. The others were authored by Albert Camus (1913-1960), a French author whose works are often described as existentialist. His works gave rise to a movement known as absurdism, with a theme that happiness is fleeting, and that the human condition is one of mortality.

126. B: Laura Ingalls Wilder (1867-1957) wrote the Little House on the Prairie book series detailing her life growing up in a pioneer family. The nine-book series traces her family's travels through Wisconsin, Kansas, Minnesota, Iowa, and South Dakota.

127. E: Clarissa Dalloway is the title character in Mrs. Dalloway. Septimus Warren Smith appears in the novel as well. Mrs. Ramsay is a character in To the Lighthouse. Both books were written by Virginia Woolf (1882-1941), an English novelist regarded as one of the 20th century's foremost modernist authors.

128. D: Noah Webster (1758–1843) wrote textbooks used by most American students in the 1800s. At age 43, he began writing the first American dictionary, because he noted that Americans in different parts of the country spelled, pronounced and used words differently and he wanted to remedy this. He has been called the "Father of American Scholarship and Education."

129. E: George Plimpton was an American journalist and writer best known for his sports writing. Charles Darwin originated the concept of natural selection and wrote numerous scientific books about his theories. Stephen Hawking is a British theoretical physicist known for his popular science books as well as for his contributions to cosmology and quantum gravity. Richard Dawkins is a British biological theorist famous for his popular science books focusing on evolution. Carl Sagan was an astronomer, astrophysicist and author, famous for his popular science books.

130. C: General Psychological Theory was written by Sigmund Freud, founder of the psychoanalytic school of psychology. Charles Darwin wrote the remaining titles. He was an English naturalist who made popular the theory of evolution resulting from a process called natural selection.

131. A: Samuel Pepys's diary, written from 1660-1669, is one of the most important primary sources for the English Restoration period. He includes eyewitness accounts of and contemporary reactions to historic events such as the Great Fire of London, the Great Plague of London and the Second Dutch War.

132. B: Night is the first of a trilogy of books by Wiesel reflecting Wiesel's thoughts during and after the Holocaust. Night tells the story of Wiesel and his family being sent to Buchenwald and Auschwitz concentration camps during World War II. The other books in the trilogy are titled Dawn and Day.

133. E: Samuel Johnson, also known as Dr. Johnson, was a British author and lexicographer, called "arguably the most distinguished man of letters in English history." His Dictionary of the English Language was published in 1755. William F. Buckley, conservative author and commentator, founded the National Review magazine. Gloria Steinem, co-founder of Ms. magazine, is an American feminist, journalist and activist. Steven Pinker is a Canadian-American scientist known for his works in psychology. He wrote How the Mind Works. Andrea Dworkin was an American feminist best known for her criticism of pornography. She authored several nonfiction books, among them Heartbreak: The Political Memoir of a Feminist Militant.

134. B: Plato (427-347 B.C.) was a classical Greek philosopher who was inspired by Socrates. Plato's work laid the foundation for natural philosophy, science and Western philosophy. His Theory of Forms asserts that non-material forms or ideas, not the material world, possess the most fundamental form of reality.

135. D: Rationalism is a philosophy in which the criterion of the truth is not sensory but intellectual and deductive. Rationalist philosophers vary from feeling that reason takes precedence over other ways of acquiring knowledge, to promoting the more radical view that reason is the unique path to knowledge. Noted rationalists include Descartes, Leibniz, and Spinoza.

136. D: Rene Descartes, "the father of modern philosophy," was a French philosopher, mathematician, and physicist. His famous statement cogito ergo sum was written in Discourse on the Method (1637), and summarizes Descartes' belief that his existence is proven by his thoughts and consciousness.

137. B: Adam Smith (1723-1790) was a Scottish philosopher and political economist. His book The Wealth of Nations is considered the first modern work about economics. It posits that the free market, while appearing chaotic, is actually guided by an "invisible hand" to produce the right quantity and type of goods.

138. A: Georg Wilhelm Friedrich Hegel (1770-1831) was a German philosopher and one of the creators of German idealism. He is famous for his theory of the dialectic, on which Marxist writings and the Soviet Union were based. The theory uses the combination of a thesis and its antithesis to create a synthesis.

For instance, if a person's idea of freedom conflicts with another person's idea of freedom, then neither person can be free until everyone agrees to slavery.

139. E: Existentialist philosophy was popular during the 19th and 20th centuries, particularly after World War II as a means of reasserting the importance of human freedom and individuality. Existentialism suggests that the focus of philosophical thought should be with conditions of the individual and his emotions, responsibilities, and acts. Existentialists believe that individuals have sole responsibility for shaping their own lives.

140. C: Aristotle was a third century B.C. philosopher from Greece, not Rome. His writings, only a third of which are estimated to still survive, created a comprehensive system of logic, politics, and Western philosophy. Aristotle found the universal in particular things, which he called the essence of things. Plato found that the universal exists apart from particular things, and is related to them as their prototype, which he exemplified in his Theory of Forms.

141. B: Utopia, by Sir Thomas More, is largely based on Plato's Republic. It describes life on an island with seemingly perfect social, political and legal systems. It is widely speculated that More wished to use the book as a platform for discussing social issues in his native Europe, and not as an ideal.

Online Resources

Due to our efforts to try to keep this book to a manageable length, we've created a link that will give you access to all of your online resources:

mometrix.com/resources719/ftcehumank-12

It's Your Moment, Let's Celebrate It!

Share your story @mometrixtestpreparation